W9-BXX-965

The Stranger Guide to Seattle

the Stranger Guide to Seattle

The City's Smartest, Pickiest, Most Obsessive Urban Manual

Paula Gilovich, Traci Vogel, and *the Stranger* staff

SASQUATCH BOOKS
SEATTLE

Cover design: Hank Trotter
Cover illustration/photograph: C. Taylor
Interior design: Hank Trotter, Kelly O'Neil
Interior maps: Maps.com
Copy editor: Melody Moss
Indexer: Nanette Cardon

Library of Congress Cataloging in Publication Data
Gilovich, Paula.
The Stranger guide to Seattle / Paula Gilovich, Traci Vogel, and *The Stranger* staff.
p. cm.
Includes index.
ISBN 1-57601-256-0
1. Seattle (Wash.)--Guidebooks. I. Vogel, Traci. II. Stranger (Seattle, Wash.) III. Title.

F899.S43 G55 2001
917.97'77204444-dc21 00-068024

Sasquatch Books
615 Second Avenue
Seattle, Washington 98104
(206) 467-4300
www.SasquatchBooks.com
books@SasquatchBooks.com

contents

Contributing Writers

. . . with many thanks to Jennifer Vogel, who provided valuable editorial input

Jim Anderson
Megan Austin
Paul Axelrod
Brandy Chance
Novella Carpenter
Rob Crocker
Bret Fetzer
Ellen Forney
Erin Franzman
Eric Fredericksen
Gillian Gaar
Brian Goedde
Diana George
Paula Gilovich
Adriana Grant
Meghan Haas
Emily Hall
Kreg Hasegawa
Jonas Hinckley
Jamie Hook
Rachel Kessler
James Kirchmer
Stacey Levine
Min Liao (Restaurant
Consultant)
Scott McGeath
Jeremiah McNichols

Charles Mudede
Melody Moss
Mike Nipper
Matt Obst
Jason Pagano
Mark Pilder
Mark Pinkos
Stephanie Pure
Trisha Ready
Bruce Reid
Courtney Reimer
Riz Rollins
Charles Rosenburg
Adrian Ryan
Dan Savage
David Schmader
Megan Seling
Andy Spletzer
Matthew Stadler
Brad Steinbacher
Ali Stewart
Evan Sult
Nathan Thornburgh
D. Travers Scott
Jan Wallace
Kelly Williams
Kathleen Wilson

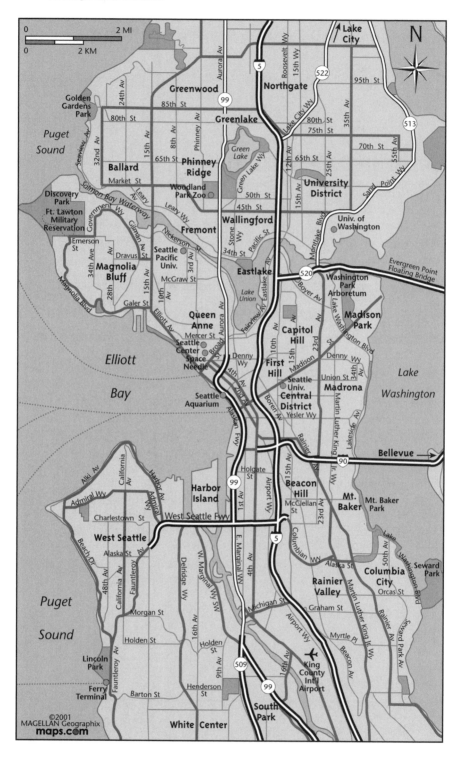

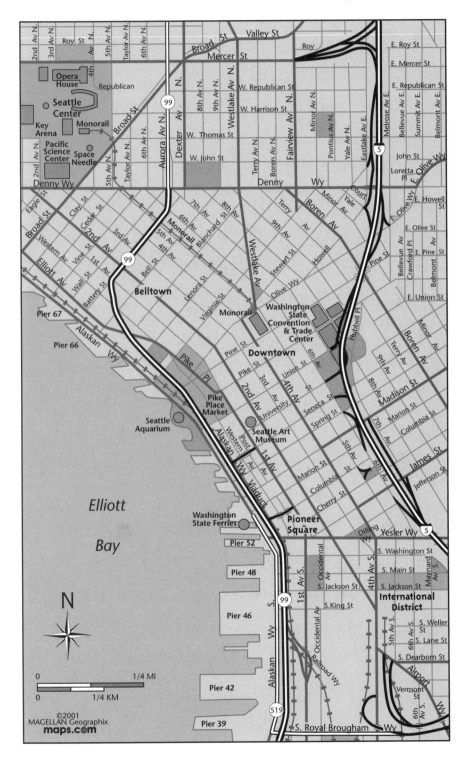

Introduction

We're living in a dump, trying to figure out what sex we are, trying to bargain for a better future.
—David Byrne, "A Self-Made Man"

WHEN TIM KECK LEFT WISCONSIN FOR SEATTLE in March of 1991, he arrived in a city newly cranked up on the software industry, the myth of grunge, and several "best places to live" nominations. There was one weekly newspaper in town, a centrist, mainstream affair. Keck, who had helped co-found the satire tabloid *The Onion*, recognized that there was an entire wash of younger people who were not being represented in print, and that the city was blooming around them uncommented on. With a few thousand dollars, working from the kitchen table of a rat-infested rental on Latona Street in Wallingford, with his roommates as editorial staff, Keck pumped out the first issue of *The Stranger*: cover by James Sturm, the first-ever "Savage Love," and a review of *Barton Fink*.

The name, *The Stranger*, came not only from Camus' novel and the Orson Welles movie, but from the sense Keck had that he was a stranger in mist-ridden Seattle—a sense that was shared by an influx of new arrivals and cultural iconoclasts. However, the name has also come to embody a sense that the city's transformation is unreal, that ground-level discourse has gone the way of the old orange Space Needle: "updated," glassed-off, made expensive. The new hierarchy in Seattle pits neighborhoods against a distant central government, and the increasingly wealthy against the increasingly poor—which, in a way, just proves that Seattle is finally becoming a real "world-class" (a description we love to deplore) city. The process invites rebellion in the form of active redefinition.

So in this guidebook you'll find physical evidence of adolescent Seattle—its scatological, unuttered, alleyway life—alongside its less ethereal, near-glacial Zeitgeist, and its diathetic trends. These are the things we love, or that we have borne with an irritability that begins to itch like love. This is not a traditional guidebook, lest we forget that out here at the end of the continent, tradition can be tossed to the seas. There are no NikeTowns, no Beppo Big-Ass Restaurants. There is no Nordstrom. There *are* places where we have ridden our bikes and fallen off in exhaustion; places where we have eaten for $3 scrounged out of tight-fitting pockets; places we have vomited in and loved. There are essays by people like Charles Mudede and Trisha Ready that strive to style the city, and interviews with people in various professions who make up Seattle's cognoscenti.

As we combed the city for the purposes of this book, we watched many of our favorite haunts disappear. The OK Hotel, Foxes, Sammie Sue's, the 211, Pistil Books, and Jules Maes have all closed shop. This book, then, is nothing less than an effort to keep the places we love alive and kicking. Overall, this is not just a guidebook—it's a manifesto, a portrait, and a highly biased geography of the city in which one editor was born and which the other has adopted. This is *The Stranger*'s city, one that is both sublime and ugly, one prone to melancholy and folly. Welcome to it, and let us know what you think at guide@thestranger.com.

Paula Gilovich, Traci Vogel, and *the Stranger* staff

1

Bars & Clubs

CLUBBING AND BARHOPPING, in any city, is a hit-or-miss affair. It's what occurs between the hit and the miss—the swirl of a drum 'n' bass beat fading in an alley, the moon blurring, your peripatetic movements to see if you've still got your wallet—that makes the evening memorable. Seattle's liquorish establishments run the gamut from swank to sewer—and its liquor laws run the gamut from fascistic to fascistic. Remember that most establishments shut down at 2 am, although after-hours clubs are slowly cropping up—ask your bartender or cab driver, or check flyers.

Dive Bars

Bush Gardens
International District
614 Maynard Ave S, (206) 682-6830
Daily 5 pm-1:30 am
Major credit cards accepted; smoking okay; wheelchair access to bar,
none to restaurant
Though it sounds like an amusement park or a dyke resort, this bar's actually a slice of Japan: pagodas, bamboo screens, koto music, incredible and visually pleasing food, lots of high-tech cell phones. All the waitresses look like biker chicks, which makes the place even more pleasingly surreal.
Crowd: *Loudmouths and superstars—especially when the karaoke kicks in at 9:30*

Ambience: *Decoratively sterile, like a hotel bar*
Helpful Hint: *Great food*

C. C. Attle's

Capitol Hill
1501 E Madison St, (206) 726-0565
Weekdays 8 am-2 am; open 24 hours on weekends
Major credit cards accepted; smoking okay

C. C. Attle's is curiously popular, even though there's nowhere to sit, hardly anywhere to stand, and the whole place has a packed-in-like-rats-on-a-sinking-ship feel to it. If a drunken grope in a crowded room and soft-core porn played in a continuous loop are your ideas of an exciting night out, C. C.'s is the answer to your prayers.

Crowd: *Very likely to hold Will & Grace–watching parties*
Ambience: *A sardine can*
Helpful Hint: *C.C.'s serves the strongest drinks on the hill*

Canterbury Ale and Eats

Capitol Hill
534 15th Ave E, (206) 322-3130
Daily 11 am-2 am
Major credit cards accepted; smoking okay; wheelchair accessible

In keeping with its medieval pub theme, a full suit of armor (minus the knight) greets the weary traveler at the Canterbury. Inside is a varied landscape of giant chairs, pool tables, and other amusements, such as the gambling game at the bar, which offers a wide selection of knives as prizes. Featuring some of the best and toughest cocktail waitresses in town, the Canterbury pours a stiff drink with love. Stick to the basics and strike up an easy conversation with the old-timer regulars. A great place to bring a

ANNIE MARIE MUSSELMAN
The Canterbury: Great drinks since the Middle Ages

crowd, the Canterbury yields room after room dotted with hard-drinking neighborhood hipsters and oldsters reading or staring out at the rain from the tavern's labyrinthine architecture.

Crowd: *All those folks you used to see at Denny's at 3 am, grown older and wiser*
Ambience: *Casually medieval*
Helpful Hint: *This is the only place in the city serving Green River milkshakes. YUM. And order the gravy fries.*

China Gate

International District

516 7th Ave S, (206) 624-1730

Daily 10 am-2 am

Major credit cards accepted; smoking okay; wheelchair accessible, but doorframes are a little slim

It's rumored that the Chinese Mafia mingles at the China Gate. Who cares if it's true? Have a good time looking for danger: Drinks are cheap and strong. The karaoke emcee's take on Prince and Tony Bennett is priceless; the regulars sing in English, Japanese, and Chinese. The bar staff all sport darling '30s hairdos and they aren't afraid to dance when they get the chance. You won't be bored; the food's pretty damn good; and the drinks are so strong, you'll start calling yourself "Johnny Night Train."

Crowd: *Young hiphop toughs, muscled biker dudes, Chinese barflies, and attention-craving couples from Tukwila who hump in the booths. Anybody, really.*

Ambience: *This is not where you'll meet the love of your life*

Helpful Hint: *Get there early and claim the most comfortable swivel chair in the city*

The Cuff

Capitol Hill

1533 13th Ave, (206) 323-1525

Daily 11 am-2 am

Major credit cards accepted; smoking okay; wheelchair accessible

The Cuff has recently exploded in size, more than doubling its former dimensions. It's bigger, brighter, and airier, but it's still as satisfyingly sleazy a bar as can be found in Seattle. The Cuff boasts a restaurant, three fully stocked bars, a huge outside porch, and a dance floor.

Crowd: *Trendy slummers and Leather Daddies*

Ambience: *The pretty kind of sleaze*

Helpful Hint: *Bring moist towelettes*

Dynasty Room at the Four Seas

International District

714 S King St, (206) 682-4900

Sun-Thurs 11 am-midnight, Fri-Sat 11 am-2 am

Major credit cards accepted; smoking okay; wheelchair accessible

"Our customers are spoiled," confides generous bartender Ariel Storm. Ariel wishes her name were Autumn Devonshire; she also wishes her smoky, paneled, old Vegas-style bar played music besides Elvis, candy rock, and jazz. There's a deep-sea glow to the Dynasty Room, tucked like a dreamy bubble into the vastness of the Four Seas: Here you can stay lost, forever if you'd like, in the bar's dark privacy.

Crowd: *Ariel promises a friendly, if motley crew of regulars*

Ambience: *Low lighting helps along the alcoholic haze*

Helpful Hint: *"Bring in CDs," Ariel encourages, and she'll play them*

Earl's on the Ave
University District
4720 University Way NE, (206) 525-4493
Daily 11 am-2 am
Major credit cards accepted; smoking okay; wheelchair accessible

ADAM L. WEINTRAUB

One of the more appealingly schizophrenic bars in town. To your left as you enter: pool tables, video games, laminated booths, and a sports-bar-lite feel, that invites you and your friends to sit down with a pitcher and an order of fries (though food service can be rather slow). On the right: a series of low tables and faux-leather chairs, plus the cramped bar itself *Nobody we know; but don't you wish you did?* that, like the best dives, encourages solitary drinking. Two large TVs are invariably broadcasting sports, but even when on, they're drowned out by your fellow midday drunks.

Crowd: *Hardcore regulars*
Ambience: *All-day drink festival*
Helpful Hint: *This bar is ripe for taking over*

Frontier Room
Belltown
2203 1st Ave, (206) 441-3377
Daily 10 am-2 am
Major credit cards accepted; smoking okay; wheelchair accessible

An uneasy truce between punk-rock and frat-boy drunks, the dark and sticky Frontier Room pours the kind of drinks that make you wonder whether the house rum is actually cheaper than the Coca-Cola. Well drinks are served in a small glass filled to the brim with booze, topped with a delicate float of mixer. If there is a jukebox, it doesn't get heard much; likewise, if there's a décor, it doesn't get seen much. This is, after all, a drinking bar.

Crowd: *Got the spins*
Ambience: *Lost in the haze*
Helpful Hint: *A good place to go when no other bar will serve you*

Ileen's Sports Bar

Capitol Hill
300 Broadway Ave E, (206) 324-0229
Daily 8 am-1:30 am
Cash only; smoking okay; wheelchair accessible

A sports bar in name only, Ileen's is the wretched hive of scum and villainy that Obi-Wan was talking about. Broadway's premier rat hole is a greasy breakfast bar in the morning and a hooky-player's watering hole after that. At night, it's loud, smoky, dark, and crowded, exactly as a low-rent drinking bar should be. Ideal situation: Meet up with a bunch of friends, take over a booth, and revel in your youth before you wind down like that guy in the corner.

Crowd: *Broadway punks and lifer drunks*

Ambience: *Loud*

Helpful Hint: *The cigarette dangling from the mounted moose head's lips has been there since before you were born, so don't smoke it*

Jimmy Woo's Jade Pagoda

Capitol Hill
606 Broadway Ave E, (206) 322-5900
Sun-Thurs 5 pm-2 am, Fri-Sun noon-2 am
Major credit cards accepted; smoking okay; wheelchair accessible

Let this review be a tribute to one of the best dive bars in Seattle, and definitely *The Stranger*'s all-time favorite: Pearl, Burt, John, and Rock, take a bow. The Jade's bartenders know how to serve up the right amount of sass

---

BIO

Burt Clemans

Who is he? Bartender, cocktail server, waiter, short-order cook, janitor, artist at the Jade Pagoda, 606 Broadway Ave E, (206) 322-5900.

If water is the "lesbian cocktail," as you're fond of saying, what's the gay man cocktail?
"A cosmopolitan. Which I hate making."

How do you feel about making lemon drops?
"After the first one, I tell them I won't make another

C. TAYLOR

until they lick every last bit of sugar off the rim!"

What would you like to see more of in the bar?
"Alcoholics ordering drinks with the ingredients right

in the name, like a rum and Coke."

How do you deal with unruly drunks?
"We mostly just have happy drunks here."

How do you like to announce last call?
"'You've got 15 minutes to get your hairy asses outta here.' Or maybe, 'Suck like you know how to suck.'"

What is the worst experience you've had here?
"Getting slapped by a drag queen after I told her not to snort so much crystal before she went out in public."

with their sweetness; owner Pearl Woo is an absolute dear. The Jade is a generous bar: Besides satisfyingly strong and cheap drinks, the Pagoda has the biggest—and best—burger in town. The Jade Pagoda has been here since the late '40s, and Pearl has been overseeing it every single day since the '70s; she obviously takes great care with her restaurant and bar, though unscrupulous urchins ripped off most of the decorations long ago. Somehow the simplicity of the place makes it seem even more welcoming. Burt, Rock, and John will charm your pants off as you sip, giggle, and gossip until last call; regulars get to know each other across the bar in no time. There's something cozy and almost womb-like about the barroom, and in the summer, the back porch is the greatest. The Jade could quickly become your favorite habit.

Crowd: *Middle-aged gay men and hipsters lying low*

Ambience: *Chinese restaurant blues*

Helpful Hint: *Please, please don't steal flowers, vases, glasses or anything else from Pearl's bar and restaurant; she does notice, and it does make her sad*

Monkey Pub

University District

5303 Roosevelt Way NE, (206) 523-6457

Mon-Sun 5 pm-2 am

Major credit cards accepted; smoking okay; wheelchair accessible

Don't let the '80s strip-mall exterior fool you: The Monkey Pub's interior is punk rock. Though proud of their Pabst on tap and cans of Schmidt, the Monkey Pub hosts a full array of microbrews, which you can enjoy while shooting pool or just looking at the junk hanging from the ceiling. On the weekends, the Monkey Pub hosts up-and-coming local bands, and the jukebox is one of the best in the city when it comes to indie rock.

Crowd: *Crusty punks and young'uns putting their drinking prowess to the test against the mellowed-out pros*

Ambience: *Dirty but fun*

Helpful Hint: *The frat boys and punks have an understanding. Don't rock the boat.*

Perry Ko's Dragon Room and South China Restaurant

Beacon Hill

2714 Beacon S, (206) 329-5085

Daily 11 am-2 am

Major credit cards accepted; smoking okay; wheelchair accessible

There aren't many options for drinking on Beacon Hill, which explains why the neighborhood's beautiful people, cops, thugs, and derelicts all congregate in Perry Ko's Dragon Room. This grotto offers many fine things, including a comfortable, multi-ethnic vibe; stiff-ass drinks brought to you by the friendly waitstaff; and a happy hour that'll make even the most hardened drinker weep with joy. Especially good are the Manhattans, double martinis, and nudie video games. Walk in with 10 bucks and walk out shit-faced. The bad news? The food is raunchy!

Crowd: *Beacon Hill's finest*
Ambience: *Murky*
Helpful Hint: *Red Apple is across the street if you'd like some tasty chicken*

Seattle Eagle

Capitol Hill
314 E Pike St, (206) 621-7591
Daily 2 pm-2 am
Cash only; smoking okay

The city's most down-and-dirty faggot fuck bar is also the only gay bar where DJs play rock. Tweakers and trendy tribal boyz cluster around the pool table while horned-up twinks drunkenly stumble the cruise circuit up and down the balcony. Fetish groups hold monthly socials here, and there's always something . . . interesting . . . going on out on the back patio.

Crowd: *Beers and queers*
Ambience: *Fucked right up*
Helpful Hint: *Beware the barber chair in the far back corner upstairs*

Shorty's

Belltown
2222 3/4 2nd Ave, (206) 441-5449
Daily noon-2 am
Major credit cards accepted; smoking okay; wheelchair accessible
(though the bathroom isn't)

Hot dogs, pinball, and video games—Shorty's is a perfect place to spend a quiet weekend night, especially if you're flying solo. It sponsors regular pinball championships for you pinball wizards. The small, quaint bar in the back is perfect for intimate conversation without the hassle of having to shout over loud music. Located just down the street from the Crocodile, it's a great place to dash for a quick hot dog (meaty or non-meaty) before, during, or after a rock show.

Crowd: *Pinball wizards!*
Ambience: *Coney Island*
Helpful Hint: *Try the vegetarian chili dog. Or if ya gotta have real meat, get it Chicago–style (the fresh tomatoes are the secret).*

Sonya's

Downtown
1919 1st Ave, (206) 441-7996
Daily 11 am-2 am
Major credit cards accepted; smoking okay

Sonya's was once the premier downtown homo haunt, open at 6 am for addicts, hustlers, and career alcoholics. After selling their old location to ritzy Pacific Place, they relocated, upscaled, and reopened, despite opposition from local politicos. The crowd has cleaned up—but not as much as the owners had hoped. Still a lovable, if no longer scary dive; the spectacular sunset-over-the-Sound view casts everyone in a dark silhouette.

Crowd: *Beware!*

Ambience: *Not really*

Helpful Hint: *Smoke your head off—the ventilation system is top-notch*

Sorry Charlie's Restaurant

Lower Queen Anne

529 Queen Anne Ave N, (206) 283-3245

Daily 6 am-2 am

Major credit cards accepted; smoking okay; wheelchair accessible

Minus the eerie soundtrack and the midget, this place is a lot like the television show, *Twin Peaks*. From the wall-sized waterfall picture to the grumpy waitresses and the "damn good pie," everything is Lynchian. Sorry Charlie's is a piano bar in the lost tradition. Pay close attention to Howard Bulson, who's been playing at Charlie's for 15 years. It's rumored that he declined a regular gig at Canlis because he couldn't bring along "his singers," the large number of regulars who get up and perform for each other every night. They range in age from 21 to 80: old jazz singers, Vegas stars, show-tune aficionados, and even opera buffs. If you can sing and you'd like to give your voice a try, just ask Howard politely. He even has a nice selection of songbooks you can root through.

Crowd: *Young and old*

Ambience: *Lounge*

Helpful Hint: *Don't talk or laugh loudly while Howard's around. This isn't just any bar; you come here to sing and be sung to. And don't forget to try the onion rings.*

NICOLLE L. FARUP

Storeroom

Eastlake

605 Eastlake Ave E, (206) 345-9041

The Storeroom: Oh, the angst

Mon-Fri 1 pm-2 am, Sat-Sun 6 pm-2 am

Cash only; smoking okay; wheelchair accessible

The term "hole in the wall" has never described a more fitting establishment. Located in the netherworld that lies between Capitol Hill and downtown Seattle (just down the street from the monolith known as REI), the Storeroom is a squalid little blemish—dark, musty, tiny—and one of the last places in town that can honestly call itself punk.

Crowd: *Punks!*

Ambience: *Punk!*

Helpful Hint: *Don't wear a suit*

Cool Bars

Cafe Septieme

Capitol Hill

214 Broadway E, (206) 860-8858

Daily 9 am to midnight

Major credit cards accepted; smoking okay; wheelchair accessible

C. TAYLOR

Cha-Cha: Serving drinks that will wrestle you into submission

Cafe Septieme brings everything you love and hate about France right into the heart of Capitol Hill. You'll come for the high ceilings, white table-cloths, and giant cafe art, but later feel the sting of utter indifference as the waitstaff blinds you with their cool, unconcerned glances. No matter: You came to experience a certain elegance, and Septieme has that in spades. The drinks are decadent and the lights are low, and really, you wouldn't have it any other way.

Crowd: *Everyone who can't leave Capitol Hill*

Ambience: *The wall-to-wall, oxblood-red paint job gives you a sense of being in Paris for about three seconds*

Helpful Hint: *The waitstaff is befriendable, and the place is even more enjoyable with them on your side*

The Cha Cha Lounge

Capitol Hill

506 E Pine St, (206) 329-1101

Daily 4 pm-2 am

Major credit cards accepted; smoking okay

This is where you will discover that the new beauty standard for boys is just as severe as for girls. Very clearly, boys are expected to have cinched waists and wear tight, tight T-shirts. It's more of a clubhouse than a bar and so only if you can handle the hipster glare you will make it in here. Everyone looks bored, tired, poor, and disenfranchised. Certain *Stranger* staffers have probably been keeping this place afloat for years.

Crowd: *Murder City Devils*

Ambience: *Blood red*

Helpful Hint: *It's so, so dark in here*

Flowers Bar and Restaurant

University District

4247 University Way NE (206) 633-1903

Daily 11 am-2 am

Major credit cards accepted; no smoking before 3 pm; wheelchair accessible

Flowers is an elegant island surrounded by frat bistros, loud sports bars, dark dives, and dubious restaurants. Inside this fragile island of hope is a mirrored ceiling, which reflects the entire bar, the well-used reading chairs near the entrance, and all the pretty tables, both large and small. If you must live or work in the U-District's grime, you can overcome it by drinking well here.

Crowd: *Anyone who enjoys eating decent vegetarian food and drinking good wine, while watching students race up and down the Ave*

Ambience: *The owner of this restaurant is from Lebanon, so there is a Middle Eastern mood about the place*

Helpful Hint: *Go there on Sunday afternoon for brunch: The waitresses and food are superb!*

Fort St. George

International District

601 S King St, Suite 202, (206) 382-0662

Mon-Thurs 11 am-midnight, Fri-Sat 11 am-2 am, Sun noon-midnight

Major credit cards accepted; smoking okay

The Polaroid collection of the numerous parties held at this tiny, enchanting bar suggests that the clientele is mostly hip, young Asian folks. Sit at the bar and chat with the sweet waitstaff and watch soundless sports television, or retreat to one of the six tables looking out over the International District. The mixed drinks feature high-quality booze poured with a generous hand; the beer selection is eclectic—Lobro dark lager, Kirin, Sapporo, and Guinness in bottles, Bud and Heineken on tap, rounded out by several sake and wine choices. Unlike most bars, the food is actually quite tasty—try the miso soup and rice. Of course, everyone smokes heavily. If you get bored, there's a large collection of Japanese fashion magazines to peruse.

Crowd: *Hello Kitty*

Ambience: *Small and smoky*

Helpful Hint: *Green-tea ice cream*

Habana's Fine Cuban Cuisine

Pioneer Square

210 S Washington St, (206) 521-9897

Major credit cards accepted; smoking okay; wheelchair accessible

Habana's is the promised land: Here the parched throat will be hydrated, the tongue tantalized, the stomach sated, the embittered spirit rejuvenated. Habana's *mojito* (rum, mint, and the secret stuff), fried plantains, and crab

fritters will rekindle your sodden passions. Habana's will give you back your strength, the strength to rise up and bellow, "¡Cuba Libre!"
Crowd: *¡Muy Cubanismo!*
Ambience: *High ceilings, good souls, live hiphop*
Helpful Hint: *Spanish and Cuban Spanish are two very different things*

Hattie's Hat
Ballard
5231 Ballard Ave NW, (206) 784-0175
Mon-Fri 3 pm-2 am, Sat-Sun 8 am-2 am
Major credit cards accepted; checks okay; smoking okay; wheelchair accessible
This cozy restaurant and bar was once a popular watering hole for seamen and the neighborhood's Scandinavian population. When new ownership took over in 1996, care was taken to restore, not redesign the establishment, which enabled Hattie's to hang on to its down-home charm. The wall's autumnal colors give the joint a ready warmth, and the loving restoration of Fred Oldfield's scenic mural of the great outdoors adds character. The menu includes items ranging from burgers and sandwiches to heartier meals such as catfish and meatloaf. Do not leave the Hat without committing yourself to pie! Fudge brownie and coconut cream are excellent choices.
Crowd: *Neighborhood folks, rockabilly types*
Ambience: *Unpretentious, unbearable when crowded*
Helpful Hint: *Famous and not-so-famous musical folk make appearances as "guest bartenders"*

Lava Lounge
Belltown
2226 2nd Ave, (206) 441-5660
Daily 3 pm-2 am
Major credit cards accepted; smoking okay; wheelchair accessible
Once just a knockoff of popular Linda's Tavern, the Lava Lounge has grown into one of Belltown's best places to drink—if you're cool with the overt Tiki theme. Dim and quiet, it's a place to converse around candles, and maybe play a game of shuffleboard or pinball. During the weekends, the place is packed, but on weeknights you can usually find a table.

CURT DOUGHTY

Lava Lounge: Where the kitsch hits the fan

Crowd: *Hipsters and condo owners, living (and drinking) together*
Ambience: *A squalid Gilligan's Island*
Helpful Hint: *Wednesday night is punk rock night: The Briefs play their dusty record collection*

Linda's Tavern

Capitol Hill
707 E Pine St, (206) 325-1220
Daily 4 pm-2 am
Major credit cards accepted; smoking okay; wheelchairs accessible
Some bars are just built right. Since its opening night, February 12, 1994, Linda's has been a perfect good-time bar: it's small but not cramped, features a punk and country jukebox and large, comfortable booths. The Western theme is friendly not forced, and extends right into the menu full of culinary Americana: meatloaf sandwiches, good burgers, and occasionally chicken-fried steak. In the summer, Linda's backporch is one of the city's pinnacle experiences, and sometimes they even play movies out there. It was also one of the last places Kurt Cobain was seen alive, if you're feeling ghoulish.
Crowd: *OK, this is where the word "hipster" applies*
Ambience: *Your home away from home on the range*
Helpful Hint: *Weekend breakfasts here are basic, satisfying, and never overcrowded*

DIANA ADAMS

Manray: Hollywood on Pine Street

Manray

Capitol Hill
514 E Pine, (206) 568-0750
Mon-Sat 4 pm-2 am, Sun 10 am-2 am
Major credit cards accepted; smoking okay; wheelchair accessible
Eurotrash lives! Strutting fags chatter away amid retro, minimalist décor, à la the space station from 2001. Crammed with video screens and white lights, Manray is the brightest fag bar in the city, but the designers thoughtfully incorporated some orange undertones to keep everyone looking good (or, in the case of tanning-booth abuse, looking much, much worse). If you get desperate for some shadows to slink into, there's a patio out back.
Crowd: *Great butts, exposed biceps*
Ambience: *Spotless '60s space age swirled with Menudo*
Helpful Hint: *Not a lot of seating, but the '80s music videos will keep you entertained while you stand*

Mars Bar at Cafe Venus

Eastlake

609 Eastlake Ave E, (206) 624-4516

Mon-Fri 11:30 am-2 am, Sat 5 pm-2 am, Sun 6 pm-2 am

Major credit cards accepted; smoking okay; wheelchair accessible

You'd never know there was a hopping little watering hole in the back of this charming restaurant—unless someone clued you in. Full of personality, with a great jukebox stocked with all the basics (including, at the time of this writing, the Holy Texan Trinity: the Rev. Horton Heat, Willie Nelson, and the Butthole Surfers), the Mars Bar is just the sort of charming hideaway every neighborhood should have.

Crowd: *People you never see anywhere else*

Ambience: *Like a shared secret*

Helpful Hint: *Spend one night a month here; it will restore your belief in neighborhood friendliness*

Nite Lite

Downtown

1926 2nd Ave at Virginia, (206) 443-0899

Mon-Fri noon-2 am, Sat-Sun 10 am-2 am

Cash only; smoking okay; wheelchair accessible

With its bare linoleum floor and fake stone paneling, this no-fuss joint appeals to the full spectrum of liquor lovers—from the young and attractive to the dusty and pickled. But the best part isn't the booze, the food (hot dogs, piles of fries, chicken strips, etc.), or even the kitschy look. The highlight of the Nite Lite? Those endearing bartenders—friendly grandmas with soft sweaters, lots of eye shadow, and kind smiles—who pour quickly and leave you alone. Sure, weekends can be annoying; the place is no secret. But for quiet bliss at the end of a long midweek night, head down here to nurse one last drink with no ice before you head back out onto the cold, wet streets, with Tammy Wynette still ringing in your ears.

Crowd: *A successful blend of scensters and lifers*

Ambience: *Cute early '60s, bathed in neon*

Helpful Hint: *Don't be an ass—avoid ordering cosmos, caipirinhas, chocolate martinis, or other trendy drinks*

Panther Room at the Cyclops Cafe

Belltown

2421 1st Ave, (206) 441-1677

Tues-Fri 4 pm-2 am, Sat-Sun 9 am-2 am

Major credit cards accepted; smoking okay; wheelchair accessible

A seat at the bar of the Cyclops gains you entry into bartender Tatchyana's wonderful world, where vodka is the correct answer to "What would you like?" The Cyclops is eye-centric, as it ought to be: Bright jumbles of eye candy offer constant distractions. Yes, go ahead and get drunk at the Cyclops.

You can sop up the liquor in your belly with the hearty food next door, revel in your seat here in Hiptown, and, later, hang off the edge of the pier screaming, "My eye has been opened!"

Crowd: *Hipsters and their parents*

Ambience: *As noisy and colorful as Sesame Street*

Helpful Hint: *If that large man wearing a dress and sparkly antennae on his head walks up and starts to clear your table—that's his job*

R Place

Capitol Hill

619 E Pine St, (206) 322-8828

Daily 2 pm-2 am

Major credit cards accepted; smoking okay; wheelchair accessible (if you want to go upstairs, ask the bartender to show you to the elevator)

An average evening at R Place consists of a hundred or so J. Crew types standing around pretending they haven't slept with each other. But if you have a hankering to enjoy a beer with a friend, R Place is a good bet. Stuffed with pool tables, pinball machines, dartboards, and computer games, R Place has an extensive selection of beers on tap and is staffed by the most adorable and friendly beertenders ever to pump a keg.

ANNIE MARIE MUSSELMAN

R Place: Where gay boys go to relive their frat days

Crowd: *Frat boys with a dirty little secret*

Ambience: *Dirty little frat house*

Helpful Hint: *Sitting near the green neon sign on the second floor makes one look like a seasick lizard*

Rosebud

Capitol Hill

719 E Pike, (206) 323-6636

Daily 11 am-1 am

Major credit cards accepted; no smoking; wheelchair accessible

Even though the prices for the Rosebud's very tasty food have skyrocketed, it is a great place to get a break on drink prices. Come here for happy hour and experience the unabashed beauty of $2 well drinks. The striped couches might not fit into your personal aesthetic, but they sure are comfortable and difficult to get out of. For the non-smokers in the city, this is one of the only bars that caters to you. For the smokers, bring a jacket because you are definitely standing outside.

Crowd: *Gays and straights*

Ambience: *No cigarettes*

Helpful Hint: *When it's crowded, it is unbearable: no seating and lots of waiting in line at the bar*

Vito's Madison Grill
First Hill/Downtown
927 9th Ave, (206) 682-2695
Mon-Fri 11 am-2 am, Sat 3 pm-2 am, Sun 5 pm-2 am
Major credit cards accepted; smoking okay; wheelchair accessible

Sip strong cocktails in the dark, sit in a big red booth, and set your cigarette to smolder in a giant ashtray. Opened in 1953, Vito's used to be the hot spot on the hill, where shady lawyers mingled famously with politicians and criminals. Now it's revamped Italian with an overstated pink disco light. Before nine it's cozy; after nine, it's a confusing party, featuring karaoke, dance lessons, and house music.

Crowd: *Lounge scene*
Ambience: *A lot like New Jersey*
Helpful Hint: *Everyone slips into a Mafia accent at some point during the evening*

The Wildrose
Capitol Hill
1021 E Pike St, (206) 324-9210
Sun-Mon 3 pm-midnight, Tues-Wed 3 pm-1 am, Thurs noon-1 am, Fri noon-2 am, Sat 3 pm-2 am
Major credit cards accepted; smoking okay; wheelchair accessible

The Wildrose is a lesbian landmark: It's Seattle's longest-running dyke bar. The Rose a great place to go if you're a new dyke in town who needs a job, a drink, or a date. It's also a great place to finally come out, dance, play pool, and dump your husband. The room itself is comfortable; check out the art and the antique bar accented with neon lights, rainbow flags, and sports trophies.

Crowd: *Butches, baby dykes, femmes, trannies who only talk about submarines*
Ambience: *Polyamorous*
Helpful Hint: *Best to look like Joan Jett*

Swank Bars

Alibi Room
Downtown
85 Pike St (in Post Alley, underneath Pike Place Market), (206) 623-3180
Daily 11:30 am-2 am
Major credit cards accepted; smoking okay

It's all about choices here. You must choose to ignore the imperfections and focus on the cozy, candlelit room where tourists, young locals, and Seattle's

Beautiful People gather long after the fishmongers above have gone home. The waitstaff can be distracted; the noise level soars after 10 pm; and the entire place can feel a bit disheveled, with its haphazard maze of tables. But bring a deep secret and a very close friend, and you'll love the sheer anonymity of it all. The Alibi Room is a favorite of Seattle's film community; it features frequent lectures and workshops for local film buffs and aspiring screenwriters. And there's a library of screenplays for customers to study at their tables.

Crowd: *Urban and pretty, with a fair amount of goatee-stroking*

Ambience: *Semi-Manhattan–casually sophisticated, with exposed brick, and art on the walls*

Helpful Hint: *Bring your patience and Marlboros. Salads, pasta, sandwiches, and other menu items can be pricey for the amount you get.*

Art Bar

Downtown

1516 2nd Ave, (206) 622-4344

Mon-Fri 4 pm-2 am, Sat-Sun 6 pm-2 am

Major credit cards accepted; no smoking; wheelchair accessible

If your go-go boots are made for walking, hike to the Art Bar. The neighbor-

DAVID BELISLE

Baltic Room: Where the stars come out at night

hood can be a little sketchy, but the Art Bar isn't. It sports a cozy dance area, cheap food, and a diverse mix of classy people. Open for all ages until 9 pm, the Art Bar is run by women and has 100 percent fewer frat boys than an Irish pub. Note to wallflowers: Seating is limited, so claim a velvet couch early.

Crowd: *Hiphop hangout*

Ambience: *Quintessential '90s*

Helpful Hint: *Wear something black or sparkly*

Baltic Room

Capitol Hill

1207 Pine St, (206) 625-4444

Daily 5 pm-2 am

Major credit cards accepted; smoking okay; wheelchair accessible

The '90s romantic style smushed in with some '20s and '30s creates the chichi essence of the Baltic Room. The aesthetic is a little overwhelming at the same time that it is cold. Career types have pegged this as the "hip bar," so some nights can be a little disappointing if one spends it listening in on marketing conversations. But some nights are a whirlwind. There's often a quirky piano man, great jazz shows, and one night is reserved for a DJ. Like any swank bar, the bathroom is really where it's at.

Crowd: *People with salaries*
Ambience: *Moody, yet successful*
Helpful Hint: *Get there earlier in the evening to snag a seat*

Barça
Capitol Hill
1510 11th Ave, (206) 325-8263
Daily 4 pm-2 am
Major credit cards accepted; smoking okay; wheelchair accessible

Oh how lovely it is to sip wine from giant glasses while sitting in a velvet booth that dwarfs your entire party, under a ceiling that seems as tall as the heavens. Upon opening, Barça was an immediate success. Even though it is situated across the street from those gauche condos, the Monique Lofts, this place has a soul while maintaining airs about itself. The bartenders and wine maids are truly wonderful. They notice when you've gussied up a bit just to come down. A bottle of the Shiraz is a nice choice. The tab can add up to something monstrous, so beware, and even after you've put too much on your bankcard you are going to have to go somewhere else to get a nibble of dinner. No snacks other than chips (which do not go with wine, come on) are available. Still, Barça is a place to adore. If you are a lady, spend some time in the bathroom smoking a cigarette on the couch.

Crowd: *Everyone is here to woo the tall, foxy cocktail waitress*
Ambience: *Dark, chatty, but not cozy*
Helpful Hint: *Eat before you come here*

Bookstore
Downtown
1007 1st Ave, (206) 382-1506
Daily 11:30 am-midnight
Major credit cards accepted; smoking okay

If you savor cigars and single-malt Scotch in a library ambience, or have to pacify someone who does, the Bookstore does the trick without overbearing snottiness. You might even spot a touring celebrity writer staying at the adjoining Alexis Hotel. The tourists stumbling in and the incongruous music (Chic's "Yowsa! Yowsa! Yowsa!") may spoil the mood somewhat, but the staff is friendly and attitude-free. Panini, espresso, and books on beer and gardening are also available.

Crowd: *Not as wealthy as it looks*
Ambience: *Like a library with a liquor license*
Helpful Hint: *Best as a weekday bar*

Capitol Club

Capitol Hill

414 E Pine St, (206) 325-2149

Daily 5 pm-2 am

Major credit cards accepted; smoking okay upstairs; wheelchairs can access restaurant and tearoom downstairs—the bar is logistically off-limits

C. TAYLOR

There isn't a higher point in Seattle's nightlife than the Capitol Club. With two floors (upper bar, lower restaurant), it is a den of decadence. The restaurant below is intimate and dimly lit; the bar above is public, with two long benches where the plush pillows are heaped high. The balcony hangs over Pine Street like voluptuous breasts. This is the "lush life," as Billy Strayhorn once put it.

Capitol Club: Like Morocco, with microbrews

Crowd: *Good-lookin'*

Ambience: *A lot like Joseph Von Sternberg's* Morocco; *it's all very fake but looks great*

Helpful Hint: *The sumptuous Turkish tearoom can be reserved (for free) by groups of beautiful people intent on having their own space*

Hunt Club Lounge & Fireside Room at the Sorrento Hotel

First Hill

900 Madison, (206) 622-6400

Daily 11 am-midnight

Major credit cards accepted; smoking okay; wheelchair accessible

Ah, the Sorrento. Back in a previous, more civilized time (say, 1909, when the Sorrento was built), couples might have waltzed around its circular lounge, diamonds flickering in the firelight. Now, lesbians lean back on the couches, sipping softball-sized goblets of bourbon, as bad jazz spritzes through the speakers overhead. Golden paneling and sweeping columns surround the tiled fireplace and overstuffed couches. The Sorrento is a good place to go when you want to do the cocktail thing without the pretense—or rather, when you want to do the cocktail thing with pretense, but you don't want any of your friends to see you.

Crowd: *Cultured visitors to our fair city*

Ambience: *Sedate, kind of scruffy elegance*

Helpful Hint: *Wear your fake pearls*

Zig Zag Cafe
Downtown/Pike Place Market
1501 Western Ave, (206) 625-1146
Daily noon-2 am
Major credit cards accepted; smoking okay

Run by three super-cool guys from Sosia, Bulgaria, this attractive yet wholly affordable bar and restaurant features live music every other night, and a menu riddled with Southern European–styled tapas—or mezzetas, as they say back home. There's great pizza as well, along with plenty of American fare for the ever-present Pike Place Market tourists. In typical European fashion, this unpretentious gem of a hangout aims to please everyone—and succeeds.

Crowd: *Languid, sophisticated night crawlers*
Ambience: *The very essence of a downtown bar*
Helpful Hint: *Introduce yourself to the owners*

Taverns

Al's Tavern
Wallingford
2303 N 45th St, (206) 545-9959
Daily 3 pm-2 am
Major credit cards accepted; smoking okay; wheelchair accessible

Owned by Max now, the same guy who owns the Sunset Tavern. Al's used to be owned by some guy named Herb. No one knows who Al is or was. This bar's been here forever. Bud in a bottle and Rainier pitchers are the bestsellers, and they sell in unbelievable amounts. Al's cool black facade with silver stars makes you think you're headed for some hipsters, but once inside, pretension evaporates. Projectionist union members, ferry workers, and stage technicians make up the regular clientele here. The true glory of this simple neighborhood bar is the long wall dedicated to a portrait of the Sound from the Discovery Park vantage point. Twenty-five-cent pool is available on a couple of tables.

Crowd: *No Microsofties here*
Ambience: *The essence of a regular bar*
Helpful Hint: *Save a buck for the jukebox, because it'll buy you 11 songs*

The Beacon Pub
Beacon Hill
3057 Beacon Ave S, (206) 726-0238
Daily noon-2 am
Cash only; smoking at bar okay; wheelchair accessible

If Perry Ko's Dragon Room is Beacon Hill's lecherous, hard-drinking uncle, the Beacon Pub is Beacon Hill's sweet, comforting auntie. Since the Beacon was remodeled by its new owners, it has become a classic hangout with a pool table, an unhip jukebox, and a room in back that looks like a sitcom living room. The bartender is spunky and fun.

Crowd: *Working class*

Ambience: *Mashed potatoes*

Helpful Hint: *Use the stubby pool stick for those wall shots*

Big Time Brewing Company

University District

4133 University Way NE, (206) 545-4509

Daily 11:30 am-2 am

Major credit cards accepted; smoking okay; wheelchair accessible

Delicious beer and a laid-back collegiate feel make the Big Time Brewery (mere blocks from the UW) one of Seattle's best places to enjoy a drink. Not just a bar, but also a complete brewery, the Big Time's microbrews are top-notch—from the deep porters to the light ales, the place certainly makes some heavenly beer. Though the roomy hardwood floors and the air of sportsiness make the place look a bit like a frat annex, the Big Time's been around long enough to win the respect of old-school Seattle musicians and lifer college rats.

Crowd: *Grad students, Greek Row, and laid-back locals*

Ambience: *Warm, comfortable*

Helpful Hint: *Avoid the weeks around college finals, or you'll be hard-pressed to find a seat*

Blue Moon Tavern

University District

712 NE 45th St, (206) 633-6267

Daily noon-2 am

Cash only; smoking okay; wheelchair accessible

Many radical, artist, beatnik and hippie keisters have graced the Blue Moon's deeply grooved wooden benches. It's been the popular watering hole for famous local poets and legendary drinkers (such as Theodore Roethke and Richard Hugo). The tavern was an instant hit with students when it opened in 1934—at the time, state law mandated that students trek at least one mile from campus to buy a beer. It was spared from demolition in 1989 by a popular uprising that forced the public's recognition of the Blue Moon as an unofficial cultural landmark. The music tends to lean toward Grateful Dead crowd-pleasers, but many nights feature live local bands or readings by bad-ass poets, writers, and performers—with no cover.

Crowd: *Rowdy and cozy all at once—tavern-wide conversations, diatribes, debates, heckling, and, if you're lucky, revolutions*

Ambience: *Smoky, dark, and comfortable, the Blue Moon is the kind of place where it's okay to spill your beer*

Helpful Hint: *Although the tavern's lit mag,* Point No Point, *is no longer around, the bathroom stalls continue to offer some of the best and wittiest poetry in town. And don't miss out on the notorious Duct Tape Wine $1.50 schooner.*

The Buckaroo Tavern
Fremont
4201 Fremont Ave N, (206) 634-3161
Daily 11 am-2 am
Checks okay; smoking okay; wheelchair accessible

The quintessential neighborhood establishment—from the pinball to the pool tables to the satisfactorily amusing bathroom limericks—the Buckaroo is a prime location for an evening of relaxed, alcohol-soaked camaraderie. While a bit on the small side, there are usually enough booths and bar stools to go around. Scenes from 1997's *Prefontaine* (starring dreamboat Jared "Jordan Catalano" Leto) were shot here, making it the closest you'll ever get to Claire Danes.

BOOTSY HOLLER

The Buckaroo: Cowpokes and pinball

Crowd: *Local folk, motorcycle enthusiasts*
Ambience: *Late-20th-century neighborhood bar*
Helpful Hint: *A good bar for sampling—there are 24 beers on tap, and 60–70 bottled brews available*

Changes Tavern
Wallingford
2103 N 45th St, (206) 545-8363
Daily noon-2 am
Cash only; smoking okay; wheelchair accessible if someone clears the drunks, stools, and piles of pull-tabs out of your way

Changes is one of the last unpretentious neighborhood fag bars in the city . . . and it's not on Capitol Hill! Friendly, fabulous, and fairly out of control, trannies belt out Led Zeppelin karaoke while neighborhood guppies and drunks chat up wide-eyed UW students. With darts, pool, and a secluded back patio, Changes is a great place to arrive, cut loose, get really drunk, and sleep with someone, which you'll later regret.

Crowd: *Not so pretty*
Ambience: *Not so pretty*
Helpful Hint: *Check your insecurities at the door*

College Inn Pub

University District

4006 University Way NE, (206) 634-2307

Mon-Fri 11:30 am-2 am, Sat 2 pm-2 am, Sun 2 pm-1 am

Major credit cards accepted; smoking okay

This basement pub in a semi-historical landmark whispers "comfortable," from its low ceilings to its scratched-up tables. The pub focuses on regional microbrews, which rotate monthly, though there are imports on tap as well. A clumsy layout creates more nooks and crannies than the space should allow, making the bar more suitable for small-group conversations than large-group socialization. It's the place where people go to shift down after an aborted evening elsewhere. The crowd is an endearing mix of misfits and neighborhood types who are probably going to turn in soon, anyway. But first—talk, talk, talk.

Crowd: *College kids and people not threatened by them*

Ambience: *You do your thing; I'll do mine . . . but in a nice way. It's a little nostalgic, too, if you're a UW grad.*

Helpful Hints: *The chili is the best item on the bar-food menu, but that's only compared to dorm fare. There's a reasonably large, private room that can be reserved for free.*

Comet Tavern

Capitol Hill

922 E Pike St, (206) 323-9853

Daily noon-2 am

Cash only; smoking okay; wheelchair accessible

The Comet Tavern is one true remnant of old-school Seattle, a lovingly defaced hole filled with regulars, both grumpy and jubilant. Large tables hunkering beneath their beer stains welcome large groups of carousers. Most bars have graffiti in the bathroom, but the Comet's graffiti has grown completely out of control, spilling out of the bathrooms and over the walls of the always-crowded pool room. Anything that can happen in a bar has happened here.

Crowd: *Bike messengers, slumming suburbanites, and junkies*

Ambience: *Like your buttrock older brother's creepy bedroom*

Helpful Hint: *Look up and you'll see hundreds of stained and crusty dollar bills mysteriously stuck to the ceiling*

Dante's Steak & Grog

University District

5300 Roosevelt Way NE, (206) 525-1300

Daily noon-2 am

Major credit cards accepted; smoking okay; limited wheelchair access

With its exposed-timber and tri-level design, Dante's resembles a cut-rate ski lodge. It has a party-boy-on-a-budget atmosphere, reinforced by the video and hoop-toss games dominating the sunken game room. The games are the only reason to come here. Darts, foosball, pool, Pop-a-Shot, and pinball are a lot to choose from. College-friendly heavy metal blares from the jukebox, and the service leans toward the brusquely efficient side of things—never more so than at last call, the announcement of which is squawked over an intercom. Still, the drinks aren't offensively watered down, and the cubbyhole layout allows for a nice feeling of solitude during the quieter hours—though you wouldn't want to be caught dead here during rush week.

Crowd: *Dumbfucks mostly, and sometimes Budweiser girls*
Ambience: *Nah*
Helpful Hint: *Don't come here before, during, or after a Huskies game*

The Double Header

Pioneer Square
407 2nd Ave, (206) 464-9918
Sun-Thurs 10 am-midnight; Fri-Sat 10 am-2 am
Cash only; smoking okay; wheelchair accessible

This quaint little anachronism located in colorful Pioneer Square is rumored to be the oldest gay bar in Seattle. The Double Header inhabits an enormous space that was obviously gorgeous in its heyday but has suffered from decades of abuse, and now resembles an eccentric garage

sale. The place has the capacity to seat 500 easily, but the scant few regulars are usually cowering timidly in a small corner of the bar.

Crowd: *Friendly but fossilized*
Ambience: *Homoerotic ghost town*
Helpful Hint: *Come for the historical value, stay for the microwaved hot dogs*

ANNIE MARIE MUSSELMAN

The Double Header: Really old gays

Eastlake Zoo Tavern

Eastlake
2301 Eastlake Ave E, (206) 329-3277
Mon-Fri 11:30 am-2 am,
Sat-Sun 1 pm-2 am
Cash only; smoking okay; wheelchair accessible

The Zoo is full of nice little details to warm the cockles of your heart. For instance, you could spend a year as a regular before you ever noticed the shiny little blue Christmas ornaments hanging in a pattern above the entrance. Likewise, the bar's possibilities unfold gradually—there's pool, but there's also a snooker table in back; there's shuffleboard, pinball, video games, and darts. Only through dedication will the pleasures of the bar unfurl for you.

Crowd: *Frat boys, hardcore drinkers, and scenesters—oh my!*

Ambience: *Timeworn wood*
Helpful Hint: *Avoid the pool tables and head straight for the shuffleboard*

Galway Arms
University District
5257 University Way NE, (206) 527-0404
Daily 4 pm-1:30 am
Major credit cards accepted; smoking okay; wheelchair accessible

We've listed the Galway under "Taverns" because it feels like a tavern, but they do have a full bar. Maybe it's all the dark wood and the old Guinness posters, but Irish pubs in America carry a much more "mature" vibe than the average neighborhood bar. Such is the case with the Galway Arms, a gathering place for older Irish blokes and those who want to sop up their vibe, not to mention sop up some slow-poured Guinness or Irish whiskey. Instead of a jukebox, the Galway plays a steady stream of Irish music (from traditional to U2), with live music on the weekends. Instead of darts, the Galway has video golf.

Crowd: *Busy mooning over their Irish heritage*
Ambience: *The boys back home would be proud*
Helpful Hint: *For those feeling adventurous, the menu includes island delicacies ranging from shepherd's pie to bangers and mash*

Knarr Tavern
University District
5633 University Way NE, (206) 525-3323
Daily 2 pm-2 am
Major credit cards accepted; smoking okay; wheelchair accessible

An unholy union of frat-row sports bar and aging hippie hangout, what really saves this place is the Viking longship that is part of its sign and identity. The Vikings—now they knew how to drink, and in that spirit, so do the patrons of the Knarr. Activities (besides drinking) include pool, pinball, video games, shuffleboard, and, occasionally, live music.

Crowd: *University riffraff*
Ambience: *Pure longship revelry*
Helpful Hint: *Beware of "Kill the Keg" Wednesdays*

Little Red Hen
Green Lake
7115 Woodlawn Ave NE, (206) 522-1168
Mon-Fri 6 am-2 am, Sat 8 am-2 am, Sun 9 am-2 am
Major credit cards accepted; checks okay; smoking okay;
no wheelchair access to bathrooms

A real, live, country-and-western bar! Live country music and line dancing! Free dance lessons! Texas Lone Star beer! It may not be the best country music you'll ever hear, but it's homey, unpretentious, and free. You might as well dance, because the music wails along at a geriatric-level volume. Most bands will honor reasonable song requests. The drink specials are fun and the staff is delightful.

Crowd: *Friendly and patient with the aspiring dancer; most of the regulars will take you for a spin on the miniature dance floor*

Ambience: *Country enough that you'll forget all about being in the heart of Green Lake*

Helpful Hint: *Please be respectful—wear your shirt tucked into your Wranglers, and put boots on. Hats are optional.*

Owl & Thistle Irish Pub

Pioneer Square
808 Post Ave, (206) 621-7777
Daily 11 am-1:30 am
Major credit cards accepted; smoking okay; wheelchair accessible

The Little Red Hen's beer of choice

Although the Owl & Thistle is at street level, walking into it is like descending into underground Seattle: Raw-brick tunnels connect a casual, well-lit pool room, an antique barbershop, a dim restaurant, and a dark bar. The stage is low and softly lit, but this is undeniably a musicians' hangout. Known for its acoustic sets (Portland legend Pete Krebs sometimes sets up shop down here), the O&T also hosts jazz, hiphop, and blues. In fact, the jukebox in the pool room features a copy of a CD called *At the Owl & Thistle*, featuring local musicians' live sets. Best detail: the restaurant's moderately impressive law library. (P.S. This is a full bar; however, like all Irish pubs, it feels like a tavern.)

Crowd: *Pioneer Square locals, folk-rock hipsters, and Navy assholes*

Ambience: *Old-Town grit*

Helpful Hint: *Check the crowd before committing for the night. Some nights are great; some are Pioneer Square spanky-homo-fratboy nightmares.*

The Ravenna Tavern

Ravenna
2258 NE 65th St, (206) 729-9083
Daily 10 am-2 am
Cash only; smoking okay; wheelchair accessible

The Rav Tav's logo says it all: It's a drunken fish flat on his back, chugging from a stein wrapped in his tail fins. The door opens at 10 am; by 10:15 am every bar stool has a butt on it. All the action centers around the single pool table, though the pull-tabs and video poker get a real workout, too. There's something so rascally about this dive that you have to give it some respect.

Crowd: *Count upward from 35 years old. Keep counting. . . .*

Ambience: *A bar's bar—every scrap of furnishing promotes one of five brands of beer*

Helpful Hint: *It'll cost you 50 cents in the scratch jar every time you knock the cue ball off the table. But if you sink the eight off the break, you win the pot!*

Summit Avenue Tavern

Capitol Hill

601 Summit Ave E, (206) 324-7611

Daily 4 pm-2 am

Major credit cards accepted; checks okay; smoking okay; wheelchair accessible

The Summit Avenue Tavern is where neighbors commingle and discuss their distrust of landlords, the petty nickel-and-diming antics of telephone companies, and those miserable boys who keep dropping the pool cues. The cues are wonderful and shouldn't be dropped, ever, lest they become nicked, warped, and totally useless. Please don't drop the cues here—enjoy them. They're fiberglass, and they're perfect. And they'll be instrumental in your running of the table, which will make you a legend in the watering eyes of your friends.

Crowd: *Neighborhood folk, scenesters between scenes*

Ambience: *Enthusiastic euphoria*

Helpful Hint: *Hot and cold sandwiches are available until 9 pm; hot sausages are sold all night long*

Sunset Tavern

Ballard

5433 Ballard Ave NW, (206) 784-4880

Daily 10 am-2 am

Cash only; smoking okay; the front door requires a step, otherwise wheelchair accessible

There was a point when hip in Seattle meant the confluence of West Coast hippie and biker cultures, and the music scene was a series of no-name bar bands forming and re-forming on a whim. Some neighborhood bars, like the Sunset Tavern, still have that feeling. The weekends are the best—darts and games during the day, music at night.

Crowd: *Neighborhood regulars, known by name*

Ambience: *They may know everybody's name but yours, but you won't be treated that way*

Helpful Hint: *Rockaroake!*

Teddy's

Roosevelt

1012 NE 65th St, (206) 526-9174

Daily 1 pm-2 am

Major credit cards accepted; checks okay; smoking okay; wheelchair accessible

Teddy Roosevelt paraphernalia covers the wooden walls of this stalwart neighborhood tavern. As you walk in, you'll naturally gravitate either to the two pool tables or the bar, while the jukebox blares the Black Crowes. Motorcycle riders meet here the first Wednesday of every month, and in the summer there's Ping-Pong on the back patio.

Crowd: *People who live in Roosevelt*
Ambience: *Presidential*
Helpful Hint: *There's an excellent children's book about Teddy Roosevelt behind the bar*

Twilight Exit
Central District
2020 E Madison St, (206) 324-7462
Daily 5 pm-2 am
Major credit cards accepted; smoking okay; wheelchair accessible

The Twilight Exit is the first Capitol Hill–style bar (meaning it's like Linda's, the Cha Cha Lounge, and the Comet) to open outside of Capitol Hill. Located in the heart of the Central District, near Mount Zion Baptist church and the mysterious red radio towers, the bar reminds many of someplace back East. But what really comes to mind when one enters this large and uncluttered space is the feeling of walking onto a movie set. This particular film is being shot on a very small budget; the actors are unknown and the director is young and promising.

Crowd: *White hipsters drinking cheap beer, with the occasional black retirees, who are also drinking cheap beer*
Ambience: *Dark and very laid-back, with loud Sunday-night karaoke*
Helpful Hint: *This is an excellent place to drink right after you've been dumped*

Dance Clubs

Aristocrat's Club
Downtown
220 4th Ave S, (206) 748-9779
Daily 3 pm-2 am
Major credit cards accepted; smoking okay; wheelchair accessible

Featuring karaoke and exuberant dancing on select nights, the mysterious Aristocrat's is the dance club of your adolescent dreams. Drinks glow; beautiful kids dance and smile in over-the-top fashion; flashbulbs pop; and there's always a free go-go block to hop up on and shake your moneymaker. Music hovers around the tried and true: dance classics from the disco era, mixed with a tiny bit of funk.

Crowd: *Young and hip on some nights; young and stupid on other nights*
Ambience: *All fun and dance enthusiasm*
Helpful Hint: *Wear something loud*

Beso del Sol

Wallingford
4468 Stone Way N, (206) 547-8087
Dancing Fri-Sun 10 pm-1:30 am
Major credit cards accepted; no smoking; wheelchair accessible
Dancers of both genders agree that this place is the warmest, friendliest, and most humble of Seattle's salsa clubs. Regulars appreciate the emphasis on genuine salsa music, whether the night is orchestrated by DJ Fernando or a lively local conjunto. The eclectic, all-ages crowd is serious about dancing, and tuxedos and jewels can be spotted doing the merengue next to T-shirts.
Crowd: *Casual to fancy, fancy, fancy*
Ambience: *Mexican restaurant*
Helpful Hint: *Come early for dinner or appetizers and pay no cover. Friday is the most lively night.*

BIO

Donald Glaude

Who is he? Local DJ Donald doesn't use a moniker anymore, but once upon a time, he was known as "Dominator." "Back in the day when raves started coming out, everyone had a name, so I felt like I should have one, too," he says. Since he was known for his love of then rave-anthem 'One & Only Dominator,' people started calling him by that name.

Years as a DJ:
"I honestly don't know," Donald admits with a laugh. What he does know is that he started spinning at school dances and weddings more than 10 years ago. The rest is a bit hazy.

Genre of choice:
"My genre of choice is funky," Donald says. Not funk as in George Clinton or James Brown, but that ineffable quality about a record

that even Donald can't quite describe. "I mean, I'm known for hard house right now, but I spin all genres. Even jungle."

Favorite labels:
None. "Labels change. I don't like to pigeonhole," quoth the ever-diplomatic Donald, adding this piece of advice: "Keep an open mind. Something you think might be cheesy might end up surprising you."

On requests:
"I don't mind them, I suppose, but I hope people

understand that there's more to this than just playing records. Otherwise I'd still be doing weddings."

Residencies:
While most DJs have residencies on a weekly basis, Donald's busy schedule allows him to make appearances only once a month. You can catch him each month at the Showbox and I-Spy.

Favorite place to spin:
Donald's popularity keeps him busy on both sides of the DJ fence–in clubs as well as at raves. "The kids keep me on my toes, but the bar scene keeps me on my toes in a different way," he says. Though his uncanny, charismatic DJ style has taken him as far away as Toronto and Florida, Donald's favorite place to play is still here in Seattle.

Idols:
"There's a lot of people who inspire me: my kids, Carl Cox, DJ Dan. . . . I try to inspire myself, too."

Century Ballroom & Cafe

Capitol Hill
15 E Pine St, (206) 324-7263
Ballroom: Wed-Sun 6 pm-1 am (but
also open for classes)
Major credit cards accepted, checks
okay; no smoking; wheelchair
access by elevator on 10th Ave

ERIKA LANGLEY

The Century's 2,000-square-foot
dance floor is absolutely beautiful and is so worth checking
out. If you don't dance, you can
also see shows there, everything
from rock solo artists to cajun
bands. Make no mistake, the
Century is committed primarily
to the art of dancing. The dancing
schedule oscillates from swing to
salsa nights (check their website,
www.centuryballroom.com for
details). Every dancing night,
whether it's swing or salsa,
begins with a half-hour lesson

Century Ballroom: Um, how did that step go again?

that's free if you pay the cover to stay and dance the night away.

Crowd: *If you've come to swing, zoot suits; if you've come to salsa, the sexiest dresses you've ever seen*

Ambience: *Dance school*

Helpful Hint: *Don't park in the KFC lot next door unless you want to pay a huge fine and walk home. Consider yourself warned.*

Fiesta Mexicana

Greenwood
1471 85th St NW, (206) 618-0401
Dancing Fri-Sun 9:30 pm-2 am
Major credit cards accepted; checks okay; smoking okay; wheelchair accessible

The music's the thing at this full-time Mexican restaurant and part-time salsa club. True salseros will think they've arrived in Latin dance heaven as the DJ serves up the ultimate tropical mix of salsa, cumbia, merengue, and more.

Crowd: *Mexican*

Ambience: *Colorful bajo Mexican space*

Helpful Hint: *Come early with friends for dinner and enjoy the authentic cooking, free salsa lessons, and dancing*

Extra Helpful Hint: *The midsize dance floor accommodates 300, so you'll be able to show off*

Illusiones Latin Club at China Harbor
Westlake
2040 Westlake Ave N, (206) 286-1688
Dancing Thurs-Sat 9:30 pm-1:30 am
Major credit cards accepted; checks okay; smoking okay; limited wheelchair access
Salsa nights at the gigantic and foreboding China Harbor are packed with Latinos and Latinas who know how to dance and aren't afraid to show a little skin. Remember, when your dance partner asks where you're from, he doesn't mean which neighborhood, he means which country, so save your life story for another time. The pace is exhilarating. No time to be shy; be prepared to look good and use your hips—that means boys, too.
Crowd: *Short, dark, and handsome*
Ambience: *Hot and sweaty discotheque*
Helpful Hint: *Women—wear heels. Men—tuck in your shirt. Everyone—practice your Spanish; you'll need it.*

I-SPY/Nation
Downtown
1921 5th Ave, (206) 374-9492
Major credit cards accepted; smoking okay
I-SPY is one of the most promising clubs in the city. They book great rock bands like Trans Am and great hiphop groups, like Blackalicious—and sometimes, on dance nights, you can witness or even partake in some breakdancing. The space's last incarnation was as the famed club The Weathered Wall, but I-SPY is eight million times better. There are two levels and upstairs holds a swanky bar with some good, but expensive food. You might say that with I-SPY, finally Seattle has a real club. I-SPY was also one of the first places to dedicate itself to doing all-ages shows early in the evenings.
Crowd: *Everyone in the city*
Ambience: *Upstairs: gauche; downstairs: louche*
Helpful Hint: *It's helpful to do a little "pre-funct"—lines at the bar(s) can be long.*

Neighbours
Capitol Hill
1509 Broadway, (206) 324-5358
Sun-Thurs 9 pm-2 am, Fri-Sat 9 pm-4 am
Major credit cards accepted; smoking okay; limited wheelchair access
Neighbours has been Seattle's queer coming-of-age bar for 16 years, and it's still the perfect spot to bump into all your ex-boyfriends, past and future. Neighbours has recently done some sprucing up in an effort to compete with newer clubs, but even with the fancy-schmancy additions, the old girl still

resembles a drag queen's basement apartment. Which is, strangely enough, a big part of its charm. Neighbours has three bars, two pool tables, and an enormous dance floor. But be warned . . . since it became cool to be queer, Neighbours' crowd often hovers around 50 percent straight, and the possibility of having a good time and/or getting some fluctuates wildly.

Crowd: *I was cruising him; he was cruising her; she was cruising me. . . .*

Ambience: *Barbizon*

Helpful Hint: *Go to the bathroom before you arrive*

Re-Bar
Downtown
1114 Howell St, (206) 233-9873
Thurs-Sun 9 pm-2 am
Cash only; smoking okay; wheelchair accessible

When the Re-Bar opened back in 1991, it was the first in a wave of cosmopolitan clubs that granted Seattle's nightlife a level of respectability. In the middle of the grunge storm, this club stood out because it played (and still plays) funk, hiphop, house, world beat, and disco to gays, straights, blacks, whites, and Asians. Amazingly, after all these years, the Re-Bar is still one of the best dance clubs in Seattle.

Crowd: *This is where all the nice people go; the Re-Bar hates bad people*

Ambience: *It is not surprising that the Re-Bar often holds small plays (directed*

....

BIO
....
Carla Schricker

Who is she? Under the moniker "MC Queen Lucky," Schricker's been spinning as a Seattle DJ for over ten years.

Genre of choice:
Funk, hiphop . . . "anything with soul."

Favorite labels:
Lucky says, "I actually am bad at paying attention to labels . . . but I suppose Jive, Rawkus, and K-Tel are a few favorites."

Wouldn't be caught dead playing:
Techno. "I know nothing about this kind of music; it bores the hell out of me. . . ."

Residencies:
Re-Bar on Thursdays and Saturdays, Thekla (in Olympia) on Fridays.

Request that most pisses her off:
"'Will you play something with a beat?' or 'Umm, can I look to see what you have?' Also the ever-charming comment, 'You're a great DJ, for a girl!'"

Idols:
"DJ Riz! One of the smartest, most soulful people I know."

In heavy rotation:
"Well . . . any disco on Thursdays. Prince is always a few songs away. On Fridays and Saturdays, 2Pac is a favorite. Also, people are liking, somewhat to my chagrin, anything on the Cash Money label . . . and we all know how I aim to please. . . ."

and written by big local names like David Schmader and Dina Martina); the place has the air of a cabaret

Helpful Hint: *Don't make a move on someone who's dancing alone. It's not that kind of place.*

BIO
Riz Rollins

ELISA SHEBARO

Who is he? Riz is a Seattle institution, having DJd for twelve years—currently, you can see him Fridays at the Backdoor Lounge.

Genre of choice: "I don't have a genre of choice," Riz declares. "I'm flexible; what I play is usually based on where I am at the time." For instance, Riz has been known to play everything from Brazilian music to "intelligent" drum 'n' bass to ska-house.

Favorite labels: "Right now, I'm goin' through a Latin thing," Riz says, adding that Ubiquity and Far Out are doing the best job of feeding this current fetish.

Idols: Henry Miller, Billy Strayhorn, Ricky Martin. "And, of course, Masa," Riz says of the local DJ and 1200 Records label head.

Wouldn't be caught dead playing: Disco. "It's a plague," he opines. "Some people won't get up unless you're playing Blondie, or even Deee-Lite, for that matter. It's a shame."

Jazz Clubs

Dimitriou's Jazz Alley
Belltown
2033 6th Ave, (206) 441-9729
Tues-Thurs 6 pm-midnight, shows at 8 pm & 10 pm; Fri-Sun 4:30 pm-midnight, shows at 8:30 pm & 10:30 pm
Major credit cards accepted; smoking okay; wheelchair accessible
Although the vibe in this pricey jazz club is far from ideal (it's housed on the ground floor of a sterile office building), there's no denying that Jazz Alley's calendar is consistently filled with world-class acts. Never mind the stuffy, suburban-like setting; dig the masters on stage. If you're on a tight budget, be sure to check out Ticket/Ticket at the Pike Place Market or Broadway Market for discounted day-of-show passes.
Crowd: *Jazz aficionados*
Ambience: *White tablecloths, intimate tables, and a dark balcony*
Helpful Hint: *The second set is often better than the first, as the musicians and the crowd get drunker and louder. So stick around and order another drink— if you can afford it.*

Tula's Restaurant & Jazz Club

Belltown
2214 2nd Ave, (206) 443-4221
Sun-Thurs 3 pm-midnight,
Fri-Sat 3 pm-1 am
Major credit cards accepted; smoking
okay; wheelchair accessible

ERIKA LANGLEY

The reasonably priced shows at this classy yet laid-back joint feature local and regional bands and lots of jam sessions, with national acts swinging through every few weeks or so. The music rarely strays outside traditional jazz boundaries, though you may run into some all-out blues or ethnic music on occasion; and if the grooves don't suit you, plenty of other entertainment options surround this comfy Belltown hangout.

Jazz and plaid: That's Seattle

Crowd: *College jazz students to old pros to first-timers*
Ambience: *A little brighter than the average jazz club, and much more spacious*
Helpful Hint: *Though it's a chatty place, show the musicians some respect by keeping your voice in check*

Rock Clubs

Breakroom

Capitol Hill
1325 E Madison, (206) 860-5155
Mon-Sat 4 pm-2 am
Cash only; smoking okay; wheelchair accessible

The arrival of the Breakroom in Seattle originally heralded the return of obscure hard-core punk in Seattle. Soon, though, the club's great location and stylish booker started stealing the good touring indie-punk bands from better-established Seattle clubs like the Crocodile and Sit & Spin. By now, the Breakroom holds its own both nationally and locally, offering a constant barrage of must-see shows. Like most clubs, the Breakroom is best at half-capacity, say on a weeknight with a relatively unknown band; the intimacy of the club is unparalleled. Sadly, the Breakroom is unbearable when it sells out—there's no escape from the music, access to the bar is impossible, and the Breakroom's unique ventilation keeps even the hardiest smokers' eyes watering. So plan carefully, and know that you can always slip around the corner to the Sea Wolf if you need a break.

Crowd: *Spanning the spectrum from indie rocker to indie rocker*

Ambience: *Tobacco sauna*

Helpful Hint: *If you can't stand smoke, don't bother*

Crocodile Cafe

Belltown
2200 2nd Ave,
(206) 441-5611
Mon-Sat 11 am-1:30 pm
Major credit cards
accepted; smoking
okay; wheelchair
accessible

JEFF STEWART

Crocodile: Blowing more than smoke up your ass

If Seattle is the record, the Croc is the turntable. Despite the inevitable complaints a town will have about any venue, it's undeniable that the Croc has the best sound and hosts most of the best bands. Even the food is good, although for big shows the restaurant space gets incorporated into a larger band room. The barroom doubles as a rotating art exhibit, which is handy because the drink lines can be looong. This club is to Seattle now what CBGB's was to New York then.

Crowd: *Spans the range of local music scenes and cliques; strictly non-dancers, unfortunately. There's a better-than-average percentage of musicians standing in line for beer.*

Ambience: *A strange snake-charmer/flaming-sheep motif, but it doesn't get in the way*

Helpful Hint: *If you become an insider, there's an upper deck to the club with the best seats in the house. Those seats are often claimed by the stars of rock: Peter Buck, Kim Warnick, and Cyndi Lauper have all been found hiding up here.*

The Sound Guy: An Appreciation

by Evan Sult

"I'VE BEEN PROVIDING THE FRAMEWORK FOR THE MATING RITUALS OF WESTERN SOCIETY FOR THE LAST 20 YEARS," announces Jim Anderson, sound guy for the Crocodile since the club opened in 1991. Then he laughs kind of shyly. "That's why people are always trying to bum a pen from me: 'I need to get a phone number from this chick.' No, I don't have any pens—they've all been stolen by people like you at this time of night long ago."

At first glance, Anderson's role in local music might seem incidental—he fiddles with levers, cranks the volume up, turns down the bass—but it's not. One of the crucial components of any real music town is at least one club where both audience and musician can reliably expect great sound. That's actually a pretty rare occurrence, and there aren't many clubs able to meet the challenge: The Croc ranks up there with the 9:30 Club in D.C., the Troubadour in L.A., and the Bowery Ballroom in New York. Anderson is attentive to his job in a disarmingly charming manner; he has a spotless memory for

CURT DOUGHTY

Jim Anderson: Attentive and prepared, with duct tape

musicians—local and national—and their sound-related quirks, as well as all the various bands and projects each has performed in at the Croc.

A big guy with a full beard, baseball cap, and strict band-shirt-and-flannel wardrobe, Anderson's easy to mistake for an old-school metalhead. Actually, he started in music as a touring trombonist in a drum-and-bugle corps. Eventually, a friend brought him to see the Dead Kennedys at the Showbox, where he cowered in the farthest corner of the room. That was when he went "from Chick Corea straight to hardcore," as he puts it. He missed classic rock entirely, which was probably for the best.

"If anything, it might actually help me," Anderson figures, "because I don't have any preconceived notions about the way rock should sound. I let the band define it for me. I can take an individual approach to every band, not like, 'These guys should sound like this'; I let 'em sound like what they want to sound like." That's an impressive statement, considering that the club hosts all sorts of bands, from ultra-loud blowouts like Juno and Six Finger Satellite to exercises in near-silence like Low, Elliott Smith, and Cat Power.

CURT DOUGHTY

The delicate touch

"That's the beautiful thing about what I'm doing at the Croc," says Anderson. "It's never the same two nights in a row. Just this last week, I had a beautiful, mellow female vocalist with acoustic guitar—Martha Wainwright—on Wednesday, and the Head Trauma Coalition, a couple of death metal bands, on Thursday. Country rock with the Picketts and Road Kings on Friday. Saturday was whatever you want to call Juno. They hate the word 'emo-core,' but that's some pretty powerful rock. I get to be a chameleon. Each different style of music requires a different approach from me. Solo acoustic guitar, I've got to use a very delicate touch; power rock, rock bands, I'm doing something completely different."

Anderson says he doesn't read a bunch of rock magazines or even follow music culture outside the Crocodile's front doors. So how did he know Juno hates the word "emo-core"?

"Oh," he laughs, "because Arlie said it onstage last night."

A sound guy who listens to the musicians so closely he can quote between-song banter the next day? Damned impressive.

Gibson's Restaurant

Downtown

116 Stewart St, (206) 448-6369

Daily 11 am-2 am

Major credit cards accepted; smoking okay; wheelchair accessible

Liquor + Chinese food + LOUD rock = Gibson's. Come nightfall, this venerable old restaurant undergoes a dramatic transformation: Rusty vans full of beat-up gear and amped-up young'uns start pulling up, in preparation for yet another night of blue-collar, punk-rock mayhem. Many a band has played its first gig here. And many a drunken singer-wannabe has debuted at Gibson's infamous punk-karaoke nights.

NICOLLE L. FARUP

Gibson's: That's some tongue

Crowd: *Fucking punk*

Ambience: *Punks fucking*

Helpful Hint: *Fuck off*

Graceland

Denny Regrade

109 Eastlake Ave E, (206) 381-3094

Daily 4 pm-2 am

Major credit cards accepted; smoking okay; wheelchair accessible

The walls are black; the floors are black; the bar is, yes, black. Elvis aficionados will find no blue-suede fix here. But the booker, Jason, is doing one hell of a job. Some of the best nights of your life will happen in this inefficient, charmless space: Blond Redhead, The Jicks, Hell's Belles, etc. If you have no phobia of concrete, scrape some clothes off the floor and bring enough friends to fill a leopard-print booth.

Crowd: *Indie teens by day, rock regulars at night*

Ambience: *This used to be the Off-Ramp, and beer spilled during those days is still stuck to the floor*

Helpful Hint: *Get there early to score one of the booths. Sit down and watch your favorite rock stars (you weren't going to dance anyway).*

Moore Theatre

Downtown

1932 2nd Ave, (206) 443-1744

Hours vary for specific shows

Cash only; smoking okay in lower bar only; wheelchair accessible if you call ahead

In 1907, the Moore Theatre was state of the art: marble columns, carved wood panels, vaulted ceilings with all the trimmings. Surprisingly, almost all the goodies have remained, giving shows at the Moore (especially under the influence of hallucinogens) a gothy, fantastic feeling. The site of Sub Pop's first Lame Fest; Alice in Chains, Mad Season, and Heart have all filmed concerts here.

Crowd: *Not a crowd-specific venue*

Ambience: *Turn-of-the-century opulence meets crowd-control carpeting*

Helpful Hint: *Yes, these are the nooks from which Eddie Vedder plunged in the "Even Flow" video*

Rainbow Bar & Grill

University District

722 NE 45th St, (206) 634-1761

Daily 3 pm-2 am

Major credit cards accepted; smoking okay; wheelchair accessible

'Twas a sad day back in the late '80s when this venue (then known as the "Fabulous Rainbow") changed hands. All manner of greats had graced its stage, from local upstarts such as Robert Cray and Soundgarden to now-legendary outta-towners such as the Neville Brothers and the Ramones. Even Sun Ra made an appearance. Subsequent transformations (strip club, Irish pub) gutted the room of its once ideal ambience, but the shows are back—along with the anything-goes bookings.

Crowd: *This crowd has one thing in common: marijuana*

Ambience: *Dive hippie joint*

Helpful Hint: *Comfortable venues for experimental jazz/avant-garde greats like Nels Cline and Eyvind Kang are rare; this is one of them*

Showbox

Downtown

1426 1st Ave, (206) 628-3151

Doors open an hour before showtime

Major credit cards accepted for drinks; cash only for tickets; smoking okay; wheelchair accessible

The Showbox is always a brides-maid, never a bride in the Seattle club scene. While it's the choice

ANNIE MARIE MUSSELMAN

Showbox: Curvy, bubbly, never a bride

venue for midsize national acts, it's not a destination when nobody good is playing. Which is a shame, because the room, with its curvilinear bar space, high ceilings, and gold-tipped columns, has the potential to be the most decadent club in town. But it often feels dingy or faded at the Showbox—like the old girl's let herself go a little saggy 'round the middle. And as beggars can't

be choosers, the Showbox mixes genres from roots to rock to rap and throws in dance nights weekly, leaving it without a loyal crowd of regulars. The place gets positively bubbly, though, when the door count inches toward capacity, and the Showbox's sound system can flex its considerable muscle.
Crowd: *Depends on who's playing, though downtown foot traffic adds unpredictability*
Ambience: *A little over the hill, but still making the effort*
Helpful Hint: *Parking down here is the worst. Figure out a ride, take the bus, or leave yourself an extra 45 minutes.*

Sit & Spin
Belltown
2219 4th Ave, (206) 441-9484
Sun-Thurs 9 am-midnight, Fri-Sat
9 am-2 am
Major credit cards accepted; smoking okay; wheelchair accessible
Popular opinion is divided on Sit & Spin's band room. Some folks call it intimate and homey, others liken it to being locked in the trunk of a compact car with a sub-woofer. The sound at Sit & Spin is always impeccable, even when it's loud, despite the cramped quarters and low ceiling in the band room. Unless you're lucky enough to score a booth, Sit & Spin's tiny floor, long bar lines, and red lights can be a claustrophobe's nightmare. There's an outer cafe space where you can sit and catch your breath, and—for the bold— wash your skivvies in the adjacent laundry room, just inches from the prying eyes of the Seattle music scene.
Crowd: *Slightly punk to stinking drunk*
Ambience: *Nope—it's a laundromat, remember?*
Helpful Hint: *Forget most of the board games; they're missing pieces*

Tractor Tavern
Ballard
5213 Ballard Ave NW, (206) 789-3599
Doors open an hour before showtime
Major credit cards accepted; checks okay; smoking okay; call in advance regarding wheelchairs (there's a step between the door and the show space, but the staff can lead you around the back way)
"The Trac," as it's affectionately known, is an unreconstructed, un-ironic retro rockabilly bar and club where the last half of the 20th century is generally frowned upon. The wood-plank floors and timber pillars only reinforce the country-dive-bar ethic of the patrons, who eschew most modern costumes in favor of head-to-heels vintage '50s clothes and accessories. Music is y'alternative, rockabilly, and swing, and the Trac is an internationally renowned folk joint. Be warned: If you're not in artfully scuffed leather cowboy boots and a checked shirt, and if you can't coax your locks into an Elvis pompadour or a prim flip, you might stand out a bit. The good news is,

folks gather at the Trac to have fun, and regardless of the pedigree of your ensemble, you'll be welcome to join the fast and furious swing dancing that erupts at most shows. Don't worry if your lindy hop is sloppy; just let the mood take you.

Crowd: *Expensive-vintage-clad rockabilly hipsters*
Ambience: *Is that Buddy Holly?*
Helpful Hint: *Most of the great folk musicians—the international legends— make it a point to play here. So does Mark Kozelek.*

Zak's Fifth Avenue Saloon

Downtown
206 Fifth Ave N, (206) 448-0961
Daily noon-2 am
Major credit cards accepted; smoking okay; wheelchair accessible

The lack of hard liquor puts Zak's a few notches below Gibson's on the dive-punk-bar scale—but only a few. Zak's picks up some slack with the sheer volume of no-name DIY bands that it books. Zak's also offers pool—and a basketball hoop! If delusions set in after a few, and you end up trying to dunk drunk, watch your step, and don't let yourself be hustled by any of the hard-up H-O-R-S-E sharks hanging around.

Crowd: *Something has already gone wrong in their young lives*
Ambience: *Dirty and loud*
Helpful Hint: *Here's where you'll be most likely to find the members of your next punk project*

....

BIO

....

Dan Cowan

Who is he? The Bill Graham of Ballard (Tractor Tavern and Hattie's Hat impresario)

Why "The Tractor"?
"Well, we first opened as the 'Old Town Music Hall,' partly to appease our rock-fearing landlord—but soon found the name too limiting. We wanted to go beyond the traditional music the room was known for, and found our new moniker thanks to the painting by the bar."

CURT DOUGHTY

You've had some greats on your stage. Any favorite nights come to mind?
"I don't know where to start—there's so many, including most of the Americana/No Depression groups. . . . But some of the Citizens' Utilities shows were certainly special, because they were one of the first indie rock bands to come in and pave the way for others."

So what's your secret? Ballard Avenue's hopping these days!
"Things were quiet for a long time. We just persevered, and gradually things picked up. Fortunately, we don't have to deal with troublemakers or fights like they do downtown. That helps us keep it simple and direct our energies toward more important concerns— like the music."

All Ages

Liquor laws restricting minors from attending shows in Seattle will probably never catch up to the rest of the country; there's just some weird insecurity in this city that keeps adults from trusting kids. So, while kids all across the United States are getting stamped, strapping on wristbands, or otherwise abiding by liquor-control laws that allow minors, adults, and bands to peacefully coexist, Seattle's youth will have to take solace in the fact that, well . . . Seattle used to be an even worse place to be a young music fan. The Teen Dance Ordinance was a huge ball and chain on the ankles of show promoters, bands, and music fans for the last 15 years. While it's not gone, the TDO has been altered enough to make independent shows more likely—finally. Also, a recent change in the way clubs are allowed to do business made it possible for local rock venues to start offering early-evening all-ages action.

SAMANTHA APPLETON

Old Fire House Teen Center: Fun for under 21

ANNIE MARIE MUSSELMAN

Early Sets or Occasional All-Ages Shows:

Breakroom
Capitol Hill
1325 E Madison St,
(206) 860-5155

Crocodile Cafe
Belltown
2200 2nd Ave,
(206) 441-5611

DV8
Downtown
131 Taylor Ave N,
(206) 448-0888
(Not exactly all-ages;
this is Seattle's "premier
18 and over club")

Graceland
Denny Regrade
109 Eastlake Ave E, (206)
381-3094

I-Spy/Nation
Downtown
1921 5th Ave,
(206) 374-9492

Seattle Art Museum
Downtown
100 University St,
(206) 654-3100
(Saturday-night shows)

Showbox
Downtown
1426 1st Ave,
(206) 628-3151

Sit & Spin
Downtown
2219 4th Ave,
(206) 441-9484

All Ages Clubs

Dimitriou's Jazz Alley
(all ages except second set on Fri & Sat)
Downtown
2033 6th Ave, (206) 441-9729

Ground Zero
Bellevue
209 100th Ave NE, (425) 452-6119

Hi*Score Arcade
Capitol Hill
612 E Pine, (206) 860-8839

Moore Theatre
Downtown
1932 2nd Ave, (206) 448-4852

Old Fire House Teen Center
(a.k.a. Redmond Firehouse)
Redmond
16510 NE 79th St, (425) 556-2370

Paradox Theater
University District
5510 University Way NE, (206) 524-7677

Paramount Theatre
Downtown
911 Pine St, (206) 682-1414

Second Avenue Pizza
Belltown
2015 2nd Ave, (206) 956-0489

The Vera Project at Local 46
Belltown
2700 1st Ave at Cedar,
www.theveraproject.org

Breakdancers: Miguel and Marcus

by Brandy Chance

MIGUEL AND MARCUS SIT WITH ME AT THE ROUND TABLE READY TO TALK SHOP. "I've been dancing since I was six years old. Everything from jazz to hiphop," Marcus says. His passion for break-dancing began with the old movies: *Breakin' I, II,* and *III*. Marcus' older twin brothers were in the Seattle hiphop scene: "They introduced me to their friends and took me to the Powerplant," he says. At the age of 12, Marcus engaged in his first battle. The "Break-Aways" only had three people in their crew, but they were ready to battle. "I thought I was sup-

posed to dance like the movies," Marcus says. "I thought I was supposed to be '80s." Only after he'd faced his first battle did Marcus realize that the art of breakdancing had moved far beyond the movies he'd seen. He had some practicing to do.

Breakdancers in Seattle practice Mondays and Fridays at Jefferson Community Center on Beacon Hill. They occupy Hassleburg Hall, a large room walled with mirrors. The breakers scatter the room by skill level:

MARK DANCEY

It's an unspoken rule. The dancers range in age from five to 30 years old. Girls are becoming more involved in crews. They aren't there to look pretty; they're there to break.

Marcus is currently in Mad Crew, though he was never really accepted, while Miguel is in the Massive Monkees (a graffiti group). These two crews got beef with each other, Marcus says. Miguel says, "No man, the Mad Crew is just jealous."

Marcus and Miguel don't want the general public to know about their scene or to get involved; they want to keep it underground. They don't want people who don't understand their scene to start coming to events, just to watch the kids dance. "We don't want to see it become commercialized," they say. "We teach ourselves. We spend hours practicing, figuring what works and what doesn't. Bruising our entire bodies. It's an individual endeavor."

"People talk about hiphop like it's just music," Miguel says. "As the great KRS-One said, 'Hiphop is not something you listen to, it's something you live.'"

ERIKA LANGELY

Hiphop Clubs

Aristocrat's Club
Downtown
220 4th Ave S,
(206) 748-9779

Art Bar
Downtown
1516 2nd Ave,
(206) 622-4344

Bohemian Cafe
Downtown
111 Yesler Way,
(206) 447-1514

Cafe Arizona
Federal Way
2012 S 320th St,
(253) 529-0553

Doubletree Hotel Lounge
Sea-Tac
18740 International Blvd,
(206) 246-8600

DV8
Queen Anne
131 Taylor Ave N,
(206) 448-0888

HD Hot Spurs
Kent
315 Washington Ave S,
(253) 854-5653

I-Spy/Nation
Downtown
1921 5th Ave,
(206) 374-9492

Last Supper Club
Downtown
124 S Washington St,
(206) 748-9975

DJs & Hiphop Clubs

DJ nights are as ephemeral as summer around here-they flare up; they blossom and sparkle; and then they fade to a sweet, hay-scented memory. Several residencies have proven their staying power, however, and these tend to be linked to DJs whose personalities dictate the scene. There are a few clubs around Seattle you can count on for hiphop. Everything from clubs that are so terrible they're great (the lounge at the Doubletree Hotel in SeaTac) to truly terrific clubs (I-SPY) that give the city a heartbeat, in included in this list. But to know exactly what you're in for, call the clubs to inquire and check *The Stranger* for weekly updates.

DJs

Brian Lyons—House. Since he's the in-the-know proprietor of one of our city's best record stores (Beats International), Lyons tends to spin the best and brightest of what's out on vinyl right now. House is his first love, but he's not afraid to venture into other territories as well.

Donald Glaude—Breaks, House. Donald has gained quite the name for himself on the national rave circuit. His enthusiastic sets and penchant for hootin', hollerin', and shakin' his booty behind the tables surely contributes to his notoriety. He's booked for one-offs every time you turn around. Check your local rave-flyer source for details.

Eva—Drum 'n' Bass. She may be tiny, but listening to Eva deftly maneuver the needle from one hard jungle record to the next, you'll agree that girlfriend is one tough bitch.

Ginger Vaughn—House. She's come all the way from Indiana to spin the funky tech house. There's just one thing—please, no requests: "It's not that I don't want to play what the crowd wants to hear; I just like to be able to concentrate on the task at hand."

LSDJ—House, Breaks. LSDJ is not, as it may sound, some tripped-out rave DJ. Quite the opposite. LSDJ is one of the city's finest scratchers, and he can mix just about anything you put in front of him.

McGowan's Restaurant and Lounge
Renton
317 S Main St,
(425) 271-6644

Re-Bar
Downtown
1114 Howell St,
(206) 233-9873

Royal Esquire
Rainier Beach
5016 Rainier Ave S,
(206) 723-2811

Showbox
Downtown
1426 1st Ave,
(206) 628-3151

Sit & Spin
Downtown
2219 4th Ave,
(206) 441-9484

GRAFFITI ART: CAUSE B
PHOTO: ADAM L. WEINTRAUB

Lord Chillum—Drum 'n' Bass, Disco. Inspired by the royal first names of Count Basie and Prince Busters, Damion chose Lord for the first half of his DJ handle. Chillum "refers to the dub and down-tempo music I was playing at the time I created the name." Since then, Damion has mixed these genres and more, including soul, funk, reggae, and, in the last few years, drum 'n' bass.

Maxx Alexander and Alo—Drum 'n' Bass. If you have yet to check out the most consistent drum 'n' bass night in town, you're among a pretty small minority. The word has definitely gotten out about this gig, which features the loud, crowdshaking jungle of DJs Alo and Maxx Alexander. These two manage to draw a crowd that is both extremely devoted to the music and also interested in checkin' out the beautiful people who pack it in each week. A rare feat, indeed.

M.I.A.—Drum 'n' Bass. "Three and half years ago, I heard drum 'n' bass for the first time and it was like meeting the man I was going to marry," says Seattle junglist M.I.A. "I just knew. I was in love instantly, and my life has centered around this music ever since." If you're a voyeur, and I know you are, you won't want to miss M.I.A. and her true love in the throes of passion at various clubs around town every week.

DJ Naha—Hard-core, Techno, Breaks, Hiphop. As you can see, Naha's favorite genre is actually a mishmash of several. Hardcore, which she is notorious for spinning, is her pet project. "I'm going to prove to people that it's not all demonic and monotonous." Catch her Tuesday nights at Graceland.

Nasir—Down-tempo, House, Drum 'n' Bass. Thanks to Nasir, this city's mission to shirk its reputation as an all-rock, all-the-time town is well under way. Along with his Sweet Mother label and music collective of the same name, Nasir's doing more than his fair share of dance music P.R. here in Seattle. Oh, and he's a favorite wax master as well.

DJ Netti—Jungle, Drum 'n' Bass. Netti refers to his favorite genre, jungle, as his "weapon of choice." What a badass. You can find him brandishing this weapon at his old standby, Mondays at the Lobo Saloon, which Netti is proud to announce is now an open turntable night. That's right, kiddies, time to lug your crates on down and have a go at the wheels of steel.

ANNIE MARIE MUSSELMAN

Tits and ass on the dance floor . . . oh, baby!

MC Queen Lucky—Funk, Hiphop. "Anything with soul" spins Queen Lucky's wheels; and she's been spinning for quite a long stint at the Re-Bar. Thursday is Queer Disco, Saturday is Dyke Night. Just don't tell her she's a great DJ "for a girl."

Riz—Eclectic. Riz has been known to play everything from Brazilian music to "intelligent" drum 'n' bass to ska-house in the course of a single week. You can catch him on-air: KEXP 90.3 FM (7 pm-1 am Wednesdays); and on the station's electronic music specialty show, Expansions (Saturdays 9 pm-11 pm and Sundays 8 pm-10 pm).

Shane Hunt a.k.a. DJ Sureshot—Old-School Funk. "I like reggae; I like hiphop a lot; but mostly, it's old-school funk." DJ Sureshot has been preachin' the funky gospel since his first steady gig way back when (he played opening night at Re-Bar) and continues to spin the rare groove three nights per week.

Spencer Manio a.k.a Suspence. Known to simultaneously DJ and do the running man, Spencer is willing and able to spin any kind of wax, from Guitar Wolf to Neil Young to Jurassic 5. No matter what he's got rolling though, he'll be flipping it raw, creative, and underground hiphop style.

Tamara—Drum 'n' bass, Eclectic. Outside of her signature drum 'n' bass, Tamara plays, in her own words, "all sorts of down-tempo, weird, intelligent stuff. I'm also really into minimal techno right now." Don't go pigeonholin' this girl! Of her Eclectic night at Art Bar she says, "Last Friday was amazing! It just keeps getting better and better. We all get drunk together and have a good time." Can't beat that.

Trent Von—'80s, Disco, Top 40. There're plenty of people in town who think dance music's glory days began and ended in the 1980s. DJ Trent Von fuels their flame not once, but thrice weekly—every Tuesday, Wednesday, and Thursday—at Neighbours. Don't be mistaken, though: The man surely knows his way around current Top 40 dance music, too. Whatever makes for a good time makes for a set of Mr. Von's.

Wesley Holmes—House. One way to judge a DJ is by whether or not you can leave the dance floor when he or she is on the decks. Each weekend, Wesley challenges audiences to resist his charming, bouncy house mixes. As the packed dance floors that accompany all of his sets will attest, the man's a damn good DJ.

Hell for Leather!
My First Rock Show
by Dan Savage

"I'm getting sick of L.A. I'll be back soon."
—Courtney Love, to the crowd at KeyArena

A lot of people backstage at the Hole/Marilyn Manson show were wearing leather pants. I don't have anything against leather pants per se; on the right guy, leather pants give me the vapors. But leather pants are difficult

TIM SILBAUGH

to pull off, which makes them a fashion-don't for most people. And most people backstage at Key-Arena definitely fell into the leather-pants-fashion-don't category.

When she ran onstage, Courtney Love was wearing leather pants. Courtney, of course, falls into the leather-pants-fashion-do category, by virtue of her celeb status. The glitter in her hair and the droopy, sheer-black shift she was wearing over her pants, however, made her look like a young Stevie Nicks—at least that's what John Roderick (formerly of Western State Hurricanes and currently of Harvey Danger) told me. John was backstage, standing off to the side with me, and to his credit, John was not wearing leather pants. Since I'm not sure exactly who Stevie Nicks is or was, I had to take John's word for whether

Courtney looked like a young Miss Nicks.

I don't know much about rock and roll. Before Everett True talked me into seeing Hole live at the KeyArena, I'd somehow managed to avoid witnessing an entire live performance of that rock-and-roll music you kids today—like kids for the last 40 years—seem to like so much. Living in Seattle in the '90s, I occasionally stumbled into bars or clubs where a band happened to be playing, but I would stumble right back out as soon as the music started. A million years ago, I was at the Crocodile when that band-that-would-be-world-famous-and-whose-lead-singer-would-later-blow-his-brains-out-making-a-widow-of-Courtney-Love got up and played. I got up and left.

I've never paid much attention to the music that shaped and defined my generation's adolescence and young adulthood. When I listen to music, I listen to KIXI, or to my small collection of Broadway show tunes. I know,

TIM SILBAUGH

I know: I'm the world's biggest cliché, the fag musical theater queen, but what can I do? I like the original-cast recording of *Gypsy*. I find Ethel Merman's voice soothing. When I've had a crappy day, Stephen Sondheim lyrics make me feel better.

I think a lot of kids get into rock music the same way they get into cigarettes and coffee: They feign an interest. Wanting to seem older and more interesting, youngsters force themselves to consume coffee or cigarettes or rock music. They do it to fit in. After a while, they acquire a taste for black coffee or black lung or Black Sabbath. Aware that I was a hopeless geek who would never fit in, I stayed at home. I drank tea, didn't learn to smoke, and listened to show tunes. I never came to appreciate coffee, cigarettes, or rock and roll.

Something I do appreciate, however, is showmanship. The two things I enjoy most about Broadway musicals are the spectacle of the shows and the joy that musical comedy performers clearly derive from their work. When you watch pre-*Murder She Wrote* Angela Lansbury play Mrs. Lovett in Stephen Sondheim's *Sweeney Todd*, she looks like she's having fun, even when she's being thrown into an oven.

The same can't be said of rock-and-roll performers, judging from what I've seen flipping past MTV, and from what I saw at the Hole concert. Courtney and her band looked alternately indifferent and annoyed at having to perform. I didn't know quite what to expect from Hole, but I expected them to do more than just stand there and play. The only real performers at KeyArena were the lights, which jumped and turned and spun, and Courtney Love's personal assistant/flying monkey, a cute boy with long hair who ran onstage whenever Courtney needed a new guitar or a mic adjustment.

I stood by the side of the stage for her set, sometimes watching Courtney sing, but mostly checking out the cute boys being passed over the heads of the crowd. And even then I was bored. Who knew a rock-and-roll concert could be so dull? Why go to all the trouble of building a set (a couple of drops—one a red curtain, the other a garden with a fountain) and throwing all that light around if the performers are just going to stand there, doing nothing? I'll take a couple of comedic secondary characters and a cheesy kick-line over Ms. Love, her bandmates, and their unhummable "music" any day of the week.

Courtney did work the crowd like a Vegas pro, though. "We like Seattle," Courtney told us, and when someone tossed a flannel shirt onstage, she picked it up and put it on. "You guys, come on!" said Courtney, standing there in leather and flannel. "We can't do flannel anymore!" Very Wayne Newton.

Even the crowd's conspicuous displays of rebelliousness were lifeless: heavily controlled and choreographed. And the control was made possible by the cooperation of the "rebellious" crowd. A line of what looked like Marines stood along the front of the stage, separated from the crowd by four-foot-high metal barricades. Whenever the crowd tossed fellow audience members over the barricades, the Marines would stand them up, turn them around, and point them to the door. The tossed audience members would then dutifully march out.

A few people did get hurt, and halfway through Courtney's set, I wandered back into the first-aid area. Seven kids suffering from broken noses, jammed fingers, overdoses, and concussions were all laid out on couches. As I chatted with a paramedic, a girl was carried in by a couple of Marines: She'd been raped in the crush of the crowd. How often is someone raped at the Fifth Avenue or the Paramount? I wandered back out to the show, where cannons had shot brightly colored confetti all over the crowd.

Besides being bored out of my show-tune-loving gourd, I looked and felt out of place at KeyArena. I wasn't dressed for Hole or Marilyn Manson, so imagine my surprise when a sweaty, shirtless boy in the crowd leaned over the barrier and asked me—in my tennis shoes, unfashionable blue jeans, and Gap-fag T-shirt—if I was "with Marilyn Manson." This boy had a message for someone named "Twiggy," and wanted to know if I could deliver it. Twiggy would be in Manson's dressing room, he told me. Not knowing who Twiggy was, and knowing I'd have an easier time getting into the Navy SEALs than getting past Manson's security detail, I told the nice young man—blue hair, black lips, and pierced nipples—that I wasn't "with" Manson. I was "with" Courtney.

"Fuck her!" he screamed at me, giving me the finger. "Fuck Courtney Love! Fuck her! You tell her I said, 'Fuck you!'" (Hey, Courtney: The blue-haired boy with pierced tits in the audience said, "Fuck you!")

Courtney seems to have that effect on young misogynists. On our way into the concert, we spotted a few straight-boy picketers outside KeyArena handing out Courtney-killed-you-know-who fliers. During the show, someone threw a shoe at Courtney. In a rare unscripted moment, she picked up the shoe and asked how its former owner was going to get home in the rain with one shoe on.

Eventually I positioned myself at the exit from the mosh-pit cattle chute, where all the boys tossed over the barricades had to pass to get back into KeyArena's seating area. The stink of teen B.O. was heady (all that Mountain Dew and pizza passing through their pores), but the highlight of my evening was getting to meet Matt Cameron, the drummer from the late Soundgarden. I'd seen some pictures of Soundgarden around the office, and always thought the drummer was really cute.

Besides Courtney, Matt was the only person at KeyArena who could have pulled off leather pants. But alas for me, he was in wool.

Restaurants

SEATTLE REMAINS SUCH A SNUG LITTLE TOWN that the owners of Capitol Hill's Satellite Lounge can get away with describing the BLT on their menu as "Brian Leroy Taylor's favorite sandwich," and feel comfortable that you will know who Brian Leroy Taylor is (he's the owner of BLT Screenprinting, which silkscreens a lot of rock posters). We present these listings as a conglomeration of some tried-and-true favorites in our small town, mixed with some new restaurants that seem as though they might stick around. Of course, the scene is also notoriously fickle, so be sure to call first and check whether these places actually still exist. Prices reflect menu price range, from the cheapest morsel—including appetizers and side dishes—to the most expensive meal on the menu.

Quick Fix

Abe's Place
West Seattle
2310 California Avenue SW, (206) 933-7398
True, meatballs are not usually considered a Turkish culinary staple. If you ask Mehmet Ocak, the owner and sole proprietor of Abe's Place restaurant in West Seattle, where he got his fabulous recipe, he'll grin coyly and say, "I made it up." About an inch and a half in diameter, and aglint with an

orangish-yellow patina of savory sauce, Ocak's delicately-seasoned pure-beef orbs are studies in righteous simplicity. Ocak's famous sandwiches receive two each of these wondrous meatballs, heaped up and then smashed down between two toasted French buns slathered in a melted cheddar-mozzarella melange. Ocak's Barbecue Beef sandwich is, alternately, piled high with only the tenderest, juiciest chunks of marinated meat and swimming in a tangy sauce, presenting a tantalizing vision of excess. Ocak also makes a nice pepperoni sandwich for $3, as well as offering side orders of hot cheese and/or garlic bread. Abe's Place (named in honor of Ocak's son Abraham, who passed away in 1999) is an entirely outdoor eatery. The spacious patio is surfaced in beautiful old red brick, and bordered by a low wooden gate that fronts the street.

$2.50-$4; daily 11 am-8:30 pm; checks okay; smoking okay

Aladdin Gyro-Cery
University District
4139 University Way NE, (206) 632-5253
Wedged tightly into a narrow space on University Way ("the Ave"), the Gyro-Cery turns out supercharged gyros, which stand with military pride as the finest available in the metropolitan area. Brown, steamy meat shavings lie within the omnipresent paper gyro wrapper, a warm, beige pita wrapped like a blanket. Could all this flavor come from just yogurt, cucumber, garlic, and parsley? Ponder this question while strolling the garbage-strewn Ave or sitting in the fake grotto at the back of the Gyro-Cery. Throw in the Gyro-Cery's ample-portioning philosophy, and you've got a true value blowout.

$3-$6.99; daily 11 am-2 am; major credit cards accepted; smoking okay

Bimbo's Bitchin' Burrito Kitchen
Capitol Hill
506 E Pine St, (206) 329-9978
Velvet paintings, giant papier-mâché puppets, enormous plastic fruits, and other garage-sale miracles deck out this tiny burrito shack that shares a door with the Cha Cha Lounge. Burritos do the job and fill the belly. The peppered shredded beef and garlic rosemary potatoes stand up and shout. Food arrives quickly and is cheap and generally filling, albeit uneven in quality. Be sure to check out the black-lit bathroom. The folks who run this place are hip, honest, and sassy: highly specialized, like the décor. Do not, as did one potential customer, ask the underpaid cooks to play your new Gipsy Kings CD or to turn down the hiphop—they will tell you, in their very truthful way, exactly where the Gipsy Kings can stick it. Bimbo's is a great place to hang out on the cheap and hide from the rain, nursing a Tecate and a taco.

$1.95-$7.95; Mon-Thurs noon-11 pm, Fri-Sat noon-2 am, Sun 2 pm-10 pm; major credit cards accepted; full bar available from the Cha Cha Lounge next door; no smoking

Catfish Corner

Central District

2726 E Cherry St, (206) 323-4330

Even with a worn-out facility, Catfish Corner continues to dish out dependable and satisfying Southern cooking. With Southern farm-raised catfish as the showcase item, the food's quality remains consistently high, while prices hover at bargain levels. The mild catfish fillet dinner shows off a generous portion of fish jacketed by a crunchy cornmeal coating, free of greasiness and dry without being burnt. The usual Southern sides dot the menu: A nice serving of fries runs 75¢; cornbread muffins are a steal for a mere quarter; and the tasty collard greens are far less buttery and salty than on previous visits, marking the Corner's ability to adapt to customers' changing expectations. Dinner items allow a choice between potato salad (yay!) or coleslaw (boo!), and come with slow-cooked beans of which legends are made.

75¢-$9.95; Mon-Fri 11 am-10 pm, Sat noon-10 pm; cash only; no smoking

E&M Grocery

Central District

1123 Martin Luther King Jr. Way,

(206) 323-8360

Ethel and Melvin specialize in Cajun deep-fried catfish and cod. Sidle up to the takeout window and inhale the abstruse scent of chitlins, mountains of hush puppies, and fried okra rising hot and crisp. The sides that Ethel doles out exceed side-size portions in every way. Gumbo is brewed so deep and dark that crab legs clack, and sausage appears more frequently on the spoon than rice. There's enough meat to stand up to the 22-ouncers available at the connecting grocery. Made to order and not overly greasy, E&M's fried chicken confidently balances the meat-to-crispy-skin ratio.

DAVID WALEGA

E&M: Soulful recipes straight from Alabama

And the seasoned fries are no garnish. These people are professionals.

$1.85-$8.99; Mon-Fri 10:30 am-10 pm, Sat-Sun 10 am-7 pm; cash only; beer available at grocery

Hall's Mister Bar-B-Que

Ballard

7302 1/2 15th Ave NW, (206) 706-9429

When you walk into Hall's Mr. Bar-B-Que, you're hit by the aroma of greens, corn bread, and sauce. With Phillip "Dino" Hall standing behind the counter, you'll feel like you just got home. The ribs ($6 for a half-pound)—prone and dark from their time well spent in Dino's smoker/roaster—shimmer in the bright Ballard sun. The chicken (a steal at $4.95 for a semi-bird), cut attractively to offer a tempting white-meat cross section, looks as though it were laid out by a food magazine designer. Also worthy of mention is the appropriately peppery potato salad, long on flavor and short on mustard—the natural enemy of any potato salad.

$4.95-$8.95; Tues-Sat 11 am-8 pm; cash only; no alcohol; smoking okay

Honeyhole Sandwiches
Capitol Hill
703 E Pike St, (206) 709-1399

You think it's silly to get all excited about a dinky li'l sandwich shop? Trust us. Two of the cutest boys God ever dropped on this Earth invaded the former home of Beyond the Edge Cafe, a stomping ground for Seattle's SM community, and they scrubbed it free of mysterious stains and bondage accoutrements, painted it yellow, and commenced making sandwiches. Really good sandwiches. *Really* good—certainly tasty enough to obscure the fact that people used to hang by their nipples from the ceiling of this very restaurant.

JOEL SCHOMBERG

Hot dogs: You know you want one

Some of these luscious little gems are (too) cutely named after *Happy Days* references, e.g., "The Gooch" (hot roast beef, red onions, and smoky cheddar on a French roll) and the downright deelish "Chachi's Favorite" (pepper turkey, Havarti, tomato, and ranch on a French roll). You can also opt for the soup 'n' half-sandwich combo, or one of the six all-veggie options. Potsie would be proud.

$4.95-$6.25; daily 10 am-5 pm; major credit cards accepted; bottled beer; smoking outside

Hot Dog Stands
A few hot dog stands around Seattle warrant mention. The first is the stand in front of the Showbox. Operated in the evening hours when drunken show-goers crave something they can cradle, this stand consistently offered up well-cooked, beefy dogs on every one of 15 or 20 trial visits. Not only that, but they make something which, when first described, sounds repulsive, but turns out to be sublime: the cream cheese hot dog. This hot dog, nicely

cooked, appears in a crispy bun smeared with cream cheese—simple enough to hold up as a ritual, rich enough to visit unexpectedly, like the Holy Ghost.

Second place mention goes to the **Wonder Freeze** booth found in the North wing of the Pike Place Market. This window, usually manned by a salesperson of New Yorkian impatience, serves up juicy, nitrite-bursting Kosher and Chicago style dogs, with piles of pretty much whatever traditional condiment you could hope for. They also offer fine milkshakes. If you are a vegetarian, you will have to wait several long, agonizing minutes for the tofu dog to cook up, and you will also have to suffer the salesperson's contempt.

Other fine hot dogs can be found at **Shorty's Coney Island** in Belltown, and up on Madison and 10th, at the little hut outside The Paint Box. Hot dogs found at bars, like **Linda's**, are often quite good in a traveling-salesman-dinner kind of way (eaten on the run and with lots of beer). The hot dog, like faith, can be carried with you wherever you go.

Madame K's Pizza Bistro
Ballard
5327 Ballard Ave NW, (206) 783-9710
This narrow, hole-in-the-wall cafe is haphazardly decorated with kitchen and bordello paraphernalia, giving it a warm, sensuous character. All the details are here: twinkling lights, romantic melodies that drift through the air, charming waitresses, and cute wine glasses. As for the food? Weeks will go by and you'll still be fantasizing about the "Artie Parmie Pie," a rich, creamy pizza that drips garlic, artichokes, and parmesan. The "Saucy Sassy Angel Hair" is unusual and tasty, the salads are large and satisfying, and the "Chocolate Chip Orgasm" ($4.79)—vanilla ice cream atop a thick pancake of cookie dough—actually lives up to its name.
$7.50-$18.50; Mon-Thurs 5 pm-whenever, Fri 5 pm-10:30 pm, Sat 4 pm-10:30 pm, Sun 4 pm-9 pm; major credit cards accepted; checks okay; beer and wine; smoking on back patio

OK Corral
Greenwood
8733 Greenwood Ave N, no phone
You'll get a snootful of wonderful smoky aroma at Greenwood's friendly OK Corral, as smokers and grills are set up right in front—cooking chicken, ribs, and hot links in one of the most honored of culinary traditions. For $8 per dinner, you get a choice of smoky and moist pork ribs, tender chicken, hot links with springy exterior (they pop when you bite 'em), or fried catfish with a crunchy corn meal jacket. The ribs' slow-smoked flavor hints at the unrivaled smokiness of Hawaiian *kalua* pig. Like the chicken and links, the ribs are smooched by a remarkable and complex BBQ sauce. Lay down three more dollars and you get the "Hook-Up," a monstrous combo.
$8-$11; daily 5 pm-10 pm; cash only; no alcohol; no smoking

Pecos Pit BBQ

Industrial Seattle, kitty-corner from Starbucks headquarters

2260 1st Ave S, (206) 623-0629

Eating at the Pit is a lesson in masculinity: not so much "dining out" as "fueling up" deep in the flatlands of resolutely undecorated industrial Seattle. During every timed lunch break, a long line of people shift back and forth, hungry. There are two order-taking windows where you shout your pick of the minimal menu: beef or pork, shredded or chopped; beans or chips; fountain sodas, one size fits all. Maybe a hot link on the side or inside the sandwich. Sauce: mild, medium, or hot. Those privileged with a bit of time can sit at one of the outdoor picnic tables, eating their sandwiches with the provided plastic spork. Eat with your hands and you've got saucy carnage on your face and fingers. Pecos Pit has been making these sandwiches for 20 years—there used to be other things on the menu, like coffee, but they cut that out.

$1-$5.55; Mon-Fri 11 am-3 pm; cash only; no alcohol; smoking: hell yes

La Panzanella

Capitol Hill

1314 E Union St, (206) 325-5217

It's best to visit La Panzanella on a sunny Saturday, when the smell of freshly mown grass reminds you that there's life in the city. La Panzanella grills incredibly good and good-looking deli sandwiches on focaccia, salami on tiny baguettes, and eggplant on round Italian bread. La Panzanella is all about Italy, and Italy means cheese-rich pastas; peppers broiled until tender; miniature bottles of spicy, carbonated beverages; fruit granitas; and layered baked desserts, downy with powdered sugar. La Panzanella is a casual haven. During World Cup Soccer Championships, watch out for bitter Italian men drinking dark, dark coffee.

$2-$6; Mon-Fri 7:30 am-6:30 pm, Sat 8:30 am-5:30 pm; checks okay; no alcohol; no smoking

Paseo Caribbean Restaurant

Fremont

4225 Fremont Ave N, (206) 545-7440

Paseo's consistently laudable sandwiches and superb dinner entrées warrant multiple visits, and the moderate pricing makes coming back even easier. Sandwiches are the heart and soul of Paseo, and whether it's pork, chicken, or prawns, they all come packed with vigorous flavor, built out of fine bread, fat slices of grilled onions, and lots of deep-green cilantro, all sauced with a seasoned mayo. Dinners (also built around chicken, fish, and pork) mount the stage and present a more elegant face than the lunchtime fare, and all are accompanied by gorgeous black beans, bright white rice, a seasonal vegetable, and a small salad with punchy dressing. The restaurant's saltbox size encourages takeout, but in the summer, two outside tables are provided.

$6.95-$8.95; Tues-Sat 11:30 am-9 pm; cash only; no alcohol; no smoking (except maybe at outside tables)

Piroshki on Broadway

Capitol Hill

124 1/2 Broadway E, (206) 322-2820

A tiny little shop across the street from Dick's, Piroshki on Broadway is one of Capitol Hill's best little secrets. Besides the sweet wit of the Russian owners themselves, and the delicious pockets of potato, cheese, meats, cabbage and the like, Piroshki on Broadway has one genius stroke: it's open 'til 11 pm. Which means that you might be able to stave off yet another evening run to Dick's by stopping in here to grab some inexpensive, tasty piroshkis or pierogies, and maybe even a cup of borscht. There's a beautifully hand-lettered sign on the wall that describes how the ingredients have been modified from the traditional recipe for a more healthy meal. Throw in the clientele's propensity for loud cell-phone conversations in Russian, and you have a brilliant little shop worth making a habit of.

$1.85-$3.45; Mon-Sat 7 am-11 pm, Sun 7 am-10 pm; major credit cards accepted; no alcohol; no smoking

Red Mill Burgers

Phinney Ridge

312 N 67th St, (206) 783-6362

Burgers are possibly the world's most popular food—though around these parts they are surprisingly hard to find. Red Mill serves a burger with sautéed hot peppers, thick-sliced bacon, and grilled onions,

ELISA SHEBARO

Red Mill Burgers: Cell phone free

with a choice of regular yaller (cheddar) or pepper jack, juicy and hot. To Red Mill's credit and fame, they've got THE BEST ONION RINGS dang near on the whole planet. These corn-meal-crusty, spicy fried rings will make you forget about most folks' French fries. When that incendiary ring slides outta its crusty skin and onto your drool-soaked chin, you'll only holler with greasy-faced glee.

$2.99-$4.89; Tues-Sat 11 am-9 pm, Sun noon-8 pm, checks okay; no alcohol; no smoking; NO CELL PHONES!

Roxy's Deli

Belltown

1909 1st Ave, (206) 441-6768

Crowded and bustling, Roxy's certainly looks and feels like a New York City deli. But in a notable departure from authenticity, diners are greeted warmly. The hot pastrami sandwich pops with flavor and is served on a chewy light rye. The classic Reuben, which features corned beef, sauerkraut, Swiss cheese, mustard, and Thousand Island dressing, presents a voluminous challenge: Roxy's meat slicing is a little on the giant side, with thick-cut pieces of corned beef stacked high and proud. Each sandwich comes with stunningly crisp pickles—these are the real deal—which snap with juicy vigor. Roxy's is set up primarily for takeout, so seating is limited; but you can easily find a cozy spot to enjoy your food among the nearby parks and benches.

$5-$7; Mon-Sat 11 am-4 pm, major credit cards accepted; no alcohol; no smoking

Salvadorean Bakery

West Seattle

1719 SW Roxbury St, (206) 762-4064

The Salvadorean Bakery opens early every day, but whenever you show up you'll find the coffee fresh and hot. We counted 30 varieties of pastry being offered, including guava turnovers (with cream cheese), jalapeño rolls, Salvadorean éclairs, and relampagos (eggy, multilayered pastry puffs filled with fluffy, not-too-sweet Salvadorean custard). Along with pastries, the Salvadorean Bakery offers real breakfasts: beans and eggs with sour cream and tortillas in varying combinations. The rest of the menu includes various choices of pupusas (two for $3)—small, stuffed, rice-flour patties, which appear to be grilled, though the pert counter boy assured me that they are baked like tiny pizzas. But it's the Salvadorean Bakery's tamales ($1.75 each) that are truly dreamy. They're plump, oblong shapes of steamy, buttery masa, filled with chicken, pork, or elote—a purée of sweet corn topped with sour cream, steamed inside a banana leaf.

ANNIE MARIE MUSSELMAN

Second Ave Pizza: What you need

$2.95-$8.95; daily 8 am-9 pm; major credit cards accepted; no alcohol; no smoking

Second Avenue Pizza

Downtown

2015 2nd Ave, (206) 956-0489

Like a rabid dog needs water, like a newborn needs a hug, pizza toppings—in order to perform their gustatory rodeo antics—need a crust as good as Second Avenue Pizza's. The cheese pizza successfully balances design and flavor—no gimmicks here, just solid crafting and proper heating. Ditto for the pepperoni, which zigs and zags its way into your heart. The bountiful salad teems with tang and zest-mixed greens, walnuts, (yet more) blue cheese, kalamata olives, and tomatoes add up to one hell of a salad bargain. And it's all in the heart of downtown/Belltown madness.

$1.75-$13; Mon-Thurs noon-10 pm, Fri noon-1 am, Sat 6 pm-1 am; local checks okay; beer and wine; smoking okay

Villa Victoria Catering

Madrona

1123 34th Ave, (206) 329-1717

Snuggled up to Gene's Barber shop, across the street from Conley Hat Mfg Co in Madrona, a tiny kitchen, swampy with moist heat, is kicking out perfect tamales, boasting silky white corn dough that actually tastes like corn. Naomi Andrade Smith has run a catering business out of this compressed kitchen for the past three years, finally opening up her window the public due to overwhelming demand. In Smith's upbringing, Oklahoma's ubiquitous greens and biscuits met Mexican home cooking, resulting in the creative takes on Mexican food Smith slides out her takeout window. A glass deli case hosts hefty platters of these tasty treats, fillings ranging from black bean to fish mole. You can buy 10, or 15, or 100, and take them home and eat them every day. The more traditional shredded pork tamale flares with roasted chiles, but couldn't beat the mushroom/chile/cheese creation. For vegetarians there is an irresistible grilled adobo tofu tamale; and, finally, you can't go wrong with the tender, sweet carne asada, sliced miraculously thin by the Villa's resident butcher who also washes dishes.

$2-$24.95 [pre-packaged dinner for 4]; Tues-Sat 11:30 am-7 pm (take-out only); major credit cards accepted; no alcohol; no smoking

Ethnic

Afrikando

Belltown

2904 1st Ave, (206) 374-9714

As you enter this Senegalese restaurant, you feel that you are about to embark on an authentic African experience: music, maps, masks, pieces of art. Senegalese cooking combines the flavors and methods of preparation of many countries, including France, West Africa, and the Middle East. You might begin your foray with akra, a plate of homemade fritters made with black-eyed peas, served under a spicy red sauce with baby shrimp; or a plate of debe, nuggets of grilled lamb seasoned with an aromatic blend of cumin, coriander, and cloves. But the king of all dishes is "Thiebu Djen," a wonderful, juicy steak of pristine halibut, stuffed with parsley and habanero peppers and stewed in a delicious, rich tomato sauce with eggplant, carrots, cassava, and cabbage.

$8.95-$17.95; Mon-Fri 11 am-2:30 pm, Mon-Sat 5 pm-10 pm, Sun 4 pm-9 pm; major credit cards accepted; checks okay; no alcohol; no smoking

Bamboo Garden Vegetarian
Lower Queen Anne
364 W Roy St, (206) 282-6616

Just one street north of Seattle Center, on a lot adorned with bamboo shoots, lies Bamboo Garden. The friendly staff and comfortable, unassuming atmosphere make this restaurant a must for vegetarians and vegans, and it's an entirely worthwhile change of pace for the curious. Inside, punked-out high-school vegans and kosher-conscious octogenarian anarchists enjoy plates of "chicken" and "pork" prepared with fresh vegetables or fried taro root. The focus is on your health: All "meat" items on the extensive menu are soy or vegetable protein substitutes, many dishes are "heart-friendly," and brown rice is always available. Significantly less healthy—but much, much higher in alcohol content—is the sake, guaranteed to have you and your dining companion downright giddy about having to walk back to the bus stop in the cold rain without an umbrella.

$7.95-$13.95; daily 11 am-10 pm; major credit cards accepted; local checks okay; full bar; no smoking

Buen Gusto
Greenwood
301 NW 85th St, (206) 784-4699

No matter what, an El Salvadoran restaurant feels uncomfortably staged in Greenwood. But as soon as food is served, you'll be relieved of meditating on cultural causality. A whole fish is crispy and succulently flavored; the pupusas (appetizers) and anything with plantain in it are pleasing as punch. Carnal pleasures have a way of pacifying moral conundrums; delicious food is one such panacea. Order another beer and exchange grins with the waitress.

$1.50-$6.95; Tues-Sun 11:30 am-9 pm; local checks okay; beer and wine; no smoking

Dom Polski Zaprasza (Polish Home Association)
Capitol Hill
1714 18th Ave, (206) 322-3020

Dom Polski is not so much a restaurant as a happening. Once a week, friends and acquaintances gather to socialize, eat, and drink Polish beer at the most beautiful bar on Capitol Hill. Ordering the special Polish platter generally results in almost instantaneous service of cabbage rolls (stuffed with spiced beef and smothered in delicious red sauce), pierogis (dumplings stuffed with meat, or potato and cheese, and the very best with sauerkraut and mushrooms), whipped potatoes with dill, and kielbasa. Beefsteak tartar arrives on a paper plate, raw and red and beautiful. Perfectly crisped, deep brown on the outside, melt-in-your-mouth on the inside, the potato pancakes come with sour cream and are served piping hot. If you're lucky, you'll catch a glimpse of the fabled ham hocks, rising at least ONE FOOT IN HEIGHT from the plate.

$5.50-$14.50; Fri 7 pm-11 pm; cash only; full bar; no smoking

Doong Kong Lau Hakka Restaurant

Greenwood

CURT DOUGHTY

9710 Aurora Ave N, (206) 526-8828

Don Polski: You like meat, yes?

Doong Kong Lau's cuisine is a compromise between the spicy northern cuisine of Szechwan, Hunan, and the tamer Cantonese. The massive menu (180 items) even includes Hakka (Chinese "Gypsy") dishes. The food gets its intense flavor by using strong stocks and special seasonings, while eschewing MSG and peppers. Start with homemade vegetable pot stickers, which are aromatic and tender. The boneless, stuffed mochi rice duck arrives all brown and crispy, produced by a complicated Hakka technique of marinating and frying and hanging and marinating and frying again.

$8-$12; Mon-Fri 10:30 am-11 pm, Sat-Sun 9:30 am-11 pm; major credit cards accepted; beer and wine; smoking okay

Gyorgo's Gyros

Greenwood

608 N 105th St, (206) 781-5514

Gyorgo's Gyros sports a sign like an old movie theater marquee, has a ceiling lit like an upside-down swimming pool, and offers both couch-style seating and a soda-fountain-type bar—but when it comes to the food, Gyorgo's identity is anything but confused. Gyros, horiatiki salad, shish kebabs, and generous helpings of feta are ready to wrap your tongue in their delightful selves. Order at the counter, take a seat at a couch, and await your bacchanalia while gazing at the strange Odyssey-themed mural. This is Greek food at its simplest, cheapest, and arguably best. (P.S. Don't expect the service to be as fast as at-the-counter ordering would imply.)

$2-$7; Mon-Sat 11:30 am-8 pm; major credit cards accepted; local checks okay; no smoking

ANNIE MARIE MUSSELMAN

Hana Sushi: Let's just say the fish is very fresh

Hana Sushi
Capitol Hill
219 Broadway E, (206) 328-1187

Hana can't be beat for trustworthy, bountiful, and inexpensive Japanese food. Although sashimi, udon noodle dishes, and various teriyaki choices are offered, the bento medleys provide the best assortment of fresh, nutritious, and colorful dishes. Hana's bento is built around a centerpiece of sushi (chilled and mellow tuna and salmon, plus the perennially irrelevant California roll). The sushi is accompanied by a small and artful piece of salmon teriyaki, along with predictable yet pleasing tempura-battered shrimp, pork, and oysters. Miso soup and a huge bowl of steamed rice bookend this grand menu selection, typical in its largesse. Despite Hana's fairly hectic pace, the efficient service and elegant touches (such as the artistic flower arrangements) make it a pleasant oasis.

$5.25-$13.25 (sushi priced à la carte); Mon-Sat 11 am-10 pm, Sun 4 pm-10 pm; major credit cards accepted; sake and wine; no smoking

Il Gambero
Belltown
2132 1st Ave, (206) 448-8597

You might walk past this place a hundred times before noticing it—it's probably the only restaurant in Belltown that doesn't call attention to itself. But Italians don't need to be flashy to get respect, and Il Gambero will eventually muscle anyone into submission because they serve the best chicken Marsala in the city. Period. The chicken swims in perfectly formed red wine sauce and mushrooms, looking as good as a bodyguard in leather. You can get a side of pasta (served with just the right amount of sauce) for a little extra. Il Gambero isn't as "romantic" as it would like to think—the wine does more than the atmosphere—but if you arrive early you can have a cocktail in the Volare Room, Il Gambero's slender, low-lit side-bar with a wonderfully kitschy name.

$11.95-$23.95 entrées (seafood at market prices); Mon-Sat 5 pm-10:30 pm; major credit cards accepted; full bar; smoking okay; reservations recommended

Jamjuree

Capitol Hill

509 15th Ave E, (206) 323-4255

Lately, 15th Avenue E on Capitol Hill has been coming alive in an awkward, even adolescent way, with boutiques and junk stores vying for space. Meanwhile, Jamjuree keeps a low profile, consistently serving up great Thai cuisine to its knowing customers. The menu here is not for veg-heads: Meats reign supreme, awash in curries that seem a notch spicier than other restaurants' counterparts.

$4.95-$11.95; Mon-Fri 11:30 am-3:30 pm & 5 pm-9:30 pm; Sat-Sun 5 pm-10 pm; major credit cards accepted; beer and wine; no smoking; wheelchair accessible

The Kingfish Cafe

Capitol Hill

602 19th Ave E, (206) 320-8757

"Suhhthun"—said with a lazy drawl—is the operative word for all things at the Kingfish. The typically Southern Po' Boy here is an astonishing sandwich, served on a long roll with green tomato tartar, marinated tomatoes, and shredded lettuce arranged bright as confetti. Other items are equally

BIO

The Lovely Ladies of the Kingfish

Who are they? Sisters Laurel and Leslie Coaston are owners, sister Natalie Coaston is a co-worker, and Kenyetta Carter is the chef at the Kingfish Cafe

C. TAYLOR

What do you guys love about the business?
"We work with a young and gifted waitstaff and an incredibly involved and enthusiastic kitchen. We get the chance to introduce contemporary Southern cuisine to a broader segment of the population."

What's frustrating about running a restaurant?
"People with no sense of fun [when they're] eating out!"

It's funny that while you need customers to survive, they can also be the worst part. . . .
"But without sounding cheesy, we've made great friends in the neighborhood—our guests are the best part of this crazy business."

What inspires you?
"Mary Laura Elizabeth, [the Coaston sisters'] great-great-great-grandmother, who was born into slavery

and died a free woman, and Minnie Mitchell, [the Coaston sisters'] great-grandmother, who acquired commercial property through years of hard work and determination. And our third cousin Langston Hughes, poet laureate of Harlem. Also, working with a dynamic, almost all-woman staff. They all have something to contribute from their travels or child-hoods—[they] help define the menu."

promising: Johnny Rebel's Pork Sandwich, Down-Home Mac and Cheese, Daddy Delacroix's Mo Betta Club. Dinner can be prolonged by a generous appetizer of Black River Peel-and-Eat Shrimp, marinated in lime, allspice, and ginger, and Kingfish House Crab and Catfish Cakes. You cannot resist the My Way or the Highway Buttermilk Fried Chicken, which is as good a fried chicken as you're likely to get outside of your Auntie Vidalia's chicken…

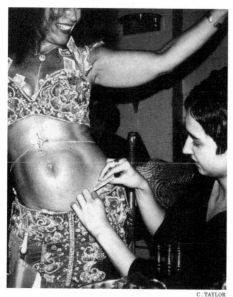

iffen you lucky enough to have one. Hint: Get there earrrrrly. $5.25-$15.95; Mon, Wed-Fri 11:30 am-2 pm & 6 pm-10 pm; Sat 6 pm-10 pm; brunch Sun 11 am-2 pm; checks okay; full bar; no smoking

C.TAYLOR

Kolbeh: That's some spicy stew!

Kolbeh

Industrial Seattle
1956 1st Ave S, (206) 224-9999
You'd hardly expect to find a sumptuously decorated Persian restaurant on the ugly strip just south of Safeco Field, but Kolbeh has been serving up its exquisite fare for the last decade, largely unnoticed by hot-dog-lovin' Mariners fans. And what a feast those baseball fans are missing: spicy stews, barbecued kebabs, slow-roasted meats, and exotically spiced beverages and desserts. The "Kabob Joojeh" is a giant skewer of remarkably tender and juicy Cornish game hen marinated in lemon, saffron, and onion juice; the "Khoresht Bomeyh," a vegetarian, chicken, or beef stew, need not be so modestly described on the menu as "maybe the best way of cooking okra"—the stewed vegetables are perfectly complemented by the intensely flavored tomato sauce. Kolbeh's Friday and Saturday nights are filled up with Iranians and others, there to enjoy the belly dancers and the amazing food (after 10 pm there is an extra $10 cover to stay for the dancing).
$5.99-$16.99; Sun-Thurs 11 am-10 pm, Fri-Sat 11 am-2 am; major credit cards accepted; beer and wine

Kusina Filipina

Beacon Hill
3201 Beacon Ave S, (206) 322-9433
New owner Jun Vicencio took over Inay's Kitchen and has since renamed it Kusina Filipina, but he's kept the emphasis on Filipino home cooking in this popular Beacon Hill joint, with food laid out cafeteria-style in a bewildering

array of colors and smells. Kusina Filipina features cuisine from the "gourmet province" of the Philippines, Pampanga, which has a strong Spanish influence and is definitely not for vegetarians: Large slabs of fish, beef, chicken, and pork abound, along with a variety of meat combo dishes. Kusina Filipina's menudo ($4.25), for example (an entrée, not the Puerto Rican boy band), is a delectable stew of pork, beef liver, raisins, potatoes, and carrots in tomato sauce. The offerings change daily, and with nearly all of the entrées priced under $5, you can afford to keep coming back to try something new. You'll probably need to make a separate trip for the gut-bomb splendor of the halo halo dessert ($2.50)—shaved ice, tapioca, beans, Jell-O, ice cream, and various brightly colored fruits, all mixed up like a milk shake.

$2.50-$5; Daily 10 am-7:30 pm; major credit cards accepted; no alcohol; no smoking

Maneki

International District

304 6th Ave S, (206) 622-2631

Maneki, Seattle's oldest sushi bar, serves up generous portions of the freshest sushi around. It's worth stuffing yourself into the sushi bar way in the back corner just to watch the chef's grace as he rolls individual pieces beautifully. A fluid list of weekly specials offers a range of Japanese home-cooking delights (best described as snacks to sustain the body while drinking), including seasonal seafood such as live sea urchin and tempura-battered smelt. Take in the nonstop Japanese television and karaoke videos in the cocktail lounge, if you can find a stool. Owner and local historian Jeanie flits from table to bar, chatting it up with dedicated customers, insuring a relaxed and comfortable atmosphere.

$3.50-$13.50;
Tues-Sun 5:30
pm-10:30 pm;
major credit
cards accepted;
sake and beer;
smoking okay

SHANE CARPENTER

Maneki: Where did I leave that smelt?

Where to Eat in the International District

by Stacey Levine

IN THE AREA AROUND 12TH AND JACKSON—dubbed "Little Saigon" by the I.D.'s neighborhood council—you can find Asian groceries, herb stores, video spots, jewelers, salons, and deli shops, all basking beneath the distant neon glare of the giant Wonder Bread factory sign to the east. But the neighborhood's real draw is its food, which can be a late-night or lunchtime lifesaver. Among the attractions are the following.

KALAH ALLEN

- **Pho Bac** at Dearborn and Jackson, serving large, pristine bowls of savory beef noodle soup and nothing else. (Pho Bac recently opened a spiffier, newer outlet at 415 7th Ave S, in the heart of the I.D.)

- **Pho So #1**, in the lively Ding How mall at 1207 S Jackson, #107, sports the same menu as Pho Bac (two sisters own these restaurants, and their soup recipes are only subtly distinct).

- In the group of stores dubbed "Asian Plaza," **Thanh Vi Vi** (1046 S. Jackson), **Saigon Bistro** (1032 S. Jackson, #202), and **A Little Bit of Saigon** (1036 S Jackson St, #A) dish out larger arrays of Vietnamese specialties.

- For deeply traditional/regional Vietnamese specialties, try **Huong Binh** (1207 S Jackson) in the Ding How mall (tropical Popsicles in flavors such as durian and jackfruit are available here).

- **Banh Mi Saigon**, the deli at 1034 S Jackson, is a social center of sorts, full of a fresh and colorful array of sweets, French bread sandwiches, banana-leaf-wrapped snacks, pastries, and the like.

- If you're looking for Chinese cuisine, head down the hill to the heart of the I.D. to find unique Cantonese small-village cooking at **L.A. Seafood Restaurant** (424 7th Ave S). Interesting, expertly made dishes are also featured at **Sea Garden** (509 7th Ave S), **Ga Ga Loc Seafood** (424 Maynard Ave S), and **Hing Loon** (628 S Weller). All these restaurants are open weeknights until 2 or 3 am.

- **China Gate** (516 7th Ave S) is a popular stop for dim sum, seafood, and hot pots; **Shanghai Garden** (524 6th Ave S) serves up unusual pickles, mushroom-based soups, and "hand-shaven" noodles, as well as brown rice.

- For excellent Chinese barbecue as well as a cheery atmosphere, try **Kau Kau Barbeque Market** (656 S King St) or **Harbor City** (707 S King St). Both spots do a brisk business in BBQ pork, duck, and spareribs (sit-down or takeout).

- **House of Dumplings** (512 S King) offers Mandarin dishes and traditional northern Chinese breakfasts, including long, lightly salted donuts. Dim sum and Chinese crepes are also sold here.

- **Raimutei**, in the Play Center Yume at 6th Ave S and S King St, offers sushi, eight types of yakitori skewers, and several different types of udon soups, if you're looking for Japanese cuisine.

- One of the oddest places in the I.D. shares space with Raimutei: a bar/restaurant dubbed **Fort St George**, 601 S King St., #202, which offers a confusion of teriyaki dishes along with little English-style sandwiches with the crusts cut away, spaghetti, and some German meat dishes. This place is the brainchild of Yuichi Maekawa, who lived in London before moving to the Northwest. He grew so homesick for his corner pub back in the U.K. that he designed a cafe with a "European" atmosphere here in Seattle's I.D.

- For more Japanese cuisine, look for extremely fresh sushi at **Yoshinobo** (520 S Jackson). This spot features strange, outsized chairs—possibly suitable for space travel—at its sushi bar, along with an astonishing assortment of appetizers listed on a separate menu. The longstanding **Maneki** (304 6th Ave S) offers very tasty sushi along with tatami rooms; **Koraku** (419 6th Ave S) is a lovely, homey lunch spot as comfortable as a grandmother's living room.

- For Cambodian dishes, try the inexpensive and phenomenally tasty **Phnom Penh Noodle House** (660 S King), and for exceptionally unique Malaysian/Indian/Chinese cooking, try **Malay Satay Hut** (212 12th Ave S); the sambal and belachan sauces here will transport you far, far away.

La Spiga

Capitol Hill

1401 Broadway, (206) 323-8881

Every native Italian who has been transplanted and is now living in Seattle eats weekly at La Spiga. And so, Italian is the first language in the dining room. La Spiga is the lesson of simplicity at the heart of Italian living and cooking; and simply by existing, the restaurant is the denouncement of excess in American culture. Even with its great success, Pietro, the charming and earnest owner, would never open another restaurant. His business is singular, and besides, he couldn't be in two places at once. Of course, all of the pasta is homemade and so is the ancient-recipe bread, the specialty of the restaurant. Pietro uses only organic vegetables to capture the best tastes for his dishes. Please order the vegetable plate as your antipasto. And please do not miss the lasagne. At some tables, just as in Italy, you could be sitting with strangers; this is an opportunity, not an inconvenience. Pietro's brother designed the iron canopy and furniture and had it shipped here from Italy. Of course, everyone who comes here is a soccer fan, and sometimes a large-screen television is brought in for special events. Pietro has also collaborated with UW Italian Professor Albert Spragia to coordinate an Italian film series at the restaurant. One restaurant holds an entire community and fulfills its responsibility as an outlet of culture. Despite the danger of sounding melodramatic, we suggest you spend some time here and feel your American shackles slip right off. With all that weight gone, you should have room for dessert.

$10-$20; Mon-Wed 11 am-3 pm & 5:30 pm-10 pm, Thurs-Fri 11 am-3 pm & 5:30 pm-11 pm, Sat 5:30 pm-11 pm; major credit cards accepted; beer and wine; no smoking; wheelchair accessible

Maya's

Rainier Beach

9447 Rainier Ave S, (206) 725-5510

Bright and festive, Maya's provides Rainier Beach with an authentic Mexican and seafood-heavy menu, a family environment, and a full-service lounge. The big menu includes appetizers, soups, enchiladas, tostadas, and plenty of seafood, lamb, beef, and chicken. With all the great selections, the bright lights, and the frisky waitstaff, Maya's has just a hint of Disney woven into its colorful fabric. The "Coctel Campechano" pleases—mixing boiled octopus, prawns, oysters, tomatoes, avocado, and cilantro. Spoon a dollop of it on the house-made chips, and you'll swear you can smell the ocean. Halibut tacos stack up with the best around, and "Camarones al Mojo de Ajo" joins pan-seared prawns and grilled vegetables harmoniously. Borrego, a marinated lamb shank wrapped in banana leaf, is so tender it will make you cry. Add it all up and it spells fresh and savory magic, whether you walk a block or drive half an hour.

$7.95-$19.95; daily 11 am-10 pm, bar until 12:30 am Fri-Sat; major credit cards accepted; full bar; smoking okay

Mesob Ethiopian Restaurant

Central District

705 23rd Ave S, (206) 860-0403

Mesob is one of the best bargains in the city. The exquisite vegetarian platter feeds two for under $10, with lentils, greens, and potatoes in a variety of colorful sauces. The beef and lamb dishes are savory and well spiced. All of the meals are served on a large round communal plate over injera, a spongy and sour pancake-like bread that is the perfect consistency for gripping fingerfuls of tibs or cabbage or whatever happens to be in front of you at the moment. The Mesob staff is cheerful and relaxed in temperament—this is not a suitable place to go for a rushed power lunch. Better to take your time and eat slowly (injera tends to expand inside your belly, so don't overdo it).

$7.50-$9.50; daily 11 am-10 pm; major credit cards accepted; checks okay; beer, wine, and Sambuca; smoking okay

DAVID BELISLE

My's Restaurant

University District

4220 University Way NE, (206) 634-3526

Popular with university folk, Vietnamese My's is crowded to capacity with bearded science researchers and students during weekday lunch hours. Noodle soup ($4.25) in beef, chicken, or vegetarian varieties, is a salty and flavorful tonic on foggy days. You can also get rice-paper-wrapped spring rolls with shrimp or chicken, and pork or tofu sandwiches on French bread for a really filling and cheap lunch.

My's: Don't get a big head about it

Other inexpensive, well-prepared items include curry chicken, warm rice noodles tucked beneath either hot pork skewers, shrimp, or saucy tofu cubes. Sometimes lunch gets so crowded here that a doleful customer or two is directed to sit at a little desk behind the front counter, alongside the owner's piles of bills and vials of prescription medicine! Such is life at this charming, family-run business.

$1.50-$6.95; Mon-Sat 10 am-8 pm, Sun 11 am-7 pm; major credit cards accepted, checks okay; no alcohol; no smoking

Nha Trang Restaurant
International District
1207 S Jackson St, Suite B101, (206) 860-0057
The Formica interior and artificial flowers tell you "yet another Vietnamese noodle shop." But a look at the elaborate menu and a taste of the fantastic food tells a very different story. This relative newcomer in the International District has some of the tastiest, freshest Vietnamese food around. Though Nha Trang has all the usual noodle dishes, there's also a lot that you won't see elsewhere, like lotus-flower-stem salad and catfish fire pot. Nha Trang has something for everyone, with an extensive vegetarian selection (15 dishes) alongside its infamous (but delicious) "Seven Courses of Beef." If you're still hungry after that, something is probably wrong with you. But do order an iced coconut, bean, and jelly drink and imagine you're on a sunny beach in Indochina.
$4-$9; Sun-Thurs 9:30 am-9:30 pm, Fri-Sat 9:30 am-midnight; major credit cards accepted; beer only; smoking okay

Noble Palace
University District
4214-A University Way NE, (206) 632-7248
Once named Proud Bird (nicknamed "Dead Bird" by Ave rats), and now renamed and relocated to a cool, spacious, haven-like room, this place is still the best bet for Chinese fare in the U-District. No frozen peas and carrots in your subgum here! Everything's fresh. Huge, outstanding soups come in many varieties, including the best-selling won ton noodle and sui kau noodle, with handmade dumplings (sui kau is a mixture of shrimp, pork, and black-elephant-ear mushrooms). At $3.95 per mega-bowl, this soup is a steamy winter favorite. Other specialties include shrimp-stuffed tofu, satisfyingly chewy chow fun, and various seafood dishes. Beer is available, and there's a large vegetarian selection. Waitresses in crisp black and white are gracious, considering how busy the place gets during weekday lunchtimes.
$1.95-$6.95; Sun-Thurs 11 am-10 pm, Fri-Sat 11 am-midnight; major credit cards accepted, checks okay; beer and wine; no smoking

Old Village Korean Restaurant
Shoreline
15200 Aurora Ave N, (206) 365-6679
With rough wooden tables and warm smiles from the proprietors, Old Village's room is like an old-fashioned roadside inn, standing beside the maniacally blundering Aurora traffic. Fresh, traditional Korean food is served with a stellar assortment of pickles and appetizers—including kimchee, seaweed salad, pickled and sauced radish, and Korean-style potato salad, replete with needle-thin carrot slivers. Rice, served in a tiny, covered silver bowl, is perfectly sticky, each grain as glossy as a tiny jewel. The large menu features "Bibimbap," a lovely combo with marinated carrots, sprouts, meat, and an egg set atop a bowl

of rice, and delicious "Chap Chae," yam noodles with a variety of stir-fry stuff (find this item in the appetizer section of the menu). Plump, tasty dumplings are also available, with or without soup. Some dishes are bathed in a thick, intense red-pepper sauce that may not please some American diners, so ask first! $2.95-$9.95; daily 11 am-10 pm; major credit cards accepted; local checks okay; no alcohol; no smoking

Panos Kleftiko
Lower Queen Anne
815 5th Ave N, (206) 301-0393

It's hard to say which is more responsible for making Panos Kleftiko one of the true great restaurants in Seattle: the food or Dimitri, the charming, foxy Greek waiter. Panos Kleftiko is a tiny little restaurant, explains Dimitri, so that Panos, the chef and owner, can cook well for a modest party instead of a big restaurant full of people. This keeps the quality of ingredients high and allows Panos to take great care with each meal. That's what Dimitri says, and it's believable, because every single visit to this restaurant is perfect, from the first hot slice of pita to the last hot cup of grainy Greek coffee. The menu is built around a long list of traditional Greek appetizers, including the kalamari salada, fassolia (a white bean salad), yigantes (an incredibly addictive plate of enormous butter beans in red sauce), and saganaki, a Greek goat cheese served flaming. All this can keep a hungry table busy for hours—Panos' pita really is the best—but there are dinner platters to be considered too, like the Kleftiko-style lamb, which is cooked with onion and feta cheese and stuffed inside a sourdough loaf. Dimitri keeps the chilled house white wine coming, and it's damn near impossible to stop eating until every single lick of food is gone.
$3.95-$21.95; Mon 5:30 pm-9:30 pm, Tues-Sat 5:30 pm-10:30 pm; major credit cards accepted; local checks okay; beer and wine; no smoking

Super Bowl Noodle House
Green Lake
814 NE 65th St, (206) 526-1570

Unlike its football-game namesake, this Super Bowl doesn't promise the moon and then leave you disappointed. A small but bright and clean joint, Super Bowl offers a variety of noodle dishes-mostly soups-that all prove satisfying and surprisingly filling. The "Turbo Noodles" are the stuff of dreams: wide rice noodles simmering in a red broth with pork, shrimp, fried tofu, won tons, fish balls (insert joke here), and more, with a hint of cilantro. A warning for the heat-shy: If you don't like your food spicy, definitely try it with "one star." If you don't like noodles, try the shrimp rice soup or seafood rice soup, the latter featuring fish, shrimp, squid, fried tofu, green onions, cilantro, and slivers of ginger.
$4.95-$6.95; Sun-Thurs 11:30 am-9:30 pm, Fri-Sat 11:30 am-10 pm; major credit cards accepted; beer and wine; smoking outside

Taste of India
University District
5517 Roosevelt Way NE, (206) 528-1575
Crowded as a village on weekends, Taste of India is one of the most sensual cheap-dining experiences in Seattle. The menu is rich in options for meat lovers and vegetarians; as you await your table, you can peer into the kitchen and see garlic naan (flat bread) being slapped into the tandoor, a clay-lined deep oven, and pans of spice-laden entrées bubbling away. Taste of India's chai, the sweetened black-tea drink, is a heavenly stimulant. Tandoori shrimp comes with perfectly done vegetables. Off the "Vegetarian Delights" section of the menu, "Vegetable Kofta" is a perennial favorite. Don't miss the large selection of microbrews. The building that houses Taste of India careers wildly from room to room, with low ceilings, walls decorated with glass-beaded quilts, and windows matched up to jutting tables. You may find yourself seated next to a UW literature professor, rendered mute by inexpressibly delicious food.
$1.95-$12.95; daily 10:30 am-9:45 pm; major credit cards accepted; local checks okay; beer and wine; no smoking

Tup Tim Thai
Lower Queen Anne
118 W Mercer St, (206) 281-8833
Although it bears a name that is comically difficult to remember and pronounce (friends are always saying, "Let's go to Tim Tup Thai, or Tip Tum Thai tonight"), this ugly little strip-mall-esque restaurant in lower Queen Anne serves up some of the most delicious and subtle Thai food found in Seattle. The menu is vast, embracing favorites and specials with equal skill. Order anything, but wear a sweater: The air conditioning is something fierce.
$7-$10.95; Mon-Fri 11:30 am-3 pm and 5 pm-10 pm; Sat 5 pm-10pm; major credit cards accepted; local checks okay; beer and wine; no smoking

Zaina Food, Drinks, and Friends
Downtown
108 Cherry St, (206) 624-5687
The decor is a jumble: Hookah pipes and Israeli postcards and all manner of Middle Eastern bric-a-brac line the walls of this lunchtime joint. Everything here is made from scratch: From the satisfyingly smoky and charred-tasting baba ghanoush plate to the succulent chicken gyro, Zaina features extremely fresh, Greek-influenced Middle Eastern cuisine. Flavors are distinct and sharp in the lovely schwarma as well as in the vegetarian platter—a huge delight featuring smatterings of cold salads, such as couscous with a chopped-greens mixture, crowded with sweet red onion. The basics here are reliable: Pita bread is moist and dense, and Zaina's hummus is truly garlicky. You'll never want to eat that store-bought pap again. There's also a Zaina in Ravenna: 2615 NE 65th St, (206) 525-7747.
$2-$14; Mon-Fri 11 am-9 pm, occasional Saturdays, call ahead to check; major credit cards accepted; checks okay; beer and wine; no smoking

Diners & Greasy Spoons

Baker's Restaurant and Famous Fountain

Lake City

12534 Lake City Way NE, (206) 365-1888

Baker's Restaurant and Famous Fountain is truly the soul of Lake City, and is a must-see for any Seattleite brave enough to cross the scary demarcation of NE 125th Street. Part candy shop, part Farrell's-style food-and-dairy shrine, and part smoking lounge for some of the hardest-smoking people in the city limits, Baker's has an attentive staff that delivers items from this massive menu with humor, aplomb, and good cheer. You'll never go wrong with a dependable Reuben, and the potato pancakes are packed with love and home-cooked goodness. The comfortable and easy-on-the-fanny booths, peeling and smoke-stained wallpaper, decaying rest rooms, and rough-hewn carpeting add color and a historic feel to this old-school establishment. Seattle loves to bulldoze places like this—God bless Baker's for surviving, and for providing inexpensive food for down-home customers who couldn't care less about the myth of fine dining.

$3.95-$12.95; Sun, Tues-Thurs 7:30 am-8 pm; Mon 7:30 am-3 pm; Fri-Sat 7:30 am-9 pm; major credit cards accepted; checks okay; beer and wine; smoking encouraged

Beth's Cafe

Green Lake

7311 Aurora Ave N, (206) 782-5588

Beth's could easily win any local "Best Greasy Spoon" contest. This place has it all, day and night: mean omelets; the greasiest, tastiest hash browns around; a jukebox full of 45s from the '50s to the '70s; and walls papered with pictures drawn by anyone who requests paper and crayons. Everyone converges at Beth's, where the style is informal, the video games are plentiful, and there's only one non-smoking table, thanks to a handy grandfather clause. During the busy graveyard shift, you'll meet

Beth's: Goes down smooth with a lil' whiskey in ya

truckers en route, students, drunks, people with hangovers, elderly couples, and hot-to-trot young people. For those who crave music, smoking, and fine food—all in the same room and in the dead of night—Beth's can be a little slice of heaven. They've also got the cheapest espresso in town.

$5-$13; open 24 hours daily; major credit cards accepted; no alcohol; smoking encouraged

Cyndy's House of Pancakes
North Seattle
10507 Aurora Ave N, (206) 522-5100
Paneled in fake woodgrain and upholstered with red vinyl, the dining room at Cyndy's invites you to mellow out while awaiting your $20 psychic-energy-reading appointment at the joint across Aurora. It may be best to sit at the bar, bolstered by swivel chairs, and view the high-talent kitchen, where they flip the fluffiest pancakes north of the C.D. The banana pancakes ($5 for a stack of six; $4 for three) float on your tongue like a tropical dream, and the bacon and eggs ($5.50) ain't half bad either. Crepes—here unpretentiously called "Roll-Ups"—are a feathery deal at $4-$6. An entire continent of hash browns comes with egg orders, and you can choose from country gravy or turkey gravy on anything.

$1.75-$7; daily 6 am-4 pm; major credit cards accepted; local checks okay; smoking okay

Longshoreman's Daughter
Fremont
3508 Fremont Pl N, (206) 633-5169
As Fremont's certified Hangover Helper, Longshoreman's Daughter has a number of ways to soothe "the morning after." First, there's the bed-headed help, who look both friendly and sketchy, much like your date last night. Then there's the fat, warm stack of buckwheat pancakes to kill the throbbing, and the real maple syrup to speed up the chemical detox. If that doesn't work, though, you can follow the yellow brick road back to sobriety with fresh-squeezed mimosas. This trendy spot is not at all your typical diner: Long-shoreman's Daughter manages to be all-natural and still have that brash, in-crowd appeal.

$4.50-$16; Sat-Mon, Wed-Fri 7:30 am-10 pm; major credit cards accepted; checks okay; full bar; no smoking

Lowell's Restaurant and Bar
Downtown
1519 Pike Pl, (206) 622-2036
"That man at the bar having a cocktail at 7 am was probably hauling produce at 3 am. His day is over already," says Mark Monroe, the general manager of Lowell's, a three-story market mainstay for 50 years. Lowell's is a destination with character, frequented by tourists, yuppies, and the working-class

Market clan whom Monroe likens to a carnival family. The food is generally good, and the regulars at the bar will happily entertain you for free. You can go for the booze or for the burgers—but if you want the best of Lowell's, go by yourself at dusk and order the clam steamers in garlic broth, sit on the first floor in front of the picture window, and watch the ferries trail back and forth across the Sound like wandering jewels.

$3.95-$8.95; daily 7 am-8 pm, bar until 10 pm; major credit cards accepted; full bar; smoking okay

Oscar's II

Central District

2051 E Madison St, (206) 322-2029

Oscar McCoy and his German wife, Barbara, opened their second bar/restaurant in its present Central District location in 1986, and Barbara is still waiting tables while Oscar cooks. Their menu focuses on good old-fashioned comfort food—Southern favorites and soul food, along with diner fare like burgers and fries. Old standbys such as the New York steak and barbecued chicken legs are done just right, and most entrées come with moist, pancake-style corn bread and your choice of two sides. Try the macaroni and cheese (creamy and delicious), red beans and rice (highly filling), or the heavenly greens: Oscar's collards are succulent and fortifying, with added crunch provided by onion and cabbage, while a meat stock contributes a deeper flavor. Go for either the food or the nightly DJ soul music—but get your butt on down to Oscar's.

ANNIE MARIE MUSSELMAN

$7-$15; Tues-Fri 4 pm-2 am, Sat-Sun 5 pm-2 am; cash only; full bar; smoking okay

Silver Fork

Rainier Valley

3800 Rainier Ave S, (206) 721-5171

The decade-old Fork is plump with warmth, gospel music, and big red booths. This is the place for bacon, although bacon is only one of the breakfast meat options: The Fork also

Silver Fork: The coffee keeps on coming

has pork sausage, turkey sausage, steak, and hot links. The perfectly salty three bacon slices, two eggs, toast, and side of grits special rides just around $5. Everything is tasty and hot. The grits are dreamy: creamy in texture and golden with butter. The "Soul Burger" with fries consists of a layer of hamburger, a layer of bacon, and a layer of hot links—all in a big bun, languishing upon a sea of golden, crispy fries as long and greasy as your hand. $3-$10; Mon, Thurs, Fri 7 am-4 pm, Sat-Sun 7 am-5 pm; major credit cards accepted; checks okay; smoking okay

Satellite Lounge
Capitol Hill
1118 E Pike St, (206) 324-4019
The Comet, that old Capitol Hill workhorse, has spawned a new offshoot just a block away: the Satellite Lounge. (It's a satellite of the Comet. Get it?) Though the Satellite is quickly on its way toward adopting the Comet's cheerily drunken regulars, it offers everything the Comet lacks: food, hard liquor, breathable air, and clean bathrooms. Burgers and sandwiches are huge and delicious, and come with tasty varieties of potato salad, coleslaw, or slim-cut fries. A regular burger with fries will set you back just $4.50; the dinner menu emphasizes comfort food like pot pies, steak, chicken, salmon, and pasta, and all are under $10. Desserts include an excellent raspberry sorbet with fruit ($3) and homemade pies ($3); if you're lucky you might still be able to nab the to-die-for strawberry-rhubarb.

$3-$11.95; Sun-Thurs 11:30 am-10:30 pm, Fri-Sat 11:30 am-11 pm, full bar; major credit cards accepted; no checks; smoking okay

Thirteen Coins
Downtown
125 Boren Ave N, (206) 682-2513
Nestled in the mysterious Denny Way trough, this bottom-feeder has been serving its mixed clientele 24/7 for 32 years. You can get breakfast, lunch, or dinner at any hour, the first two running between $8 and $15, the latter about $10-$18 à la carte. In the darkly

ANNIE MARIE MUSSELMAN

Thirteen Coins: This'll wake you up

lit interior, barflies are everywhere around you, accompanied by the subtle ice-cube clink of cocktails. There is an abundant antipasto plate, which comes automatically (and which is refreshed as you linger). Remember this place when, famished from an arduous night of drinking, you long for sustenance before you pass out.

$2.95-$22.95; daily 24 hours; major credit cards accepted, local checks okay; full bar; smoking okay

Cafes & Bistros

Agua Verde Cafe & Paddle Club
University District
1303 NE Boat St, (206) 545-8570

Agua Verde uses Baja and Oaxaca Mexican cooking styles as starting points, adds some "Northwest fusion," and ends up with an ambitious, inexpensive, flavorful menu. It's hard to know if fish tacos are in or out, but here the "De Pescado Tacos de la Casa" don't disappoint. Nestled earnestly in two tortillas, nice little pieces of grilled halibut or smoked salmon are modestly covered by shredded cabbage and then lightly sauced. The crab cakes ("Bocoles de Congrejo") are beautiful, not only in their robust and fresh taste, but in their seductive appearance as well. Whether you sit inside or out, you can't go wrong with Agua Verde's setting; you can eat next to the boats in Portage Bay, or sit inside near the big windows.

$1.25-$8.95; Mon-Sat 11 am-4 pm & 5 pm-9 pm; major credit cards accepted; checks okay; full bar; smoking okay

Asteroid Cafe
Wallingford
1605 N 45th St, (206) 547-2514

The Asteroid Cafe would like to dispel the rumor that it is merely a coffeehouse. This small storefront in Wallingford is a full-fledged, authentic Italian restaurant, focusing on the cuisine of South, Central, and Northern Italy, where owner Marlin Hathaway has spent much of his time. The Asteroid is small, and you might feel crowded if you're in a romantic mood; but the food, beginning with a stunning, complimentary bruschetta, makes up for any lack of privacy. The pastas are a work of art, and the portions are immense; but you will keep eating. A few unusual dishes, like the wild boar, have developed a following, and the daily dinner specials often feature unique seafood entrées. Hathaway is also proud of his wine list, which spans several regions of Italy but concentrates on Tuscan reds.

$5.95-$22.95; Mon-Fri 11 am-3 pm & 5 pm-10 pm, Sat-Sun 10 am-3 pm & 5 pm-11 pm; major credit cards accepted, checks okay; full bar; no smoking

BluWater Bistro
South Lake Union

1001 Fairview Ave N (in Yale Street Landing), (206) 447-0769

Diners sitting at water level at BluWater Bistro gaze out on Queen Anne Hill, which rises up like a stallion in the mist. This small room reeks of a neighborhood place, but with an inclusive "everyone's welcome" feel. BluWater, centered around its busy bar, serves simple and down-to-earth food and captures the true spirit of what a bistro is supposed to be. The "Blu New York" is a finely grilled New York steak with little blue-cheese glops. The crisp, oven-roasted, free-range half-chicken show-cases a moist and giddy texture, and seafood items abound on this crafty menu. Food is delivered to the table within seconds of being cooked, as servers practically (yet discreetly) sprint to your table. Singles action kicks in at 10 with the arrival of the Frat-Boy Patrol, so time your visit accordingly.

$9-$18; Daily 11:30 am-2 am; major credit cards accepted; full bar; limited smoking; reservations recommended

Bungalow Wine Bar and Cafe
Wallingford

2412 N 45th St, (206) 632-0254

Warm and cozy, the Bungalow is located in the snuggly upper-story den and living room of a neighborhood house, complete with happily crackling fire-place. The Bungalow is literate and sensitive—there's a poetry bookstore downstairs—but also outdoorsy, as cafe tables are available on the deck during warm-weather lunches. The cafe's staff has an exhaustive knowl-edge of wine, but is totally friendly and unpretentious about it. And when you get down to business, we're talking multiple orgasms, baby. The Bun-galow whips up hot French, Italian, and Northwest dishes with casual aplomb. Go to Bungalow and fall in love. Better yet, take a date there and make him or her fall in love with you.

$5-$25; Tues-Thurs 3 pm-11 pm; Fri-Sat 1 pm-midnight; major credit cards accepted; checks okay; beer and wine; no smoking

Cafe Lago
Montlake

2305 24th Ave E, (206) 329-8005

Some restaurants put all their energy into one aspect of the dining experience and really get it right. Cafe Lago is one of those places. Rather than waste energy on fancy décor or finding the perfect location, Lago is a clean, simple place where the focus is on the food. The cafe has raised its wood-fired pizza to an art, so you'll fight over the last piece of salsiccia—a sausage-and-red-pepper number. Lighter takes on Italian standards such as antipasto (available in vegetarian and carnivorous varieties) and lasagne might also cause squabbling. But it's the pizza that'll keep you coming back.

$5.95-$21.95; Tues-Thurs 5 pm-9:30 pm, Fri-Sun 5 pm-10 pm; major credit cards accepted, checks okay; full bar; no smoking; reservations recommended

Cafe Flora
Madison Valley
2901 E Madison St, (206) 325-9100
Cafe Flora is a sometimes-disorienting blend of yuppie upscale and hippie down-home. An all-vegetarian menu creeps from the boundaries of blandness into light pastry (the portobello Wellington in Madeira wine sauce) and pastas (a lemongrass-spiced wild mushroom linguine special). There is a non-dairy pâté platter appetizer, and delicacies such as black-eyed pea fritters. The breakfast menu is especially pleasing, in a brunchy, linen-tablecloth kind of way. And if you can, sit in the sunroom.

$5-market price; Tues-Fri 11:30 am-10 pm, Sat-Sun 9 am-2 pm & 5 pm-10 pm; major credit cards accepted; no smoking

Cafe Soleil
Madrona
1400 34th Ave, (206) 325-1126
With upscale Ethiopian food by night and classic brunches by day, Cafe Soleil is one of a strip of three restaurants that make Madrona the brunch neighborhood of Seattle. The homey living-room atmosphere and the sunny southern exposure (when there is sun) keep this small place crowded on weekends, especially with Teva-and-fleece geeks. Frittatas here are not really frittatas, just omelets laden with pesto, sun-dried tomatoes, portobello mushrooms, fresh parmesan, olives, etc. Ethiopia was once occupied by Italy, and the influence extends to pastas and mozzarella sandwiches. At night it's strictly Ethiopian fare, but better quality than you'll find at more traditional places nearby. Such authentic Ethiopian-style shrimp, salmon, and lamb can't be found elsewhere. The vegetarian combination is about twice the price of other Ethiopian places, but it feeds three and the flavors are fresh and sophisticated, ultimately making it worth the cost.

$4.50-$10.50; Wed-Fri 11 am-3 pm & 5:30 pm-9 pm Sat-Sun 9 am-2 pm; major credit cards accepted; beer and wine; no smoking

El Greco
Capitol Hill
219 Broadway E, (206) 328-4604
El Greco serves some of the best-prepared food in one of the least-comfortable rooms on Capitol Hill. The room is narrow, an L-shaped corridor with a hard tile floor. That said, you will loaf there many nights and love it. The food and wine are that good. The menu is largely Mediterranean: Pastas, panini, hummus, tzatziki, and baba ghanoush share space with lamb, pork, chicken,

and fresh fish. Basil, oregano, garlic, and tarragon are favored. Pork and lamb are invariably tender and moist, threaded with spicy marinades. El Greco also has some terrific vegetarian fare, especially their "Crispy Penne" tossed with eggplant, tomato, kalamata olives, and capers, then grilled; it's every bit as complex as the richly marinated pork loin.

$6-$16; Tues-Thurs 5 pm-9:30 pm, Fri-Sat 5 pm-10 pm, Sat-Sun 9 am-2:30 pm; major credit cards accepted, checks okay; wine and beer; no smoking

Mona's Bistro and Lounge

Green Lake

6421 Latona Ave, (206) 526-1188

How to describe the straightforward greatness of Mona's? String together a list of accolades? Well, okay: The food is impeccable, but not too pricey. It's served artfully, but generously. There's an excellent selection of fish, meat, chicken, and pasta—not too many choices, but just enough to please every kind of diner. Service is attentive, but not to the point of intrusive fawning. Even the ambience is perfect: candles on every table, low lighting and cool art on each deep-colored wall. Best of all, the live jazz trickles in from the adjoining bar to provide the perfect accompaniment to a romantic dinner. It's so damn good, you'll wish you could keep it as your little secret. Sadly, you're not alone.

$4-$22 (market-price seafood); Tues-Wed 5 pm-10 pm, Thurs-Sat 5 pm-11 pm, Sun 5 pm-10 pm, lounge until 2 am; major credit cards accepted; full bar; no smoking

Coffeehouses

Allegro

University District

4214 University Way NE, (206) 633-3030

Coffeehouses are best when they're in an alley. This is where professors fall in love with their students and vice versa. When the affairs break up horribly, you find these people retreating upstairs, where it is possible to smoke (the ritual of regret).

Coffee Messiah

Capitol Hill

1554 E Olive Way, (206) 860-7377

Established in '97 by ex-Mormon/ex-Catholic Tim Turner "to work through some stuff," Coffee Messiah features innumerable gaudy cruci-fixes (including a tortured Pee Wee Herman), pew-like seats, "Blood of Christ whole bean coffee," and a full vegan menu. Alongside neighbors Fallout and Apocalypse Tattoo, Coffee Messiah embodies Capitol Hill's dwindling sense of intimacy: Saturday features a midnight cabaret, and there are two different open mic nights, as well as occasional rock shows.

This is old-school Seattle: coffeehouse as community service.

Counter Culture

Downtown

2219 2nd Ave, (206) 441-8075

Although the decorating scheme is a little loud for some, especially in the morning, Counter Culture serves as an oasis of indie coffeedom in otherwise bland Belltown. They serve great waffles and fruit, and espresso-wand steamed eggs with biscuits.

ANNIE MARIE MUSSELMAN

Joe Bar

Capitol Hill

810 E Roy, (206) 324-0407

Joe Bar is a tiny getaway on one of the most beautiful streets in the city. Everyone who works here is cool, and the incentive cards are on the honor system, which is even cooler.

Lottie Mott's Coffee Shop

Columbia City

4900 Rainier Ave S, (206) 725-8199

If coffee is comfort food, this messy living room is a perfect place to lounge and warm up your life.

Lux

Downtown

2226 1st Ave, (206) 443-0962

Lux is the perfect Sunday morning groove spot. Triphop weaves through the morning air, and no one will disturb your hangover.

Petti Rosso

Capitol Hill

1101 E Pike St, (206) 323-4830

Petti Rosso serves up an elegant cup of coffee, silky with foam. This place used to be a coffee cart in REI; now it's a hidden gem in south Capitol Hill.

Still Life in Fremont Coffeehouse

Fremont

709 N 35th St, (206) 547-9850

The soups will make you love a pissy Seattle winter. Still Life is the perfect cafe: The food, coffee, and

Hangover Breakfasts

Beth's Cafe
Green Lake
7311 Aurora Ave N,
(206) 782-5588
Helpful Hint: *What you draw on your placemat says everything about you*

Continental Restaurant & Pastry Shop
University District
4549 University Way NE,
(206) 632-4700
Helpful Hint: *Save room for baklava*

Dick's Drive-In
Wallingford
11 NE 45 St,
(206) 632-5125
Capitol Hill
115 Broadway E,
(206) 323-1300
Greenwood
9208 Holman Rd NW,
(206) 783-5233
Lower Queen Anne
500 Queen Anne Ave N,
(206) 285-5155
Lake City
12325 30th Ave NE,
(206) 363-7777
Helpful Hint: *Opens at 10 am; why not have a Deluxe for breakfast?*

C. TAYLOR

Glo's
Capitol Hill
1621 E Olive Way,
(206) 324-2577
Helpful Hint: *Whatever you get, order the-very-best-in-the-city hash browns to go with it*

Hattie's Hat
Ballard
5231 Ballard Ave NW,
(206) 784-0175
Helpful Hint: *Best grilled cheese in town*

Kathy's Koffee Korner
Beacon Hill
4811 Beacon Ave S,
(206) 762-6261
Helpful Hint: *Bring grandma*

Shanty Cafe
Lower Queen Anne
350 Elliott Ave W,
(206) 282-1400
Helpful Hint: *Oh Lord, the Shanty knows how to bake a pie!*

Silver Fork
Rainier Valley
3800 Rainier Ave S,
(206) 721-5171
Helpful Hint: *Stick to the breakfast food*

Voula's Off Shore Cafe
University District
658 NE Northlake Way,
(206) 634-0183
Helpful Hint: *Get yourself some of Voula's Greek sausage. Beware the mushroom burger; it will become an addiction.*

atmosphere are healthy yet wonderful; even the artwork is good. When you think of a Seattle coffeehouse, this is what should come to mind.

Ugly Mug Cafe
University District
1309 NE 43rd St, (206) 547-3219
Named after the grimacing gargoyles on the outside of their U-District building, the Ugly Mug Café serves up great coffee, soups, and sandwiches in a crowded but comfy, creaky-floored room.

Uptown Espresso
Queen Anne
525 Queen Anne Ave N, (206) 281-8669
The barista will remember your name. If you think this is a good thing, you'll love this neighborhood-oriented spot. Try the scones.

Victrola
Capitol Hill
411 15th Ave E, (206) 325-6520
Until Victrola showed up, 15th Avenue E used to be a coffee wasteland. With a big space, plenty of tables and suitably rude baristas, this place is bound for greatness. The drip coffee's so strong, it really is like taking LSD.

Vivace Espresso
Capitol Hill
901 E Denny Way or 321 Broadway E, (206) 860-5869
You've found the Holy Grail of coffee.

Zeitgeist Kunst and Kaffee
Downtown
161 S Jackson St, (206) 583-0497
This has all the big-city, art-district coffeehouse feel one can take. Great nibbles and drinks. This is where the Typing Explosion (a poetry performance group) was conceived.

Zoka
Green Lake
2200 N 56th St, (206) 545-4277

A non-corporate Tully's is what this place is like. Besides truly delicious coffee, Zoka stocks toys for tots to play with.

Tea Worth Noting

Ambrosia
International District
619 S King St, (206) 622-6241
If you only come here once, order a mango milk with tapioca pearls. The giant straws allow for the tapioca pearls to shoot into your mouth, which is as exciting as a roller coaster. If this place becomes a habit, as it should, experiment with all the flavored tea. Ambrosia is so cool, you can smoke and sip at the same time.

Mr. Spot's Chai House
Ballard
2213 NW Market St, (206) 297-2424
Run by the nicest hippies this side of Portland, Mr. Spot's offers homemade chai, deep couches, and groovy ambient music.

Tea House Kuan Yin
Wallingford
1911 N 45th St, (206) 632-2055
Hippy-delicious curatives like honest ginger tea make Kuan Yin a wholesome hangout. Try the oranges with syrup if they have 'em.

ERIKA LANGELY

Mr. Spot's: Really nice hippies (really)

Open All Night
A Selective Guide to Seattle's 24-Hour Nightlife

by David Schmader

WHEN *THE STRANGER* SUGGESTED I EXAMINE THE STATE OF 24-HOUR RESTAURANTS IN SEATTLE, I leapt at the chance. Here was my opportunity to shed valuable light on the shady world of after-hours food—exalting those establishments that provide quality commerce without regard for time's arbitrary strictures, while exposing those frauds who sling crap around the clock, fully counting on their patrons to be too desperate to go anywhere else and too drunk to notice the footprints on their omelets. Here is a selective guide to Seattle's after-hours food: the good, the bad, and the smarmy.

JULIE DOUCET

The Hurricane Cafe (2230 7th Ave, 206/623-5750) A few years ago, the Hurricane Cafe stepped in to fill the sad void left by the closure of Seattle's legendary Dog House, and while the Hurricane is neither as relaxed nor as colorful as its predecessor, it has proven to be a smashing success in its own right. While certain other all-night dives (i.e., Minnie's) labor under embarrassing pretensions of quality and legitimacy, the Hurricane makes no bones about being exactly what it is: a big, noisy, sloppy, and extremely smoky dump that serves cheap food custom-made for hungry drunks. Where else can a group of smashed friends feast on a communal 12-egg omelet and all-you-can-eat hash browns for under $12? Or pork chops and eggs for $7.25? Or a bottomless bowl of oatmeal for a mere $3.50?

Verdict: Glorious trash, if you've got the stomach for it. Teetotalers and asthmatics beware.

Five Point Café (415 Cedar St, 206/448-9993) Like the Hurricane, the Five Point seems to anticipate a drunken clientele, but whereas the Hurricane draws exuberant young boozers, the Five Point caters to an older, quieter crowd—more Raymond Carver, less *Animal House*. The food is your basic greasy-spoon fare (sandwiches, fries, all-night breakfasts, all reasonably priced) with some noble forays into more imaginative culinary territory. I was initially tempted by these more exotic items (my choice: the blue-cheese omelet), but I soon learned the hard way that some places would do well to stick to basics: My omelet tasted as if it had been prepared for me by my worst enemy as part of his occupational therapy. Still, it was served promptly and with a smile, and I was happy to luxuriate in the Five Point's relaxed, intimate environment. The night I visited, the small room was filled with an assortment of people—a bleary-eyed couple, a student, some coffee-swilling truck drivers—all sitting quietly and watching Björk videos on the bar TV. And like every restaurant worth its salt, the Five Point has a bottle of A.1. Steak Sauce on every table.

Verdict: Charming atmosphere makes up for less-than-savory food. The best of the low-rent diners.

International House of Pancakes (950 Madison St, 206/322-4450; 4301 Brooklyn Ave NE, 206/634-2284) As I headed out in the middle of the night to the International House of Pancakes, I was overcome by a wave of nostalgia. In my hometown (Buttcrack, Texas), IHOP was the only 24-hour game in town, and I recall fondly the many hours I spent in that surreal fluorescent environment, patiently awaiting my pancakes and basking in the glamour of the only international place I'd ever been. But my nostalgia dissolved when I entered the IHOP on Capitol Hill and found not the hazy, slow-moving sanctuary of my youth, but a bustling circus of harried wait-staff, hollering drunks, and impending violence. During my half-hour in attendance (late on a Friday night), I witnessed two screaming matches, three forced removals of patrons, and one ferocious whisper-fight between a pair of IHOP employees. Throughout all of this, the kitchen crew and waitstaff executed their duties with the precision of a Marine drill team, shouting out orders, jogging down aisles with platefuls of food, and obeying commands from an ass-kicking night manager who deserves the food-service equivalent of the Congressional Medal of Honor.

Verdict: A Jerry Springer episode brought to life, with eight different kinds of syrup.

Stella's Trattoria (4500 9th Ave NE, 206/633-1100) Entering Stella's, the University District's premier all-night restaurant, the first thing you notice is the light. It exists in abundance, as if the owners hadn't heard of the ordinance requiring all-night restaurants to cloak their wretched patrons in darkness. Then there is the menu, displayed in the atrium and boasting an impressive selection of Italian dishes served round the clock, as well as "nighthawk specials"—from designer breakfast items (frittatas, fancypants French toast) priced six bucks and up to the student-friendly combos of two eggs, potatoes, and toast for only $4.75 (Note: breakfast served 4 am-11 am on weekdays and 4 am-3 pm on weekends). Finally, there's the maitre d', perfectly groomed and beaming, leading you to your table with a spring in his step as if . . . well, as if it weren't the GODDAMN MIDDLE OF THE NIGHT, when all decent people are at home in bed, not prowling the streets like the undead expecting quality food and service with a smile when it's the GODDAMN MIDDLE OF THE NIGHT! And that's what makes Stella's so special, and so unnerving. Because inside the walls of Stella's, time doesn't exist. Stella's is the Twilight Zone of all-night restaurants, operating on a plane beyond the temporal world—always open, always clean, always friendly. And while I was happy to enjoy tasty food in a well-run restaurant at four in the morning, I kept expecting the waitstaff to peel off their faces to reveal the robot frameworks underneath.

Verdict: A clean, well-lighted, slightly eerie place serving after-hours food you wouldn't be ashamed to eat during the day.

The Hurricane: Filling the void

Ultra-Splurge

Andaluca
Downtown
407 Olive Way, (206) 382-6999
Situated at the base of the Mayflower Park Hotel, Andaluca offers a respite from its bustling downtown neighbors. With its dark ambience and intimately small dining room, it is well suited for serious romantic or familial dining. Andaluca's cuisine reflects a mélange that is blisteringly European, incorporating flavors from Greek to Italian to Moorish Mediterranean. Dishes range from "Crisp Duck Cakes with Apricot Chutney" to "Cabrales Beef Tenderloin with Marsala Glaze, Grilled Pears, and Mashed Potatoes" to "Lamb Loin with Grape Leaves." If you get a booth, you can rub legs with your partner in self-congratulatory glee.
$7-$38; Mon-Sat 6:30 am-11 am & 11:30 am-2:30 pm, Sun-Thurs 5 pm-10 pm, Fri-Sat 5 pm-11 pm; Sun 7 am-noon; major credit cards accepted; checks okay; full bar; no smoking; reservations recommended

Avenue One
Belltown
1921 1st Ave, (206) 441-6139
You are alone, and you've found yourself a restaurant that's nice—even elegant. You are escorted past the whispering front bar, through the champagne-peach warmth of the main dining room, to an intimate back parlor. "Tuna Tartare Wrapped in Nova-Smoked Salmon with Dill-Mint Vinaigrette" comes as twin towers of seafood, on a dish dotted with discs of thinly sliced radish and lemon zest. "Potato and Salt Cod Galette with Roasted Red Peppers"—a thick cake with two stems, reaching out like antennae from a crown—arrives in a pool of warm cream and chives. You can choose from "Roasted Herb-Crusted Beef Filet on Roasted Shallots and Potatoes"—a hearty slab of beef sliced and splayed like a deck of cards in a velvet olive glaze—or the "Roasted Duck Breast and Confit with Green Peppercorn and Cherry Sauce," crisp and juicy atop a plateau of wild rice. Despite your evening's indulgences, you won't want to leave until you've tasted the fresh mango tart or the chocolat pot-au-crème.
$5.50-$27; Wed-Sun 11:30 am-2:30 pm, daily 5 pm-10:30 pm; major credit cards accepted; full bar; smoking in bar, wheelchair accessible

Canlis
North Queen Anne
2576 Aurora Ave N, (206) 283-3313
On the cusp of the Aurora Bridge, perched above Lake Union, Canlis looms over Seattle like a benevolent patriarch. Decorated in soothing earth tones, the ambience is modern classic, designed to give every table an advantageous

aspect to the walls of windows. The omniscient waitstaff describes the origin and preparation of your dish as you order it—no verbose descriptions of menu items you're not interested in—and then disappears. The menu is not elaborate and the presentation is not spectacular, but the food is superb. Grilled Alaskan weathervane scallops and "Peter Canlis Prawns" are prepared with restraint and simplicity, to highlight their freshness. Filet mignon and Wasyugyu steak (a Kobe-style, New York cut of Washington beef) also avoid the pomp-and-circumstance vulgarity so common to the presentation of premium meats. Nothing at Canlis boasts; instead, dishes arrive with confidence. That's the secret of true class: The best of everything should be assumed, not flaunted.

$8.95-$49; Mon-Sat 5:30 pm-midnight; major credit cards accepted; full bar; smoking okay (jacket recommended; no jeans, shorts, sneakers, or athletic wear)

Cassis

North Capitol Hill
2359 10th Ave E, (206) 329-0580, www.cassisbistro.com

Cassis, that royally colored liquor that sweetens French lives and French champagne, lends its name to this royally priced bistro, which offers supremely elegant French dishes. The menu changes monthly, and there is a prix-fixe menu offered Sunday through Thursday from 5 pm to 7 pm (three courses are included in the price). Although the atmosphere at Cassis is nothing special, head chef Charlie Durham's food will transport you: Creative salads vie for your palate with richly sauced meats (sometimes slightly daunting meats like calf's liver) and delicate seafood. Daily specials range from sweetbreads to rabbit. You can also go for just the cheese plate and a selection from the snooty wine menu, if you want to

play fancy without the financial backlash.
$6-$22 (fish at market prices; prix fixe $24); Sun-Thurs 5 pm-10 pm, Fri-Sat 5 pm-11 pm; major credit cards accepted; full bar; limited smoking; wheelchair accessible; reservations recommended (required for prix fixe)

ANNIE MARIE MUSSELMAN

Cassis: Make your own atmosphere

Earth & Ocean

Downtown

1112 4th Ave in the W Hotel, (206) 264-6060

Diners who can fight the urge to burst out laughing at the blatant pretentiousness that surrounds Earth & Ocean will be rewarded with delicious and weird-as-hell dishes. "Small plates" (and they're not kidding, with bread plates that could easily be mistaken for ashtrays) definitely rule. The nutmeg-seared lamb loin is compact and delicious, with a dazzling layout, and full of unusual flavor. The duck confit, formed into the sporty shape of a hockey puck, is stacked neatly atop a matching little disk of fingerling potato salad. As with other dishes, the confit's highly dense and compact nature tends to obscure its filling character. It's as though Earth & Ocean is trying to conserve space with its tiny food, perhaps making a clever environmentalist comment with their compressed and tight little packages.

$16-$26; Mon-Fri 6:30 am-10:30 am & 11:30 am-2:00 pm, Sun-Thurs 5 pm-10:30 pm, Fri-Sat 5 pm-11:30 pm, Sat-Sun 7:30 am-10:30 am; major credit cards accepted, local checks okay; full bar; limited smoking; wheelchair accessible; reservations recommended

Jimmy's Table

Madison Valley

2805 E Madison St, (206) 709-8324

Madison Valley, bordered by wealthy and not-so-wealthy neighborhoods, is a gratifyingly funked-up part of town. Chef Jimmy Watkins reflects the cultural character of the nearby neighborhoods by melding ambience and culinary elements. Thus we find a 16-ounce New York steak and baked potato on the menu alongside Southern Comfort barbecued shrimp served with grits. A nod to the nearby International District produces an udon noodle bowl with green curry and roasted tofu. But the culinary experience at Jimmy's Table isn't about cultural juxtaposition as much as it is about "fusion." As tired as the term is, the results can be sublime. Those barbecued shrimp and grits are bathed in a rich, gumbo-ish broth, with okra and slices of Asian green squash-the dish is as reminiscent of Malaysia as it is of Louisiana. Lunch is a steal, at half the price of dinner. Don't miss out on the rum chocolate cake!

$7-$24; Tues-Fri 11:30 am-2:30 pm, Tues-Sat 5:30 pm-10 pm, bar until 11 pm; major credit cards accepted, checks okay; full bar; no smoking; reservations recommended

Le Pichet

Belltown

1933 1st Ave, (206) 256-1499

Le Pichet is a work of French literature posing as a restaurant. The narrow room is warm with soft aromas from the kitchen—oregano and red wine layered with the salty, arid perfume of cured meats. In the back, there is a bar just big enough for a few young intellectuals—drinking brandy they probably can't afford—to converse about the death of God. The curling smoke from their strong cigarettes is reflected in the large mirror hung behind the bartender, who polishes a thick glass with the hem of his apron. The feeling is crowded and urban and rich, as if you were in another city in another time, an expatriate in your own town. Food comes in simple groupings: entrées, mixed plates, and specials, plus an ever-present assortment of cheeses chalked out on the cheese board. The house rightfully prides itself on its pâtés and smoked meats. Grilled fish, with the right wine, can floor you. Late-night hours and cheap wine complete this novel experience.

ADAM L. WEINTRAUB

Le Pichet: Mais, oui! We have your paté right here

$3.50-market price; Sun, Mon, Thurs 8 am-midnight, Fri-Sat 8 am-2 am; Tues-Wed 8 am-11:30 pm; full bar; major credit cards accepted; checks okay; limited smoking

Monsoon

Capitol Hill

615 19th Ave E, (206) 325-2111

Monsoon serves haute cuisine from Vietnam—a country too often associated with profligate, salty, $3-a-bowl bargains. Everything about Monsoon is gorgeously restrained, and changes seasonally. The tofu is a perennially perfect and humble dish, with the delicate flavor of fried tofu befriended by a warm spicy sauce. More complex is the wok-fried lemongrass chicken, which comes swimming in a sea of pungent spices. But for a great meal, the meal that will slap your face and tell you to shape up, pick any one of Monsoon's "Signature" dishes, which, at press time, included "Green-Tea-Baked Salmon in Banana Leaf," and seared Chilean sea bass with fresh herbs and chile pepper. Both dishes are so confidently conceived and so honestly good, you will lose yourself in their flavor.

$5-$17; Tues-Fri 11:30 am-2 pm, Tues-Sun 5:30 pm-10 pm; major credit cards accepted; beer and wine; no smoking

Sapphire

Queen Anne

1625 Queen Anne Ave N, (206) 281-1931

While the pungent aroma of hip pretense can occasionally be detected here, the food is still graceful, honorable, and marked by natural and hearty Mediterranean flavors. The chef's platter, billed as "a daily selection of little bites, antipasti, and salads," is a mammoth trough almost big enough to jump in. Cauliflower florets are lightly steamed, providing a modest counterpoint to the other more heavily flavored "little bites": Crunchy asparagus, toasted pecans, thin slices of Granny Smith apples, purple Finn potatoes, tangy golden beets, marinated ahi, baba ghanoush, and little balls of fresh mozzarella complete this exhaustively thorough appetizer. As a main course, the smartly spiced Moroccan-style lamb stew blends creamily with arborio rice, underscoring Chef Leonard Ruiz Rede's firm grasp of his "Mediterranean plus fresh Northwest" game plan.

$5.50-$15; daily 5:30 pm-1 am; major credit cards accepted, checks okay; full bar; limited smoking; reservations recommended

Tango Tapas Restaurant and Lounge

Downtown/Lower Capitol Hill

1100 Pike St, (206) 583-0382

Tango will cost you, but the chefs are true gentlemen—they don't skimp on the meat. "Ensalada Caribe," a "spice-rubbed duck confit shredded and tossed in a warm Jamaican vinagreta with seasonal greens and toasted pumpkin seeds," had about a 1:1 duck-to-greens ratio. The "Moqueca de Peixe," a Brazilian coconut and seasonal fish stew simmered with vegetables, mild spices, lime, scallops, squid, clams, halibut, prawns, and Lord knows what else, was truly enjoyable and well worth eight-fifty. The wine list here is encyclopedic, and the mixed drinks are inspired. The view of the hill-climb is entertaining, too, until you have to navigate it yourself.

$5.50-market price; Mon-Fri 11:30 am-2:30 pm, Mon-Sun 5:30 pm-11 pm, Thur-Sat 11 pm-1 am; major credit cards accepted; full bar; no smoking; reservations recommended

Eccentric Seattle

by Trisha Ready

OUTSIDE THE CITY'S CIRCUMFERENCE, hanging in that unknown space, is a constellation of heroes and demons whom we mythologize and sometimes destroy. These eccentrics—colorful drunks, religious extremists, serial killers, cornballs, rebels, medical martyrs, and cult leaders—shape a version of Seattle's history that can be gleaned from the marks left behind, the push and pull of that anarchic void. Our half-lights and hibernation winters combine with a crosshatched grid of earthquake faults and volcanoes to make a perfect environment for eccentrics. They thrive here; we thrive because of them. Here are the stories of five eccentrics who helped shape or haunt Seattle into its present cityhood.

Doc Maynard (1808-1873): For the most part, Seattle's Founding Fathers were a moneygrubbing lot of humorless religious zealots and business opportunists. Bill Speidel's infamous history, *Sons of the Profits*, finds one exception to that pack in Doc Maynard, a strapping middle-aged divorcé who blustered into Seattle with the dream of rearranging the city into a Northwest version of his own hometown—Cleveland, Ohio.

Doc was purportedly hard-drinking, funny, and generous; he parceled up his property and practically gave it to business-venturing types who were big on dreams but short on cash. Maynard's Wild West optimism and panache ran up hard against Arthur Yesler, the other big man determined to make Seattle in his own image; Speidel portrays Yesler as a cranky miser famous for filing lawsuits and amassing wealth at other people's expense.

As with all great legends, the clash between Maynard and Yesler serves as an explanation for the otherwise inexplicable: Pioneer Square. Between them, Maynard and Yesler owned the land that would become Pioneer Square, but they couldn't agree on a common grid for construction. Maynard laid his streets north-south; Yesler laid his parallel to the waterline. Neither Maynard nor Yesler budged from his plan, even where grids of streets and alleys smashed awkwardly into one another. The longstanding battle between Seattle's puritanical and wild sides began with this street battle. Yesler blamed the layout on Maynard, and he insisted that Doc was drunk the day he drew up his plan for the streets that would become the heart of Seattle.

Ivar Haglund (1905-1985): Ivar is Seattle's favorite cornball folk hero. He was a media opportunist, a clown, and a man who understood that Seattle at that time comprised a bunch of small towns strung together. A crusty, charismatic king of the wharf, Haglund's name entered Seattle's history when he started a chain of seafood restaurants named after himself.

Ivar began his career as a guitar-playing folk singer and tap dancer, and launched his first venture, the aquarium, primarily as a showcase for his own singing and guitar playing. Ivar's campy antics became his trademark: During one Christmas season, he dressed up his favorite seal, Pat, in a pinafore, and wheeled the slick baby downtown in a carriage to see Santa at the Frederick and Nelson department store.

Then came the seafood restaurants. His clumsy sloganeering appealed to the country in Seattle's city people. He promised "Acres of Clams" and urged his patrons to "Be Wiser at Ivar's" and "Keep Clam." His hokey, friendly schemes worked, and the city loved him.

Ivar didn't always abide by rules that would've made him popular with neighbors and city officials, though. While other businesses on the waterfront were banning seagulls from their piers, Ivar was welcoming the birds—"the unpaid guardians of public health"—with bread crumbs.

One of Ivar's crowning glories was buying the Smith Tower and then filling it up with odd things—such as antiques from Asia—and floating a giant wind

FRANCES FARMER © JIM BLANCHARD

sock at the top. In his later years, he became the victim of one of his own jokes: Running for port commissioner on a lark, he accidentally got the job, and was miserable thereafter.

Frances Farmer (1915-1970): All but one of the books on Frances Farmer have been stolen from the Seattle Public Library system. She's still not really embraced as a Seattle legend, though Nirvana's "Frances Farmer Will Have Her Revenge on Seattle" (from *In Utero*) did force the city to remember her. She's a tragic cult figure, and somewhere between Farmer's Joan of Arc status and the smothered silence about her life lies the true story.

Farmer was born on Capitol Hill (312 Harvard Ave), and later lived in West Seattle (2636 47th Ave SW). Gorgeous and outspokenly intelligent, she clashed immediately with her staid family, even as she achieved a reputation as an accomplished stage and film actress. The real furor around her started with the publication of her bleak essay, "God Died," which caused a citywide controversy and brought the wrath of churches and "respectable" citizens down on the teenager. When Farmer visited Russia as a UW drama student during the Red Scare, she was officially considered a menace; her mother gave an interview to a local newspaper warning other mothers to guard their daughters from the influence of Communism.

As blunt and willful as she was sexy, the young actress hopped between Hollywood, New York, and Seattle. She popped her mouth off a lot, and started having trouble with the cops. She was finally thrown in jail in L.A. for a speeding ticket. Once the state had her, it worked with her family to commit her to a series of mental hospitals, including Seattle's Harborview and Western State in Tacoma. When she finally broke out, she tried to hitchhike down to northern California, as much to get away from her family as from the institutions. She was quickly arrested and returned to Western State.

Stories of her treatment are unbearable: She was given every kind of experimental psychological treatment available, including insulin shock, electroshock, and drug therapy. The diagnoses of her "disorders" were conveniently broad and serious, and, with the collusion of Farmer's mother, enough to keep her continually committed. Farmer was treated brutally at Western State: She was raped, neglected, and humiliated. And her wild spirit was finally crushed when the infamous Dr. Walter Freeman recommended a lobotomy. On the very day of his recommendation, the lobotomy was performed. Alive but dead, she became a born-again Christian and even hosted her own TV talk show, until it interfered with her blinding, merciful alcoholism.

Love Israel [Birth date unknown] Cult leader Love Israel was actually a TV salesman from L.A. who teamed up with the son of comedian Steve Allen to form a new spiritual path for the dispossessed children of the middle class.

The Love Israel Family, or the Church of Jesus Christ at Armageddon, began as a community of young hippies who settled their cult on Queen Anne Hill from about 1970 to the mid '80s.

At its peak, the Love Family had nearly 400 members in 15 houses. The largest was a castle-like structure with turrets. The group also owned a health-food store and a woodworking shop on McGraw Avenue.

Love Israel is the eccentric center of the circle of true believers. He preached that members of his Love Family were all members of Jesus Christ's body (which member isn't clear). Cult followers changed their first names to match a virtue or Biblical figure—Serious, Logic, Love, Meekness—and took the last name Israel.

The Love Family wore robes, never cut their hair, carried cash in paper bags, and snorted Toulene.

The Love Family wore robes, never cut their hair, carried cash in paper bags, and snorted toluene (a toxic solvent) to achieve a spiritual high. This enlightenment method worked pretty well until two cult members died from asphyxiation. The Love Family's existence sparked a few other neighborhood and city controversies, such as the time a jealous Love Family man lit one of the Queen Anne houses on fire; his ex-lover and her new Love Family boyfriend were sleeping inside at the time. The cult also sparked the creation of the Citizens' Freedom Foundation, an anti-cult group designed to help cult members escape, get reprogrammed, and find happiness in a more rational fashion.

Cheryl Linn Glass (1961-1997): At the precocious age of nine, Cheryl Linn Glass was competing in go-cart races and running her own business, selling painted porcelain pottery to Frederick and Nelson. The money Glass earned enabled her to buy her first race car, and by the time she was 17 she had already won almost 500 races. When she graduated from Nathan Hale High School, she was labeled a "genius" because of her high IQ (by the late '80s, Glass had been elected one of the 100 Outstanding Women in Washington State).

Glass became a professional race-car driver at age 18—the first and only African-American female driver in the history of professional racing; her nickname in the racing circuit was "The Lady."

She turned from cars to new passions in 1983, inspired by her marriage to Richard Lindwall, the head mechanic from her racing team. She became ambitious about weddings and wedding attire, and aspired to have "a wedding the likes of which you've never seen before and maybe never will again." Her own ceremony cost 50 grand, on top of the cost of her elaborate raiment. The *Guinness Book of World Records* noted the detailed artwork of her gown: Designed by Glass, it included a 15-foot train and 40,000 pearls, 7,000 crystals, and 25,000 sequins sewn into the silk. Soon after her wedding, Glass opened her own bridal design shop in Pioneer Square on the corner of Second and Main.

But once out of the racing circuit, her life veered onto a twisted and dangerous course. Her marriage dissolved and she was harassed by racist groups at her home in Edmonds. She had repeated run-ins with the King County police and with her neighbors. Her once-bright life devolved into a mess of fear, racism, and litigation, her accomplishments obscured by the shadows around her final years. Glass jumped—or was pushed—to her death off the Aurora Bridge on July 15, 1997. She was 35 years old.

Some who were close to Glass think she was killed as part of a Mafia conspiracy: Glass had incriminating evidence, they say, about the laundering of cocaine money through the race-car industry. Others think she simply lost her mind. In her last few years, Glass' only real advocates were fringe groups and political radicals. The confusing details of her story are unresolvable; like many of Seattle's eccentrics, somehow Cheryl Linn Glass came unstuck from the city's safe orbit and headed out into the darkness.

3

Arts

SIR THOMAS BEECHAM, MUSIC DIRECTOR of the Seattle Symphony from 1941 to 1943, once said, "If I were a member of this community, really I should get weary of being looked on as a sort of aesthetic dustbin." Those involved in Seattle's art scene today can only laugh bitterly at the 60-odd years since that proclamation—because not much has changed. Seattle is still considered an artistic backwater, especially by the city's infamous nouveau riche. Resident artists either welcome the resulting freedom of expression or become as bitter as ex-Seattleite Art Chantry (who, after moving, said in a *Stranger* interview that Seattle had become "a city of assholes and whores"). Despite Mr. Chantry's charming ebullience, there are still some venues at which to find great art. In the following series of guides, the assholes are debunked and the real artists celebrated.

Art Galleries & Museums

Center on Contemporary Art (CoCA)
Denny Regrade
310 Terry Ave N (within Consolidated Works), (206) 728-1980, www.COCASeattle.org
Thurs-Sun noon-8 pm
$5 suggested donation
Until the arrival of Consolidated Works, CoCA was the venue for "fringy" art.

It's best that the two have joined forces and CoCA has been folded into the giant space that is Consolidated Works. There was, and still is, a lot of disagreement—among artists and art viewers alike—about whether CoCA lives up to its rather pretentious name: "The Center on Contemporary Art." This controversy rages no more transparently than in every year's Annual, in which a guest curator picks and chooses from local work to create a who's who of Seattle artists. Of course, the art world is never happy with the result, but the show is always interesting. If you're looking to become familiar with local art, another useful, eccentric event is the occasional 24-hour art marathon, in which artists create works on the spot and sell them for reasonable amounts. Showing up at 3 am is sure to get you a good deal.

PIER DICARLO

ConWorks: Shifting visionaries Matthew Richter and Meg Shiffler

Consolidated Works
Denny Regrade
410 Terry Ave N, (206) 860-5245,
www.conworks.org
Thurs-Sun noon-8 pm

Who knows where the vagabond Consolidated Works will be by the time you're reading this? But we hope it's somewhere, because Meg Shiffler, the director of visual arts, is putting up the most intelligent shows in Seattle: philosophical as well as visual investigations of different art forms. Within the space of two months, audiences were treated first to the obsessive focus of artists who work in ephemeral media like paper cups and their own hair, and then to a big exuberant sprawl of graffiti, sprayed right on the gallery wall. In addition to the out-and-out quality of the work, the shows have generated an interest in art that no other institution here has matched; the opening-night parties are as well attended as rock shows.

Esther Claypool
Pioneer Square
617 Western Ave, (206) 264-1586, www.estherclaypool.com
Tues-Fri 11 am-5:30 pm, Sat 11 am-5 pm

Everyone loves Esther Luttikhuizen and Brad Claypool. They're one of the scene's nicest couples, always supportive of local artists and their work. The

Esther Claypool gallery is one of the few commercial spaces to concentrate on Seattle and Northwest artists (although the gallery also puts up shows by Auslanders). The emphasis here is on works on paper, from conceptual to figurative, from watercolor to photography—there is a definite sense of craft and fun. Word is out about this gallery; it's a sea of black clothing on First Thursdays.

Eyre/Moore
Downtown
913 Western Ave, (206) 624-5596, www.eyremore.com
Tues-Sat 11 am-6 pm and by appointment
Eyre/Moore is like an adolescent girl: at times awkward and unsure, at times stunningly (and obliviously) beautiful. Having opened in 1997, this gallery hasn't been around long enough to develop a real personality, but some of the shows thus far have been refreshingly sophisticated. Owners Missi Moore and Rich Eyre have hosted a couple of philosophically driven group shows, including a fine meditation on self-portrait photography, revealing their quirky, concept-driven sensibility.

Greg Kucera Gallery
Downtown
212 3rd Ave S, (206) 624-0770, www.gregkucera.com
Tues-Sat 10:30 am-5:30 pm
Greg Kucera wears the mantle of his gallery's high-class reputation well, balancing shows by major artists (Kiki Smith, Ann Hamilton, Andres Serrano) with good local artists, such as Sally Schuh and Mark Calderon. Kucera has the pull to get the majors—but by the time Kucera's selection of "cutting-edge" work reaches the cool, clean air of his gallery space, it already seems to be institutionalized. Guess that's what happens when you get a reputation.

Henry Art Gallery
University District
15th Ave NE & NE 41st St, (206) 543-2280, www.henryart.org
Tues-Sun 11 am-5 pm, Thurs 11 am-8 pm
$3.50-$5.00 (Thursdays from 5 pm-8 pm are pay-what-you-wish)
Since its mammoth redesign in 1997, the Henry has become a real draw for its showings of edgy contemporary artists as well as full-scale retrospectives (including the beautiful exhibition last year of Andy Warhol line drawings). The space-age new building is divided into north, south, and east galleries, a cafeteria, a sculpture garden, and a gift shop. Plan to spend at least two hours wandering the labyrinth; exhibitions are frequently interactive (the video art has been particularly intriguing in this element), and the text provided is pithily intellectual, as befits the Henry's University of Washington association. For more in-depth education, check into the

Henry's lectures and workshops (206/543-2281). To schedule a guided tour, call (206) 616-8782 during business hours.

Houston

Capitol Hill

907 E Pike St, (206) 860-7820, www.wehaveaproblem.com

Tues-Sat noon-7 pm

Houston smartly fills the gap between everyday visual culture and art. The trademark of any show at Houston is a kind of witty nonchalance about "high art," but in truth it is the kind of gallery that makes you realize how much of your day is spent looking at and analyzing visual input, from graphic design to textiles to billboards. Gallery owner Matthew Houston has brought in work as varied as Barry McGee's graffiti, Simon Larbalestier's photographs for the covers of Pixies albums, and Shawn Wolfe's anti-advertising campaign, Beatkit.

BIO

Matt Houston

Who is he? The man who created and runs Houston, a gallery of graphic design, street art, and consumerism.

How did you start Houston? "It started out of the design firm/design collective I founded in 1998. But Houston has been an idea long in the making. I was at Microsoft for five years, and when I was ready to say goodbye, I started this. This place has been a dream of mine: a studio, a store, and a gallery."

Which galleries in Seattle do you like and dislike? "Billy Howard at Howard House shows a good handful of artists. Greg Kucera has been around and Jim Harris shows fresh work. I'm constantly disappointed by SAM, but the Henry

C. TAYLOR

makes up for it."

What sort of work are you trying to expose the public to? "I want to show young contemporary artists from around the world. I show what I like: pretty graphic work. I'm looking outside of Seattle for what you wouldn't see here. We have artists from Sydney, Amsterdam, San Francisco. And we are opening a Houston in Tokyo. It will be called Return to

Houston. At the gallery, technology is a subject or a theme, or a medium. Graffiti or digitally created work is also a focus. We're celebrating individual artists who create products: books, T-shirts, paintings, and stickers. And people are always asking us what we're listening to and where to go to see a show; it's a complete culture."

What's striking about this city, and what's ugly about it? "The EMP. And the inside of the EMP. It's perfectly Seattle to spend a ton of money on the outside and not pay attention to the exhibition itself. And they charge $20. The Louvre is $12. Come on. But I'm excited about the library and Rem Koolhaas. I'm very interested in the process of moving all those books out of the current library, and putting them back into the new library."

Howard House

Belltown

2017 2nd Ave, (206) 256-6399, www.howardhouse.net

Tues-Sat 11 am-6 pm

Billy Howard started this gallery in his own home (hence the name) and then moved it to the back of a hip furnishings store. This is the place to see Seattle's cleverest artists—from people working with found materials and assemblage (Robert Yoder, Jesse Paul Miller) to the artists exploring the frontiers of abstract painting (Ken Kelly, Mark Takamichi Miller). Howard's bent is toward conceptually based artists, no matter what their media, and this has resulted in show after show of really fine work. His artists also tend to hang together socially, and to find yourself in the middle of this circle is to witness the wheels of Seattle art in action.

James Harris Gallery

Downtown

309A 3rd Ave S, (206) 903-6220

Tues-Sat 10:30 am-5:30 pm

By the time you are reading this book, we hope that James Harris is back and running after the nasty little earthshaker of February, 2001. James Harris shows nationally and internationally known artists side by side with local talent, contextualizing Seattle's art in a way other galleries fail to. This opens the door for Seattle artists working in installations or in non-traditional media, and it's also a boon for art viewers, teaching them that a teacup is not always a teacup. Few other galleries will devote a whole room to one of Los Angeles artist Carlos Mollura's inflatable sculptures, or Martha Benzing's abstract, Milky-Way-like Kool-Aid paintings.

Oculus/FotoCircle

(206) 624-2645, www.fotocircle.com

Oculus has a number of strong artists, and FotoCircle works very hard to bring in a variety of photographers. The ramshackle space that the two co-ops shared under the viaduct was irreparably damaged in the 2001 earthquake, so the galleries are happily relocating—the old space was too large, anyway, to do justice to the artists' meticulous insouciance. (In the old, tiny Oculus space, Stephanie Ashby-DiRicco could fill the room with a web of wax, string, and spools, and actually change the atmosphere.) Call or check their website for relocation information.

The Pound Gallery

Capitol Hill

1216 10th Ave between Spring & Union, (206) 323-0557, www.poundgallery.com

Sat-Sun noon-4 pm and by appointment

The shows at this space rarely fall into the traditional, comfortable categories that commercial galleries tend to favor. Susan Robb's installations, for example, combine intricate and slightly icky biological sculptures fashioned out of an astonishing palette of materials (Play-Doh, fur, epoxy, her own hair) with blown-up, abstracted, deeply colored photographs. Gary Smoot's enormous mousetraps (baited with babies made of cheese) made the gallery difficult to stroll around in, a witty comment (perhaps) on art's dangerous and subversive quality. Steven Lyons often accompanies his sculpture—assemblages in a Joseph-Cornell vein, but a great deal more morbid, and often suspended in an amber-colored resin—with photographs of the very same pieces, making him a kind of flâneur of his own work. The gallery's name

Pound Gallery: Gary Smoot's "Weiner" is just one of the dogs

comes from the legion of dogs (and a tail-less cat named Bunny) who wander amiably through the gallery and the artists' studios and occasionally integrate themselves into the installations. They are friendly. Pet them.

Roq La Rue
Belltown
2224 2nd Ave, (206) 374-8977, www.roqlarue.com
Tues-Fri 2 pm-6 pm, Sat noon-4 pm, and by appointment
No one else shows the kind of art Kirsten Anderson does at her ballsy little gallery in Belltown. Anderson's selections have a hard urban edge, featuring paintings inspired more by comic books and album covers than by Rothko and Newman—meaning, you won't see art-school exercises here. The work is not always gorgeous; more often than not it leans toward the gritty and confrontational, which makes Roq La Rue a kind of conscience for Seattle's art world.

Seattle Art Museum
Downtown
100 University St, (206) 654-3100 recorded information, (206) 654-3255 information desk, (206) 654-3121 box office, www.seattleartmuseum.org
Tues-Sun 10 am-5 pm, Thurs 10 am-9 pm
$5-$7 (First Thursday of every month is free)
There it is, at the heart of downtown: slick, tall, and fronted by the enigmatic Hammering Man. The Seattle Art Museum is, in every way, an Institution. The shows curated here tend to be creaky and uninteresting, and the permanent exhibits change so rarely and invoke so little passion that locals rarely

frequent the place. However, every once in a while something great comes through—recently, the architecture- and graphic-arts-inspired shows have been the winners. Also worth noting is SAM's lecture series, which imports speakers such as Henry Louis Gates Jr., art historians, and archaeologists to discuss topics in-depth. There is a yearly noir film festival, which is both little-known and great, and sometimes there's even the odd all-ages rock show.

SOIL Artist Cooperative
Capitol Hill
12th and Pike St, (206) 264-8061
Thurs-Sun noon-5 pm
SOIL is enormous—at any given time there are 20 to 30 participating members, which in the past has created some bureaucratic difficulty. (The politics of an artist co-op can be as intricate and brutal as anything plotted in the palaces of the 16th-century Mughals.) The payoff of SOIL's size and frequent turnover, however, is an equally enormous range of work, some of it very good. Most young local artists pass through SOIL at some point in their careers, either as members or as guests. The best shows here tend to be thematic: a group of artists meditating on home, or plaster, or the color pink. And SOIL throws great opening parties.

C. TAYLOR

Gallery openings: Where the free booze flows (this one is at Roq la Rue)

Suyama Space (aka George Suyama Architects)
Belltown
2324 2nd Ave,
(206) 256-0809
Mon-Fri 9 am-5 pm
This is one of the most gorgeous art spaces in Seattle; not coincidentally it's in the middle of an architect's office. Curator Beth Sellars has a penchant for installation and conceptual art, and she invites artists to respond to the space itself, rather than simply hang their work, and some of the resulting exhibitions have been stunning: Trimpin's sound-oriented installation of "Conloninpurple," Victoria Haven's rubber-band sculpture climbing up the side of a wall, Deborah Aschheim's universe of textured and epoxied shapes hanging from the ceiling. The gallery's mid-office location can make visiting a little tough, but you should never, ever pass up a show at Suyama.

Theater

A Contemporary Theatre (ACT)
Downtown
700 Union St, (206) 292-7676, www.ATCTheatre.org
Since moving into its new, $30 million-plus facility a few years go, ACT has been trying to balance fiscal responsibility and aesthetic adventure by countering riskier work (such as *Quills*, the comedy-drama about the Marquis de Sade that has since been made into a movie) with the hoariest theater chestnuts (such as Neil Simon's *The Odd Couple*). The former Eagles Hall now holds three performance spaces: a traditional thrust stage, a theater-in-the-round, and a smaller cabaret space, which is often rented out to smaller theater groups (such as the incomprehensibly popular Late Nite Catechism, which will probably still be running as you read this). Tickets are pricey, but production quality is consistent. Occasional big-name touring acts add extra variety to the programming.

GREGORY WHITE

Annex Theatre: Held captive by skyrocketing property values

Annex Theatre
Downtown
1916 4th Ave, (206) 728-0933, www.annextheatre.org
A company focused on new and developing work, Annex is also notable for being an all-volunteer collective that has survived since 1987. One of the city's most prominent "fringe" theaters, Annex considers itself a flagship for "big, cheap theater," and is noted for the exuberant musicals of playwright/composer Chris Jeffries as well as other large-cast spectacles. It seems likely that Annex will soon lose its current space due to rising property values; how a transition to a new space will affect its identity remains to be seen.

ArtsWest
West Seattle
4711 California Ave SW, (206) 938-0339, www.artswest.org
Arts West is West Seattle's only resident theater, with an impressive performance venue. Relatively new, programming here has been wildly varied, which is a sign of both an eclectic mindset and a still-forming identity.

Book-It Repertory Theatre

Seattle Center, 305 Harrison St (offices), (206) 216-0877, www.book-it.org

Book-It adapts literature to the stage with rigorous—some would say excessive—fidelity. But even critics would agree that Book-It's adaptations of novels have grown more creative, veering away from the inclusion of every single word, which was the theater's original policy. Book-It has a loyal subscriber base, and its performances are often shockingly successful—a few years ago, *The Awakening* really rocked the house. Performances are staged at various venues.

Consolidated Works

Denny Regrade

410 Terry Ave N, (206) 860-5245, www.conworks.org

A recent and highly ambitious addition to the Seattle arts scene, Consolidated Works houses a theater, art gallery, and cinema, and produces multidisciplinary series in which the work created in all three media relates to a theme. Consolidated Works' capacious building is in constant danger of being yanked away, but executive director Matt Richter seems to be operating on the idea that if the place is beautiful enough, the landlords won't be able to bring themselves to pull the plug on it. So far, he's succeeded.

Empty Space Theatre

Fremont

3509 Fremont Ave N, (206) 547-7500, www.emptyspace.org

For several years, the Empty Space was dominated by wacky comedy of the high-camp, chain-saw-and-smoke-machine variety. More recently, and under new direction, its programming has become more diverse, ranging from a surprisingly sincere and affectionate *Of Mice and Men* to *The Texarkana Waltz*, a cowboy musical about a catatonic youth's fantasy life. Though the actors' backstage facilities are notoriously cramped, the theater is very comfortable; the vertiginously slanted seating ensures a good view for every audience member.

The Fifth Avenue

Downtown

1308 5th Ave, (206) 625-1900, www.5thavenuetheatre.org

Looking for Broadway hits performed by second-rate touring stars? Look no more! But even theatergoers who hate musicals will marvel at the theater's architectural majesty; built in 1926, the Fifth was Seattle's first theater to be designed with an Asian motif. Symbols cover everything, particularly the main domed ceiling, which is an exact replica of the dome in the throne room of the Forbidden City's imperial palace! Another fancy feature is the fully restored Wurlitzer pipe organ, which rises dramatically from the orchestra pit when used to accompany the occasional vintage silent film.

The Fifth is often used by groups as diverse as Seattle Arts & Lectures, Seattle International Film Festival, and the Burien Dance Theater.

House of Dames
Capitol Hill

1017 E. Pike St, (206) 720-5252, www.houseofdames.com

Basically, House of Dames is maverick director/producer Nikki Appino, who likes to work on a large scale. Previous work has ranged from the adaption of the French novel, *Djinn*, the production of which sprawled throughout an abandoned warehouse, to *Rain City Rollers*, a musical set in a women's roller derby; gender-bending and mythology are frequent sub-

ject matter. The shows are sometimes uneven, but are always worth seeing. Unfortunately for Appino's fans, these ambitious projects take time and a lot of fund-raising to put together, so House of Dames rarely mounts more than one show per year.

SARAH HARLETT

House of Dames: Monica Appleby as Rosie in Rain City Rollers *shows her fighting spirit*

Intiman Theatre
Queen Anne

Seattle Center, 201 Mercer St,

(206) 269-1900, www.intiman.org

For years and years, Intiman has been Seattle's "classic" theater—that is to say, it puts together serviceable productions of plays that you read in college drama class. Intiman has occasionally broken away from this formula, as with its production of Tony Kushner's *Angels in America*. And new artistic director Bartlett Sher promises to move the theater in new directions. Whether this will result in renewed vitality or a further elimination of any distinction between Seattle's biggest theaters (ACT, the Rep, and Intiman) remains to be seen. Intiman's theater space has the potential to provide for glorious entertainment: It features a lovely 446-seat thrust-stage playhouse, a cushy lobby, and plenty of parking.

New City Theater
Capitol Hill

1632 Broadway, (in First Christian Chruch), (206) 328-4683, newcity@accessone.com

Once one of Seattle's most exciting and experimental companies, noted for collaborations with Maria Irene Fornes and Richard Foreman, New City went into a slump for several years, during which it sold its home (which has now become the Richard Hugo House) and produced infrequently at best. More recently, artistic director John Kazanjian seems to be bringing the organization back to life; Seattle will benefit from a revitalization of this theater's adventurousness and intelligence.

Northwest Actors Studio
Capitol Hill
1100 E Pike St, (206) 324-6328, www.nwactorsstudio.org
Primarily an acting school, Northwest Actors Studio is also available for rent, and in recent years has begun to mount its own productions with greater frequency. Sightlines are not the best, but it's a fairly comfortable space.

Northwest Asian American Theater
International District
409 7th Ave S, (206) 340-1049, www.nwaat.org
NWAAT produces a wide range of stuff, from re-interpretations of standard fare like *The Fantasticks* to experimental performance art in its annual A-Fest. They're in residence at Theatre Off Jackson, a comfortable and versatile venue in the International District.

Open Circle Theater
Denny Regrade
429 Boren Ave N, (206)382-4250
One of several relatively recent "fringe" theaters, the Open Circle is together enough to have its own space, a reasonably comfy theater in the Denny Regrade area. An energetic group, this theater's programming falls into a mix of original work by company members and productions of plays by contemporary playwrights, in a similar vein to Annex and Printer's Devil.

ANDY PAPADOTOS

Open Circle Theater: Is that the Fringe out there?

Printer's Devil Theatre
(206) 860-7163,
printersdeviltheatre@hotmail.com
Printer's Devil Theatre was the darling troupe of Seattle for a while, blessed by the likes of Eric Bogosian. Now wending its way through an awkward organizational adolescence, Printer's Devil continues to apply its energy and commitment to a mix of new work (such as plays by Erik Ehn and Lawrence Krauser)

and reinterpretations of classics like Ibsen's *Hedda Gabler*. One of many theaters in town without its own venue, Printer's Devil is prone to seize on unusual spaces for its productions, such as using the Kalakala ferry for Chekhov's *The Seagull*.

Re-Bar
Denny Regrade

1114 Howell St, (206) 223-9873

One of the few places in town where you can drink, smoke, and watch theater simultaneously, Re-Bar is home to a mix of cabarets and plays, with an emphasis on lurid, campy romps. Productions tend to be hilarious, irreverent, messy, drunken, and inexplicably successful in some truly fucked-up way.

DAVID BELISLE

Seattle Fringe Theater Festival
Everywhere

Dina Martina at the Re-Bar: Those eyes, those lips. . . .

1415 3rd Ave, (206) 342-9172

Once a year in September, several venues around town (including bars and churches, which indicates the level of madness) host tiny productions by unknowns. Advocates argue that this event is a truly democratic forum for performance; critics snipe that its structure discourages more skilled performers from taking part, resulting in a mishmash of beginners and degrading the whole fringe theater scene. Still, every year a handful of acts rise to the top, pulling in crowds and good press. Trying to find something good can be maddening, but this may be the most audience-interactive theater event you'll attend in Seattle.

Seattle Public Theater
Greenlake

7312 W Green Lake Dr N, (206) 328-4848, www.seattlepublictheatre.org

Seattle's most politically minded theater has taken over the former Bathhouse Theater in the Green Lake district. SPT is greatly influenced by Augusto Boal's Theater of the Oppressed, with its practice of involving the audience in the narrative of the productions.

Seattle Repertory Theatre
Queen Anne

Bagley Wright Theatre and the Leo K. Theatre in the Seattle Center, 155 Mercer St, (206) 443-2222, www.seattlerep.org

It's rumored that artistic director Sharon Ott spent close to $1,000,000 on the

Rep's lavish production of *As You Like It.* True or not, it's indicative of this company's approach: large, lavish productions of middle-of-the-road fare, such as last season off-Broadway hit, or something featuring politically correct, "controversial" themes. But the results are solid (the Rep won a 1990 Tony for Outstanding Regional Theatre) and there are signs of fresh energy, such as the Rep's production of a play by a local writer, Elizabeth Heffron, in the 2000-2001 season—a first for a large equity theater in Seattle. The Rep has a substantial and esteemed educational program as well.

Taproot Theatre
Greenwood

204 N 85th St, (206) 781-9707, www.taproot.org

A Christian theater company that isn't as close-minded as you might expect; productions range from safe, religious-themed crowd-pleasers like *Mass Appeal* to chancier stuff like an original adaptation of H. G. Well's *The Island of Dr. Moreau.*

Theatre Babylon
Capitol Hill

Union Garage, 1418 10th Ave, (206) 784-8647, www.theatrebabylon.org

Focused on original work by its own members, Theatre Babylon's productions vary in quality but can be surprisingly rich in emotion. They co-habit the Union Garage with A Theatre Under the Influence, a small but comfortable and versatile performance space that has recently been expanded.

Theater Schmeater
Capitol Hill

1500 Summit Ave, (206) 324-5801,

www.schmeater.org

Theater Schmeater began with a focus on the classics, which didn't stop them from turning stage versions of *Twilight Zone* episodes into a popular cash cow. Artistic director Sheila Daniels has begun pushing in different directions, including plays by contemporary playwrights and late-night satires. And risks have paid off: Theater Schmeater's remount of Larry Kramer's *The Normal Heart*, an AIDS drama considered by many to be hopelessly dated, turned out to be a smash success and surprisingly resonant.

MEGAN JOPLIN

Theater Schmeater: Risks have paid off

theater simple

109 N 58th St, (206) 784-8647, www.theartery.org/simple

The adaptation of Bulgakov's *The Master and Margarita* by theater simple's was so successful, it led to a tour all over the United States, Canada, and Australia. Though other productions haven't made such a splash, they're an inventive troupe prone to spare but imaginative stagings.

A Theatre Under the Influence

Capitol Hill

Union Garage, 1418 10th Ave, (206) 720-1942

This troupe specializes in lesser-known works by notable playwrights, ranging from Edward Albee to Caryl Churchill. Their choices have been intriguing, and the direction and acting are dependably solid and perceptive. A Theatre Under the Influence co-habits the Union Garage with Theatre Babylon.

BIO:

Amy Fleetwood

Who is she? Actor/managing director at Theater Under the Influence

How long have you been married?
"Gosh, when did I get married... three and a half years, I think."

Is marriage everything you thought it would be?
"Oh dear. Uhm... my, my, my. Marriage is many things."

Name a few.
"Oh god. Well, it's interesting being married to Craig [Bradshaw, director of The Provok'd Wife] . . . ."

What's interesting about Craig?
"Craig is a man of strong opinions. And so am I—a woman of strong opinions. I like being married to Craig, but it's all over the place."

KELLY O

Where do you go?
"We go turtle-watching and we go bird-watching and bear-watching. And we go to loggerheads about running a theater company, at which point we go back to see the turtles."

And you have a baby now?
"Yes, Sarita. I'm finding that having a baby is making the doing of theater very difficult. None of us gets paid for doing this play, and we're spending a lot of money paying for a baby-sitter at a time when I've left work and am

staying home with the baby. So the doing of theater ends up costing a lot, in all kinds of ways."

You should put your baby in the show.
"When she was five days old, Craig was going to put her in the show we were doing, *Light Shining in Buckinghamshire.* There's a scene where a woman is so poor that she's starving to death and has no milk, so she's leaving a baby on the steps of the mayor's house and trying to tear herself away. Craig thought we could put Sarita in for the baby."

And you decided against this?"
I nixed the idea. She can go on stage when she chooses to, and not before then.

Because an actor's life is so hard and you didn't want to fill Sarita's head with glamour?
"Exactly. I'm hoping she'll be a botanist."

Dance

Amii LeGendre Dance

Capitol Hill

Velocity Contemporary Dance Studio, 915 E Pine, (206) 325-8773

In short: Amii LeGendre kicks ass. A former gymnast, her work is characterized by athletic movement and wicked quirks. A slight hand flicker here, a head roll there—her stuff is not for the novice. LeGendre is a regular instructor at Velocity Dance Studio and an emerging local choreographer; her work can often be seen at On the Boards and other venues around town.

The Chamber Dance Company

University District

Meany Theater, University of Washington, 4001 University Way NE, (206) 543-9843

To order tickets, call the UW Arts Tickets Office at (206) 543-4880

ALICE WHEELER

Amii LeGendre Dance: Kicking ass—but subtly

The Chamber Dance Company features local dance favorites, each of whom are earning advanced dance-related degrees at the University of Washington. This company boasts the unparalleled Rob Kitsos, a tremendously talented choreographer and dancer who most often injects humor into his work, a rarity in modern dance. His previous work featured the recitation of cornball self-help clichés while he and fellow dancer Ryan Corriston floated around the stage in orange flight suits. (And you thought modern dance was already funny looking!)

Lingo dancetheater

Capitol Hill

Velocity Contemporary Dance Studio, 915 E Pine, (206) 325-8773

As the co-founder of Velocity: A Contemporary Dance Studio, and as the leader of Lingo, KT Niehoff is the Seattle dance scene. *Emma Was Attracted to Accidents*, one of her best pieces, was a gale force of athleticism and rock 'n' roll, and there seems to be no stopping her energy.

On the Boards

Queen Anne

100 W Roy St, (206) 217-9886, www.ontheboards.org

Box office: (206) 217-9888

On the Boards provides Seattle with a steady stream of high-quality contemporary works from a wide variety of artists in dance, music, and performance art. Especially notable is the fabulous 12 Minutes Max, held every six weeks. For five bucks, you can see six short pieces, each of which has survived a

....

BIO

....

KT Niehoff

Who is she? Dancer/choreographer/administrator.

What brought you to Seattle?
"A desperate need to get out of New York City. [Choreographer] Pat Graney brought me here—a job with Pat."

What keeps you here?
"You get entrenched, right? What keeps me here—my company, the momentum of Seattle—I think we all feel it. There's a national attention to Seattle at the moment, and it feels like a pregnant place to be making work. Maybe ripe is a better adjective; I don't know about that pregnant part."

What's wrong with pregnant?
"Pregnant's all right; ripe is better, I thought. There's all this opportunity—there's funding; there's On the Boards—it seems like ever since I got here there's potential for things to happen. It's still a bit of a frontier land."

KELLY O

And New York is not?
"No. New York is the Boston Tea Party. The economy is set there; the establishment has its clutches in. Here, you say, 'I'd like to do X, Y, and Z,' and people come back at you with 'That's a great idea!' There's still an entrepreneurial spirit, whereas in New York, you put an idea out there and it gets squashed. It's just more difficult."

What have you got in the works?
"Well, we've just changed the company name. The group is now called 'Lingo dancetheater.' That took fucking forever."

Why?
"Well . . . it's permanent. You have to imagine yourself as a 60-year-old choreographer, and you have to imagine that you can live with that name."

What were some other candidates?
"'Other Alphabets.' 'Spill/Response.' 'Strong House.' It was all over the map. 'Badass Dancers.'"

That's the one I like!
"'You Really Should Hire Us,' that was in the running. 'Seattle's Number One Dance Company' was another candidate, but we opted out."

And you just revamped your performance space?
"Yes, the Velocity Main-Space Theater. We're starting a bunch of programming and hope to pick up the contemporary performance presentation ball."

Are you trying to compete with On the Boards?
"God, no. There's a lot going on—there's Consolidated Works; there's OTB; we're just hoping to add to the pool of places to perform."

quality-assuring audition process. The showcase features dance, puppetry, humorous monologues, and just about anything else you can think of. A chance to see great art without all the commitment.

Pat Graney Company

911 E. Pike St, (206) 329-3705, www.patgraney.org

Pat Graney has been described as one of the best modern dance choreographers in the country. For the past 20 years, she and her company have captivated audiences with visually stunning pieces and intellectually driven imagery. This is modern dance at its best.

ALICE WHEELER
Pat Graney: Not like any choreographer you've seen

Spectrum Dance Theater

800 Lake Washington Blvd, (206) 325-4161

Audiences who love jazz love Spectrum. This professional company has gathered a sizable audience in a short amount of time. The company's work is accessible and appealing to the average viewer, and though you won't be as moved as at a modern dance performance, you might be lifted to your feet and compelled to shout "Encore!" You can take your mom to a Spectrum Dance Theater performance.

Summer Arts Festival

University District

University of Washington, (206) 685-6696, artsfest@u.washington.edu

To order tickets, call the UW Arts Tickets Office at (206) 543-4880

This relatively new festival featured the Chamber Dance Company its first year, promising many other notable dance performers to come.

33 Fainting Spells

(206) 568-8640, www.33faintingspells.org

The spell cast by 33 Fainting Spells, Seattle's dance theater group (made up of Dayna Hanson, Gaelen Hanson, and Peggy Piacenza), seems to be concocted of one part nostalgia and two parts innovation. Consistently witty and beautifully narrative, the group's pieces—which have included *Sorrow's Sister* and *Maria the Storm Cloud*—simultaneously evoke a dusky European fin-de-siècle romance and a manic, austere modern psychology, employing cryptic but gorgeous movement, peculiar props, and arcane, wide-ranging music. The group is Chekhov in tank tops.

UW World Series

University District
Meany Theater, University of
Washington, 4001 University
Way NE
To order tickets, call the
UW Arts Tickets Office at
(206) 543-4880

ANNIE MARIE MUSSELMAN

33 Fainting Spells: Peculiar props and Chekhov

Featuring internationally known companies such as: Pappa TARAHUMARA, Paul Taylor Dance Company, Trinity Irish Dance Company, Ballet Hispanico of New York, Garth Fagan Dance, and Mark Morris Dance Group. If you know these names, you know the caliber of dance the UW World Series presents. It's some of the best modern dance in the world.

Music

Death Cab for Cutie
by Erin Franzman

BEN GIBBARD, CHRIS WALLA, AND NICK HARMER MET ME AT THE GREEN LANTERN TAVERN IN WALLINGFORD, where they've been holding most of their band meetings. My mother would say they look like nice young men in their short pants, white socks, and Converse sneakers. The scene is wholesome: We drink bottled beer and lean back against the blond wood paneling of the Green Lantern. The light is low and warm. Nick fidgets and sits on the chair-back, his feet on the seat, but he gives long and thoughtful answers. Ben grows expansive after the second round and illustrates his speech with gestures. He is the only one who bothers with sarcasm. Chris is serene, except for a steady toe-tapping that he keeps up almost without fail for the two and a half hours we are there.

What would be the title of your autobiography?
Ben: "Mine would be *All You Need Is to Get Some Sleep.*"

What's more important: the lyrics or the music?
Ben: "The music."

C. TAYLOR

Death Cab for Cutie: Holding up the wall

Nick: "The music—it's usually what you hear first."

Chris: "'Cause if you turn the music up loud enough you can't hear the lyrics."

What is the stupidest lyric ever written?

Nick: "The worst lyric ever written was by this boy group called LFO (Lyte Funkie Ones), and the chorus is 'New Kids on the Block had a bunch of hits/Chinese food makes me sick/and I like girls that wear Abercrombie & Fitch.'"

Chris: "It was my first day at work; I'm next to this guy cleaning plates, and that Kid Rock song comes on The End. And when it comes to that part in the song, 'I'm not straight outta Compton/I'm straight outta the trailer park,' the guy goes, 'Trailer park!' and raises his fist! And then he got all stoked and was rockin' out, like he was from a trailer park."

What's the dumbest thing you've ever done while drunk?

Nick: "Every band has its roles, and my role, whether I asked for it or not, has become band Dad. So I mainly don't drink at shows, or really, at all."

Ben: "I think I peed in my laundry hamper once when I was drunk."

Chris: "I think the dumbest thing I ever did drunk was go to work the next morning. When I was still drunk."

What song will you have played at your funeral?

Ben: "I'm on a super-super big GBV kick right now, so 'Don't Stop Now,' by Guided by Voices—because I think it's the most beautiful song."

Chris: "I think for me, 'How She Lied By Living,' by the Posies."

Nick: "Because I think about how I am going to die, 'Violence,' by Low. This is a thing that I have been going around and around in my brain about. It has to do with that whole 'Do the arts make kids pick up guns and go kill themselves and other people?' question. There are artists in the world who say, 'My violent movies and violent songs don't make kids pick up guns; this is totally unrelated to what I'm doing.' But what you negate when you say that is the fact that your movies and your music make people cry, make people jealous, make people feel. Either there is an impact or not. I just want to hold those people—who say there is no connection—to what they actually mean. So if you're saying that your movie doesn't make a kid go out and kill someone, then you are also saying your movie shouldn't make me want to feel a variety of emotions—much less feel empowered to do something like pick up a social cause."

> *The worst record I've ever loved? I had a secret affinity for Poison's* Look What the Cat Dragged In.

Ben: "Like how, after *Dead Poets Society*, I got my doctorate in poetry. I was so inspired I went out and got it the next day."

What's the worst album you've ever loved?

Nick: "The worst record I've ever loved? I liked Van Halen's *1984* a whole lot, and I had a secret affinity for Poison's *Look What the Cat Dragged In*."

Ben: "I think it would have to be Daryl Hall and John Oates' *Big, Bam, Boom*. Because I have it on cassette and vinyl. It's so tight."

Chris: "I went through that whole art rock phase, when I liked Yes and Genesis. Moving into the next level of art rock, when you pass Yes and Genesis and get into the Yes and Genesis clone bands of the '70s, I skipped over Camel and Gentle Giant, but I landed on Marillion for a while. There is a reason you don't know about this record. I really liked Misplaced Childhood."

What's the most naive ideal you held in your teens?

Chris: "That Marillion's Misplaced Childhood was a really good record."

Nick: "The most misplaced ideal that I probably ever had was that socialism could work in America."

Ben: "Mine had to do with SATs and GPAs in high school meaning something. I worked hard and got good grades and stayed in. Then I realized there was no point to it. So if I have a kid, I am going to pull him aside and say, 'Listen, Ben Jr., don't worry about it—if worst comes to worst, we'll send you to a junior college and then you'll go to a four-year, but don't worry about it. In fact, don't even go to college.' Because all I did was waste $25,000 of my parents' money."

Chris: "I think mine was that alcohol is an inherently bad thing by nature. I was straight-edge until I was almost 22."

What did you want to be when you grew up?

Chris: "I always wanted to be a recording engineer. There was a time when I wanted to be an architect, but the only career that I have thought about and stuck with since I was nine or 10 was recording engineer."

Nick: "I really wanted to be a geologist."

Ben: "I was going to play first base for the Mariners. That was until I was about 19, before I realized that I hadn't played baseball in eight years."

Classical

Early Music Guild of Seattle

(206) 325-7066

This excellent organization makes possible many good things for many good people who are dedicated to "historically informed performance" (or—amusingly, since the goal is to recapture ancient sounds and styles—HIP). More to the point of this entry, the Early Music Guild is the host of a pair of fine concert series, which bring in the big guns from all over the early music world. The International Series focuses on large ensembles, the Recital Series on smaller groups or occasional soloists. If a group has recorded for Harmonia Mundi or DG Archiv, the EMG will welcome it to Seattle with arms open and appropriately tuned to A=430Hz.

Typical Programming: One of the glories of the HIP movement has been its exhumation of overlooked masters; there's also a lot of Bach.

The Esoterics

(206) 344-3327, www.TheEsoterics.org

This superb chorus, probably the premier such ensemble in Seattle, have distinguished themselves for their bold repertoire choices and their fine voices. Dedicated to 20th- (and, one trusts, 21st-) century music, the Esoterics have consistently given audiences the best gift possible: fresh discoveries. Organizing each concert around a central theme (as concrete as a single composer; as poetic as works devoted to one of the elements), leader Eric Banks casts a wide net in selecting what to perform. A standard evening can draw from Europe, Africa, Asia, and South America for its sources, not to mention your backyard—Seattle and Northwest composers are well served by this group, which has commissioned a number of works over the years. (And the group's been well served by local composers—for the most part.) The Esoterics are what the phrase "not to be missed" is all about.

Typical Programming: Diverse, with a night encompassing both the most tonal of songs and some wild, chattering weirdness.

Medieval Women's Choir

(206) 325-7066

This affiliate of the Early Music Guild has made its mark with programming every bit as original and unfamiliar as any of the new music–leaning groups discussed elsewhere—only, in this case it's showcasing composers you've never heard of who've been dead for centuries. Just one of the many contributions that founding director Margriet Tindemans has made to music in this city, the MWC can make 14th-century France sound like the most wonderful place to be.

Typical Programming: Well, medieval, of course, but mostly the forgotten and overlooked byways of the time.

Northwest Chamber Orchestra
(206) 343-0445

The busy NWCO performs not only in the pleasingly raked Nordstrom Recital Hall in Benaroya, but also at the Seattle Art Museum and the Asian Art Museum in Volunteer Park. From these latter venues, you might guess that the NWCO doesn't exactly stray far from the tried-and-true; in this

BIO

Lori Goldston

Who is she? Cellist; co-founder of Black Cat Orchestra; provider of superb accompaniment for silent films; collaborator with just about every other interesting musician in town; played cello with Nirvana for Unplugged show and recording.

BENHAM STUDIO

Silent film scoring requires a range of musical styles—popular tunes, recognizable classics, folk melodies. Has playing with **Black Cat Orchestra** encouraged your eclectic career, or did you gravitate to them because you already were attracted to such diverse influences?
"I started the Black Cat Orchestra with Kyle Hanson about nine years ago. Aside from the songs that we compose, most of the band's material comes from our record collection, which covers a whole lot of territory. I've always loved hearing and/or playing new things."

You've dueted with everything from a drummer to a koto player; are there some instruments that match better with the cello than others, or is it merely a question of the collaborators involved?
"I'm generally much more interested in a musician's individual voice than the vehicle for it. That said, I admit that I am especially partial to certain instruments, including drums."

Are your own works improvised or through-composed? Do you have a preference between these methods?
"I'm comfortable with either or both, depending on the context and the players. I have a slight preference toward improvisation, due mostly to an aversion to loose sheets of paper."

I've always loved the sound of the cello in a rock-and-roll context; am I being delusional, or do you think there's something particularly apposite

about the union?
"The cello is a natural for rock. Its sound has a broad range of really visceral textures and noises; I'm surprised by new sounds all the time. Electric guitarists run their signal through all sorts of effects boxes in order to produce sounds that cellos make acoustically: distortion, sustain, fuzz and feedback, to name a few."

Do you have a favorite venue in Seattle? Is there a particularly welcoming theater with regrettably poor acoustics, or vice versa?
"Zeitgeist's new space has lovely room sound, and is very easy on the eyes. Second Avenue Pizza's back room is very homey, like some crazy loft space. The Baltic Room is elegant and dreamy. On the Boards' studio theater has a good sound, but is not so cozy. We did play one time on the Kalakala, and the acoustics were much better than I'd expected. It would be a great place for all sorts of sound experiments. I do wish that there were more venues in Seattle with some history. For instance, I really liked playing at Jules Mae's. It would be nice if things didn't get torn down so much here."

assumption you're basically correct, despite some more interesting items scattered here and there. But for those times when a Schubert trio will fit the bill (and that should be often enough), these are musicians of the highest caliber. Tickets are a bit pricey, though, considering the familiarity of the material; then again, kids are free.

Typical Programming: Some guest performers bring in a pleasant surprise; the rest is exactly what you'd expect.

Opus 7

(206) 782-2899, www.opus7.org

The ensemble-in-residence for the imposingly towered St. James Cathedral offers a fine reminder that whatever excesses Christians of all stripes have committed in the name of God, they've also made possible some lovely

music. Dedicated to religious works, naturally, but specifically to music of the 20th century. And the group admirably manages to avoid the overfamiliar; there's Britten and Tavener, to be sure, but not necessarily the pieces you'd expect. If God is in the details, then director Loren Pontén has done full service to his deity—the group sings beautifully to a member, no matter what is set before them. Always a service worth catching; too bad about those uncomfortable pews, though.

BOB LEX

Opus 7 at St. James Cathedral: Beautiful, with uncomfortable pews.

Typical Programming: Mostly tonal (were any of the Darmstadt gang into God?), but some aggressively modern pieces are fit in (and performed wonderfully) as well.

Orchestra Seattle, Seattle Chamber Singers

(206) 682-5208, www.osscs.org

Like the ads say, if you're number two you've got to try harder. So it'd be nice to report that these fine but, well, second-tier musicians were mixing it up with innovative programming. But the occasional West Coast premiere excepted, this is your father's classical music list. There's nothing wrong with Bach's choral works, Beethoven's symphonies, or Brahms' whatever; but one doesn't necessarily need to hear them again. Prices are reasonable, however; and if you're trying to figure out what classical piece that snatch of music in the Bugs Bunny cartoon comes from, a season of OSSCS will set you straight.

Typical Programming: Nothing that would have gotten von Karajan in hot water during the war years.

President's Piano

(206) 543-4880

This annual series at the University of Washington's Meany Theater isn't cheap, but each season features at least one or two "money-is-no-object" names. If your favorite ivory tickler is on tour, this is the most likely way she'll show up in town.

Typical Programming: Up to the artist, but what do you expect from virtuosi? Lots of Beethoven, Chopin, and similar monstrous dextral workouts.

Seattle Chamber Music Society Summer Festival

(206) 283-8808

Yes, Virginia, Seattle does have a summer, and the surest sign it's here is the return of this monthlong festival, which fills July with joyous music. Several well-programmed evenings of diverse chamber works, performed by talented local artists, make the rare sweltering evening a breeze to sit through. And the budget-conscious can't do better than sitting out on the lawn; you're allowed to do that for free, and the music is piped out to you. (It may seem like a simple idea, but it's depressingly rare in classical music for anything to be free.) Bring a blanket and enjoy.

Typical Programming: Heavy on the Romantics, but some early 20th-century masters get tossed in for spice.

Seattle Composer's Salon

(206) 548-0981

A monthly forum for local composers to try out their new, often unfinished pieces on audience members who don't pay much and only sometimes get their money's worth. The downsides are immediately apparent. The good news is there are many more interesting composers out there than you might think, and it only takes a few waves of beauty to make up for a flood of depressing mediocrity. These evenings (they barely qualify as concerts) can't really be recommended to the restless or ultra-demanding music lover, but if you feel like taking a chance on something, here's your chance.

Typical Programming: Anything you can imagine.

Seattle Pro Musica

(206) 781-2766

One of the older and more venerable choruses in town—which used to mean they were one of the more staid. In the past decade, however, director Karen P. Thomas has shaken things up for the better, keeping the baroque music that brought the group acclaim but making room for modern composers as well, not the least of which is her own fine work.

Typical Programming: Chosen throughout the last millennium, though never far from hummable.

Seattle Symphony

(206) 215-4700, www.seattlesymphony.org

Under Gerald Schwarz's leadership, this ragged, rural orchestra transformed itself into a topflight ensemble—at least on record. The Seattle Symphony's CD catalog, especially those discs devoted to the then-neglected American tonalists whom Schwarz has championed—Hanson, Piston, Diamond—is full of revelations. Live, the Seattle Symphony loses a

KCTS TELEVISION

Seattle Symphony: Brass and warhorses

little of its sheen, but it's still the number-one game in town for more than just its size (or the price of a ticket). In addition to its regular concerts (a conservative but nicely eclectic collection, hitting all the warhorses but covering some unfamiliar and original territory as well), a series of special series are designed for the more focused musical listener: the self-explanatory Mainly Mozart, the Hamlisch- and McFerrin-leaning Pops concerts, and Music of Our Time. The latter has done well by Pacific Rim composers, though truth be told, it has never gotten more adventurous or audience-challenging than mid-'60s Ligeti. The Seattle Symphony's home base, Benaroya Hall, features two venues: The larger Taper Auditorium houses the big shows, and though prices can reach into three figures, the acoustics are good enough to ensure satisfaction for much less; the Nordstrom Recital Hall, which also showcases many acts besides the Seattle Symphony, generally sells for considerably less.

Typical Programming: Familiar, but with attention paid to established (and comfortable) up-and-comers and favorites of the musical director.

UW Contemporary Group

(206) 543-4880

Thorny, dissonant, polyrhythmic, difficult music of all stripes—who actually listens to this stuff? Well, some of us do like all the blares and squawks. Fortunately for us, the University of Washington' s Joël François Durand heads an ensemble dedicated to its performance. Your best chance in a still sedately tonal town to hear Xenakis and Boulez, with plenty of gleaming neoclassical pieces thrown in for the faint of heart.

Typical Programming: All the glorious, challenging stuff that was "destroying" classical music back in the '60s, plus other hard-liners past and present.

Radio

KBCS 91.3 FM

Bellevue Community College's radio station features a lovingly eccentric line-up, including a groovy soul show, a great '50s B-sides show, Appalachian Mountain music, innovative jazz programming, and music of Hawaii.

KEXP 90.3 FM

It's rumored that cities other than Seattle have more than one interesting college radio station. Since the FCC is intent on shutting down pirate stations outright, or cunningly legislating them out of existence, there's really only one station in Seattle that plays music the other stations don't: KEXP 90.3 FM.

KEXP is a new name for an old Seattle institution: in April of 2001, the Experience Music Project made a deal with the University of Washington to co-own UW's KCMU 90.3 FM. After moving to less-cramped offices off-campus, and nearly doubling the station's transmitting power, there was one last change: the call letters. KCMU—that warhorse of independent radio—officially became KEXP on April 2, 200. It will be a huge crime against the city if the policies and programming of this station are mainstreamed in any way—but so far, as this book goes to press, there have been no adverse changes.

As with most venerable nonprofit institutions, KCMU's history is strewn with attempted revolts and bitter ex-volunteers, and there is a permanent

DJ Kutfather: Seattle's only radio rap show

sense that the station isn't what it could have been if it had stayed true to itself. Somewhere there still lurks the specter of CURSE (Censorship Undermines Radio Stations Everywhere), a group of ex-DJs (including former DJ and current rock musician Mark Arm) and their supporters who banded together in the early '90s to protest changes in KCMU's fundamental programming strategies. But despite the seemingly constant internal tension, KEXP's broadcasts are the best in the city for independent and local rock, African music, rap, and general weirdness.

Audioasis is the show dedicated to local indie rock recordings, while the Live Room is where you can find live, in-the-studio broadcasts of local bands. Street Sounds, featuring DJ Supreme and Kutfather, is Seattle's only local rap show, and almost always features guest spots by local hiphop artists. Sonarchy Radio and Expansions are both live shows as well: Sonarchy features live, wild jazz–tinged improv sets by musicians, while Expansions (sometimes mixed by local legend DJ Riz) comprises layers of quietness built over jazz-tinged rhythms. The Roadhouse, Swingin' Doors, and Shake the Shack—blues, country, and rockabilly revues, respectively—are only for die-hard genre fans, but KEXP's secret treasure is the Best Ambiance, a well-curated collection of African music with an emphasis on "Zim pop," as one DJ calls Zimbabwean music.

KSRB 1150 AM

Happily, the sweet breath of soul finally blew our way. A few years ago, this small, 5,000-watt station opened up shop, and listeners from Olympia to just north of Everett are finally being graced with a daily dose of classic R&B. And not just your mainstream crossovers either—even those well versed in the soulful arts will find themselves stumped and surprised by some of KSRB's artists and their B-sides, which are rarely (if ever) heard on commercial radio. While it's not surprising that someone finally realized the huge black music niche waiting to be filled in this market, what's more surprising is where it's coming from, and who started it: Bellevue, and two very white guys.

ADAM L. WEINTRAUB

DJs: Two very white guys

A quick listen to KSRB, and you might think you're stuck in a radio time warp. Not only is the soul music dated (1960-1980), but even the DJs, bumpers, and commercials sound like they're from 1972. It's as if the music were originating from a small, worn, one-room studio way down on Rainier Avenue—but it's not. It comes from inside a glossy, copper-colored building in the high-tech mecca of Bellevue, from the plush offices of the Sandusky Radio Corporation (home of local AM radio powerhouse KIXI AM 880). Though KSRB's "soul street-cred" should crumble right there on the spot, a look past this opulence at KSRB's actual working area and staff puts those fears to rest.

KIXI AM 880

You might be soothed by the sounds of Burt Bacharach, Sammy Davis Jr., Pat Boone, Barry Manilow, Tom Jones, Dionne Warwick, Billy Joel, Herb Alpert, Frank Sinatra, Neil Diamond, or Eddie Fisher. And on Saturday nights they play some of the goofiest concept radio around. "Rainbow" radio night, for instance, is a night dedicated to songs with colors in the title.

Film

Anarchists and Independents

Beyond the established venues, Seattle is home to a bevy of bars, back rooms, and independent screens that show movies that aren't big or commercial enough to land any sort of distribution outside of self-distribution. **The Speakeasy Cafe** (2304 2nd Ave, 206/728-9770) has been host to Joel Bachar's monthly Independent Exposure series since 1996 (see Bio), as well as other film and video events. The basement of the **Alibi Room** (85 Pike St, 206/623-3180) has been the home of Reed O'Beirne's Emerald Reels Super 8 Lounge. **2nd Avenue Pizza** (2015 2nd Ave) occasionally shows Super 8 film programs, and sometimes cult movies on video. **Consolidated Works** (410 Terry Ave N, 206/860-5245) shows some adventurous film series, while the **Seattle Art Museum** (100 University St, 206/625-8900) shows more traditional series, from screwball comedies to film noir. **911 Media Arts Center** (117 Yale Ave N, 206/682-6552) is the region's premier media arts center, and presents touring programs on both film and video. **The Big Picture** (2505 1st Ave, 206/256-0566) is a place to watch TV shows in a theatrical environment, and shows occasional indie films off video and DVD. For those listings and more, consult a current copy of *The Stranger.*

Calendar Houses

Although video has essentially killed the commercial viability of repertory theaters that show different classic double features every night, Seattle is home to several theaters that program excellent art films, as well as new prints of older films. Theaters like the Egyptian, the Varsity, and the Grand Illusion—a 70-seat jewel-box theater with turn-of-the-century red velvet seats and a pressed-tin ceiling—provide one with the sense that film is as important to rainy Seattle as it is to rainy

Grand Illusion: Good coffee, great movies.

Paris. The Grand Illusion's acclaimed Weekend Rarities program features director retrospectives and archival prints from around the world. And remember, the cafe at the Grand Illusion is the only place in the University District where you can find Vivace coffee.

The Little Theatre is open for performances of all sorts: Rendezvous readings and Michael Chick plays have been performed here. And the lobby serves as one of the best art galleries in town, where you can sometimes glimpse paintings by Brian Sendelbach (of Smell of Steve Inc.) and the Typing Explosion's oversized, photocopied masterpiece poems. Local filmmaker Gregg Lachow shot most of his film *Silence!* in the alley, theater, and lobby of this building.

Egyptian
801 E Pine St, (206) 323-4978

Grand Illusion
NE 50th St at University Way NE, (206) 523-3935

Little Theatre
610 19th Ave E, (206) 675-2055

Varsity
4329 University Way NE, (206) 632-3131

....

BIO
....

Michael Seiwerath

DAVID MARCRANDER

Who is he? Executive director of Northwest Film Forum, the only local non-profit institution that makes films, sanctions grants for films, teaches, and provides production and post-production space for filmmakers.

The first movie this editor saw when she was a little girl was *Rosemary's Baby.* **What was yours?**
"It was? Really. Huh. Uh, it had to be *Star Wars.* I was dying to go to *Star Wars.* My parents went to see it before they took me. My mom came home and said she 'fell asleep in the middle of it.' I couldn't speak to her, not for at least 10 minutes."

What do you do as executive director, other than drink champagne and prop your feet up on the desk?
"Oversee the programs of

two theaters and the studio director. I also watch over grants, the program with EMP [Experience Music Project], etc."

What are you doing with EMP?
"Wednesday-Night Movie Nights. It consists of concert films, rare footage, and feature-lengths with great musical scores."

How did you get into film?
"My first love was still-photography. And during a summer in college, I was

offered free rent in Thousand Oaks, California. That's a terrible place. But I met a cinematographer and went to the Panavision studios and checked out the 35mm cameras. Then I went to South America. When I came back I went to 911 Media Arts Center to renew my membership, and they said that they didn't really do film anymore and I should talk to Jamie and Debbie [co-founders of Wiggly World, which runs the Little Theatre and the Grand Illusion]. I was Wiggly World's first volunteer. The first thing they asked me was, 'Why don't you go to the library and look up all of the organizations that give money to filmmakers?' I was in Suzzallo [Library] for 10 hours. They were surprised I went, that I did it at all. Then Wiggly World acquired the Grand Illusion and the whole thing exploded."

Film Festivals

There is no doubt that Seattle is a movie watcher's paradise. Though it may not be the first stop for foreign or independent films, most of them do make it to the Emerald City. Since its inception in 1976, the Seattle International Film Festival (SIFF) has grown into one of the largest, best attended, and most important film festivals in the world, running 24 days beginning in mid-May every year. But that's not the only festival in town. In fact, this town is festival crazy, hosting events dedicated to Polish (always in mid-November), Irish, Jewish (always in mid-March), and Scandinavian films, to name but a few. For those who like edgier fare, there's the annual Lesbian and Gay Film Festival (late October every year) and the relatively young Seattle Underground Film Festival (SUFF) held in early October each year, which has earned a strong presence. Meanwhile, the people who put on SIFF—the nonprofit group Cinema Seattle—run the Women in Cinema film festival every November.

ALICE WHEELER

Seattle International Film Festival: You'll get all wrapped up in it

SIFF

Main Box Office: Broadway Performance Hall, 1625 Broadway; Mon-Sat 11 am-7 pm, Sun noon-6 pm. **SIFF Single Ticket Outlet:** Pacific Place Concierge Desk, First-Floor Lobby, 600 Pine St (advance single tickets only); Mon-Sat 11 am-7 pm, Sun noon-6 pm; (206) 324-9996. Every spring, trumping even the enticements of nature itself, the Seattle International Film Festival brings forth a bloom of man-made diversions. Indeed, the film festival is the artistic embodiment of spring's mandate toward excess, packing 200-plus films into three crammed weeks, and drawing long lines of pasty-skinned cinephiles who are out in the withering sun to buy tickets and perspire pheromones. The mind reels as films butt up against more films, giving birth to mutant plot-line hybrids and the terror of half-remembered stories: Was last night's film a German eating drama, an erotic Chinese love tale, or (shudder) both? The liquor flows, the films don't stop, and by the end, everyone is bleary-eyed and sick of both foreign films and each other for another year to come.

BIO

John Behrens

Who is he? Experimental filmmaker; director of SUFF (Seattle Underground Film Festival).

We might as well start off by making sure we're on the same page; what, if anything, is your definition of an "experimental" film? "I think when you do something on film such as hand painting it or hand processing it or using weird filters or whatever you do that you don't know how it will turn out, you are experimenting."

Your own filmography is quite extensive; without stooping to name "favorites," are there two or three you'd consider exemplary of your vision? "The films I made in the late '70s through the mid-'80s were a lot darker than the films that I make now. If you asked me this 15 years ago I would have given you a totally different response. I like all the films that I have listed in my filmography; I also have an extensive filmography of films that I felt should never be seen so they just sit in my closet buried under comic books and stuff. But my favorite films are mostly from '93 to the present. The films that I worked on with other people, such as *Girl and a Bicycle* (1995), *Sister*

Society (1984), the film I made with Steve Creson, *Desert Abstractions* (1997), have been incredibly successful for films that are considered experimental. If you ask me the same thing 20 years from now I would most likely say the films I have made from 2010 till the present."

The Seattle Underground Film Festival managed to include Fuller and Hitchcock; is there a sense in which an "underground" esthetic that was once available to mainstream fare is now gone? Or have these works become underground in retrospect, viewed from our current perspective? "Well, I have said before that we modeled SUFF after the way SIFF was many, many, many years ago. If you recall, they used to program all kinds of stuff like that in their fest. Underground film to me just means films

that a major studio did not put out."

It is now possible for almost anyone to make their own movies, yet venues for these works remain limited. Should this situation be understood as part of the price for the independence of making your own films, or should we legitimately expect screenings of experimental shorts in Dolby Digital Sound? "I think that film as we know it is just about gone. This digital shit that people still call film is taking over. The price of doing a feature on DV is 70 percent cheaper than if you shot it on film. So, yes, anyone can make a video but not everyone can make a film. I do think that these young filmmakers who spend $20,000 on their first feature should give some thought to who actually is going to want to screen it. It is a lot easier to get short films screened, actually; there is always the festival circuit and, believe me, a bad short is more likely to be screened than a bad feature. Well, this is just my own prediction: I think that at some time filmgoers will be so burned out on this boring Hollywood shit that everyone will start seeking out films made by people like Brakhage, Belson, Kuchar, Anger; all the legends of the avant-garde and experimental film, the true pioneers of independent cinema."

Microcinema Festival/Satellites

Takes place during **SIFF**

For years now, local film programmers have been trying to negotiate the annual juggernaut that is the Seattle International Film Festival. Regardless of one's opinion of the festival itself, it's a simple fact that competing with an event that consolidates 200 films, 25,000 people, and the focused attention of every media outlet in the city is a real motherfucker.

A coalition of Seattle's finest film and video organizations, micro and

BIO

Joel Bachar

Who is he? Founder of Microcinema.com

What is your background— or, rather, what the heck did you do before you started programming short films, and before you started your website Microcinema.com?
"After holding internships and production assistant jobs on feature films and corporate video jobs for a couple of years, I bought a video camera and started Blackchair Productions in 1992. I thought I would establish myself as a production company instead of working my way up the ladder from coffee boy and gofer. I made short artsy films and videos for a few years and began sending them to festivals and screening venues that didn't charge an entry fee. My work got accepted to a few places, rejected from several, but for the most part I simply never heard back from anyone at all. So this frustration, coupled with the lack of alternative programming in the Seattle area that showed the kind of work I wanted to see,

DIANA ADAMS

inspired me to start my own show. Literally the day after I had this idea to start my own program, I heard about the Speakeasy Cafe opening up. I went down there not to talk about a short-film show but to understand more about what a cyber cafe is. Turned out, they had this "Backroom" that they wanted to do shows in, so I suggested my program, Independent Exposure. We have played there every month, January through October, for the past five years. Microcinema, Inc. and Microcinema.com were born from these activities in January 2000 when I decided I wanted to represent the under-represented filmmakers and get their works distributed and exhibited the world over,

both on-line *and* off-line."

Microcinemas have been around since the Lumiere brothers showed their first movies in the basement of a bar 100 years ago.
What was it that drew you to the idea of showing shorts, and did you know this would evolve into a full-time pursuit?
"Some have even suggested that the first microcinemas were the caves of thousands of years ago and the "films" the cave paintings. Either way, microcinemas are not new. I simply felt I could fill a niche that was lacking from Seattle's "alternative" film and video programming. There wasn't too much video art being shown in Seattle and short films simply didn't get much respect in town. The Speakeasy was a perfect venue based on its location, and the fact that it is a cyber cafe was a real plus five years ago, because who had heard of such a thing at that time? I truly never expected to make it through five years of Independent Exposure. I suspect I will be around for at least another five years, and hopefully 50 more!"

independent cinemas, and alternative exhibitors have banded together to present Satellites—not an anti-SIFF program but, rather, an adjunct festival designed to nourish the commonweal. Between the Grand Illusion, the Little Theatre, 911 Media Arts Center, Independent Exposure, and Cinema 18, all the stars of what we should call the "undie" film community ("indie" having been rendered meaningless and "microcinema" being too specific) are represented. Though the week-and-a-half-long series doesn't exactly have a unifying theme, its eclectic content and focus on alternative spaces offer up a pupu platter of the kind of alternative cinema that Seattle's underground exhibitors put on year-round.

IMAX

When big movies aren't big enough, there's always IMAX films. The gimmick here is that movies shot in the IMAX format are projected on screens so huge, you are positively engulfed in the image. The Boeing IMAX theater at the Pacific Science Center, in the shadow of the Space Needle, even has the capability of showing 3-D IMAX films, while the Omnidome on Seattle's waterfront shows the classics, both old and new.

Boeing IMAX Theater
200 2nd Ave N, (206) 443-4629

Omnidome
Pier 59 Waterfront Park, (206) 622-1868

Landmark Theaters

VICTORIA RENARD

Harvard Exit: One of Landmark's landmarks

Landmark is the name of a giant company that owns several Seattle art-film houses. The University District's adorable Seven Gables Theater is the anchor to Landmark's chain. Looking like a house on the corner of Roosevelt and NE 50th Street, the theater has a gabled roof (of course), a charming lobby, and a small theater with lights that recede into the ceiling and a medieval painting that covers the screen (painted in the mid-'70s, of course), which rolls up when the lights dim.

Not to be outdone, Capitol Hill's old-fashioned Harvard Exit contains nothing less than a grand piano in its elegant lobby. Other theaters include the nautically themed Neptune, the Egyptian-themed Egyptian (see calendar houses, above), the Guild 45th's two buildings that house two theaters (one old, one new) but share one box office, the Metro's 10 screens that mix Hollywood and art films, the Broadway Market's mall theater, which does the same, the Crest's second-run screens (see below), and the Varsity's mix of Hollywood films and calendar programming.

Broadway Market
Broadway and E Harrison St, (206) 323-0231

Guild 45th
2115 N 45th St, (206) 633-3353

Harvard Exit
807 E Roy St, (206) 323-8986

Metro
NE 45th St at Roosevelt Way, (206) 633-0055

Neptune
NE 45th St at Brooklyn Ave, (206) 633-5545

Seven Gables
NE 50th St at Roosevelt Way, (206) 632-8820

Varsity
4329 University Way NE, (206) 632-3131

Loews Cineplex Odeon
Sometimes you just want to see a Hollywood blockbuster. When that urge comes around, there's no better place for a fix than the theaters in the Cineplex Odeon chain. These soulless theaters perfectly mirror the heartless feeling of most big-budget films.

City Centre
6th Ave at Union St, (206) 622-6465

Meridian 16
7th Ave and Pike St, (206) 223-9600

Northgate
10 Northgate Plaza, (206) 363-5800

Oak Tree
10006 Aurora Ave N, (206) 527-1748

Uptown
511 Queen Anne Ave N, (206) 285-1022

Cinerama/Pacific Place

A step up from the Cineplex Odeon chain, in presentation if not content, are the Cinerama and Pacific Place theaters. The Cinerama is a Seattle institution, a giant theater that had fallen on hard times before local billionaire Paul Allen bought it and turned it into a beautiful, high-tech movie house with great sound. This is the best place in the city to see the latest blockbuster, though it is also one of only a couple of places in the world capable of showing those old three-projector Cinerama films. Pacific Place is a classy multiplex in a classy mall, which has the added distinction of having a beer garden in a reconstructed forest ranger's station, "for that Northwest feel."

VICTORIA RENARD

Cinerama: Huge!

Cinerama
2100 4th Ave, (206) 441-3080

Pacific Place 11
6th Ave and Pine St, (206) 652-2404

Second-Run

Sometimes you just don't want to pay full price for a movie, or maybe you waited too long and it moved out of the first-run theaters. Not to worry; that's where the second-run houses come in. Though increased rents have pushed these theaters out of downtown, cheap movies can still be found in West Seattle (Admiral) and North Seattle (Crest). The Aurora Cinema Grill offers the added bonus of beer and food during films.

Admiral
2343 California Ave SW, (206) 938-3456

Aurora Cinema Grill
130th St and Aurora Ave, (206) 364-8880

Crest
16505 5th Ave NE, (206) 363-6338

Literary Arts

Elliott Bay Book Company Readings

Pioneer Square

101 S Main St, (206) 624-6600, www.elliottbaybook.com

Almost always free with advance tickets

This Pioneer Square bookstore has the feel of a creaky ship, especially if you're drunk (one editor irresponsibly did Jell-O shots at the David Foster Wallace reading). Elliott Bay's reading series (curated by the upstanding Rick Simonson) usually takes place downstairs, in the tile-floored room off the cafe, with the audience seated in spindle-legged chairs and the reader set up on a stage made of shipping pallets. Nearly every major touring writer has passed an evening in the Elliott Bay basement—in the past the series has included such luminaries as Haruki Murakami, Joan Didion, Sonia Sanchez, and Stanley Crouch. Audiences get to have a say during the Q&A sessions afterward, and can stand in line to get autographs. Elliott Bay also sponsors readings in larger venues such as Town Hall or Seattle Art Museum, so check locations carefully. It behooves you to go and pick up free tickets a few days in advance. For the more popular authors, you should also show up an hour early and stand in line.

Open Books Reading Series

Wallingford

2414 N 45th St, (206) 633-0811

Free

If you like poetry, you'll eventually find yourself in the cool-lit recesses of Open Books: A Poem Emporium, the bookstore located in Wallingford below the Bungalow Wine Bar. Owners John Marshall and Christine Deavel kindly guide the poetry-overwhelmed through to revelations, making suggestions that are both elegant and democratic. Suggested reading is buffered by visiting poets in the Open Books Reading Series; these intimate events have featured the likes of Sam Hamill, Heather McHugh, and Colleen McElroy. Open Books also occasionally co-sponsors readings at larger venues.

Red Sky Poetry Theater

Capitol Hill

The Globe Cafe, 1531 14th Ave and Pine St, (206) 324-8815

Donation requested, every Sunday, sign-up at 7 pm

To many, the Globe Cafe defines hippiedom in Seattle. Small, dust-ridden, and prone to using spelt in its cookies, this vegan Capitol Hill hole-in-the-wall has hosted Seattle's longest-running and most free-spirited reading series for many years. Notables such as small-press impresario Paul Hunter frequent the mic, along with sign-up readers whose poetry occasionally approaches propaganda or scare tactics. But amid the bean sprouts, magic sometimes happens. Check out the chapbook library, too. Red Sky doesn't run during the summer. However, on Tuesdays a younger crowd shows up for another open mic—sign up at 7:30 pm. (P.S. Find a seat that allows for a clean exit.)

Rendezvous Reading Series
Capitol Hill
The Little Theatre, 610 19th Ave E, (206) 675-2055
$5 suggested donation
Readings at the Rendezvous series redefine the genre—deftly incorporating film, live music, performance, and alcohol, until the whole hootenanny fills the Little Theatre and overspills onto the sidewalk. The secret is in the curators'

Bio

The Typing Explosion

DIONA MAVIS

What is it? Who are they?
The Typing Explosion, concocted by S. P. Ocampo, Rachel Kessler, and Sierra Nelson, writes poetry-on-demand in a noisy performance art/unionized process. You can give them any title or first line you choose. And the thing is, the poetry is good.

Is this really poetry?
"It's not, in the traditional sense of poetry, because it's not boring and it's not difficult to understand. The little ditty that you get on the piece of paper is fun. It's also kind of random and chaotic and Dadaesque. At the very least, it's not just poetry. It's performance, and art, and writing—all of these things kind of wrapped up in a big fuzzy ball."

Why are you dressed as secretaries?
"I think because type-writers are traditionally the tool of the secretary. Each of us has a sort of librarian/secretary alter ego, and it helps to have the secretary uniform on and the accoutrements to get into character. Also, secretaries or clerical workers are the cogs that make the white-collar world go. It's our little comment on women's history—a lot of our mothers were secretaries, and they hated it—it's not completely straight the way that we're playing these secretaries. We're female drones, but we turn out these little pieces of poems that can be scary or subversive or have swear words in them."

What's the weirdest first line or subject you've ever gotten?
"Once, someone requested a poem about frozen peas, and the poem we wrote was about mother/daughter relationships, with parts about a dream that I used to have about an alien inhabiting my mother's skin. It turns out that not only was the poem requested by Sierra's mom, but that Sierra used to have that exact same nightmare. Since none of us can talk to each other while we're typing, weird psychic connections occur."

attention to theme: Writers are culled around a specific trope ("Crush," the annual Valentine's Day event, is a great one), and then the concept is given a couple of carefully considered, bizarre elements to flesh it out. Rendezvous co-founder Matthew Stadler says the intention was to create a series of parties; current curators continue this tradition. National writers such as Amy Bloom, Chris Kraus, Slim Moon, and James Purdy are paired with local talents at each reading; new themes are interspersed with annual traditions such as *The Stranger*'s Minor Fiction Contest, the Indie Showcase, and an annual oral history performance.

Richard Hugo House Readings

Capitol Hill
Richard Hugo House, 1634 11th Ave, (206) 322-7030
Price varies

The Richard Hugo House, named for the Seattle poet who declared, "You've found the town, now start the poem," is the hub of Seattle's literary community. A center for local, national, and international writers, the Hugo House has invented space for every possible mode of writing. Upstairs there is a well-curated library (open only to members), and the main lobby contains two performing areas: a large theater for well-known writers or local plays,

and a small space (the cafe space) for more intimate readings and Stage Fright, an open-mic, under-21 night held every other Wednesday. There's even an exhaustively collected zine library in the basement. One of the most valuable resources in this town for those aspiring to the writerly life is the Hugo House's huge reader board: On it is every job, opportunity, and contest available to writers, locally and nationally. The Richard Hugo House also offers writing classes that you won't find at the UW, taught by excellent writers whom the UW is too staid to hire. (Charles Mudede taught a course called "Writing the City"; Rebecca Brown taught a course linking fine art with text; and Sonia Gomez

ELISA SHEBARO

Hugo House: Zines, readings, and a haunted basement

taught "International Six-Pack," six writers from six different countries.) Writers-in-residence (two per year) are responsible for developing and organizing a reading series. Past series have included the Sketch Club, which sought to link writers with themes such as "Food" and "The Body," curated by Rebecca Brown; and Charles Mudede's "Hugo Talks," a series dedicated to writings about Seattle.

Roethke Readings
University District
Roethke Auditorium, 130 Kane Hall, University of Washington
Contact Sherry Laing, (206) 543-2634
Free
Named after the famous poet and UW professor, the Roethke reading series started in 1964, mostly as a benefit for UW students (students are treated to smaller Q&A sessions with the visiting poet). The main reading is open to the public, however, and usually occurs on the Thursday in May closest to Theodore Roethke's birthday (May 25). Past readers have included Gary Snyder, Seamus Heaney, and Maxine Kumin.

Seattle Arts & Lectures
Downtown
A Contemporary Theatre (ACT), 700 Union St, (206) 621-2230 ext. 10
$10-$20 per event, $175 for series lecture pass
Seattle Arts & Lectures got a shot in the arm a few years ago when it hired director Matthew Brogan away from New York's Academy of American Poets. Brogan promised to turn what many viewed as an elitist organization into a more widely appealing venue, and some of his choices have definitely moved in that direction. SAL has shifted a portion of its budget into "Writers in the Schools" programs, and has sponsored some smaller readings by local or semi-struggling writers. For its seven-part lecture series (which includes fine artists, filmmakers, and cultural thinkers), SAL gets to bring in the big guys and put 'em in one of Seattle's most glorious spaces, Benaroya Hall. Past readers have included Michael Ondaatje, Salman Rushdie, Susan Sontag, and Don DeLillo. For the poetry series (which frequently sells out), readings are held at ACT (A Contemporary Theatre). Such readings have included Philip Levine, Anne Carson, and Robert Hass. Readings are expensive, though (if you're a student, you can get in for about $8).

"Wednesday University" is SAL's newest program, designed as an inexpensive adjunct to SAL's other series. Professors from the UW teach classes to the general public, and the charge is very light compared to UW extension classes ($60 for each series; $150 for the whole year). Previous classes have included "Fiction and Family" and "Race and the American West."

Seattle Poetry Festival
Held at On the Boards and other venues around the city
Eleventh Hour Productions, (206) 725-1650
Price varies
This three-to-five-day annual event hits the city like a returning comet every spring. If you like gorging yourself on poetry as much as you like gorging yourself on strawberry shortcake at the Bite of Seattle, then by all means go. If too much poetry leaves you feeling gassy, stay home. You have to sit and sit

and listen and listen to lots of mediocre poets, who are sometimes nothing more than the not-talented friends of the directors. Big names (The Last Poets!) have proven fascinating choices in previous years. Like the Richard Hugo House, this festival tends to emphasize just how BIG Seattle is getting and how BIG Eleventh Hour is in the scene.

Eleventh Hour Productions, the Seattle Poetry Festival's parent company, frequently sponsors smaller readings that are much more interesting. Keep your eye on *The Stranger* for these.

SMELL OF STEVE

Seattle Poetry Slam

Pioneer Square
Dutch Ned's, 206 1st Ave S, (206) 340-8859
9 pm every Wed; $3 admission

Allison Durazzi has curated the Seattle Poetry Slam through recent venue changes (it used to occur, famously, at the OK Hotel) and its expansion into the 50/50 Reading Series and open-mic performances. Now, touring slam-competition winners share the stage with slam scenesters waging warfare for entertainment value. At stake is a cash prize that averages $25. It's fun to sit and watch the action, have a beer, and vote with your vocal adjectives. Seattle Poetry Slam is where Bukowski would've read, which explains its attraction to Little Bukowskis lacking talent but overflowing with theatricality.

Spoken Word

Pioneer Square
Pioneer Square Saloon, 73 Yesler Way, (206) 340-1234
8:30 pm every Thurs; Free

Take the stage in cowboy boots, so you can intimidate the judges at this weekly open mic, where alcohol-induced honesty goes hand in hand with art. There's usually a good balance of "people's art" on display from musicians, poets, and (eep!) stand-up comics. Kind of like karaoke, except without the video helpmeet.

Subtext Reading Series
Capitol Hill
Richard Hugo House, 1634 11th Ave, (206) 322-7030
Price varies

Run by a board that calls itself "The Subtext Collective," this reading series faithfully sponsors avant-garde poets and prose writers, and pairs them up with board members. As a consequence, the readings sometimes feel a little cliquish, but the material is inevitably fascinating, sometimes even brilliant, and gives you a glimpse into a literary world that is not at all commercially concerned. Readings in the past have included Alice Notley, Douglas Oliver, and Spencer Selby.

Titlewave Reading Series
Queen Anne
7 Mercer St, (206) 282-7687
Free

Titlewave Reading Series was founded six years ago by Greg Burkman and Dennis Wilkin. It is now curated by the very entertaining Doug Nufer. Titlewave ususally presents three or four writers and a musician, or as Nufer says, "on occasion, a magician." Nickie Jostol, who owns the store in Lower Queen Anne, is a great supporter of the literary arts; and unlike other bookstores and literary establishments, she does not make the reading series pay rent and therefore leaves them free from the hassle of grant seeking. If you are interested in knowing all the nooks and cranies of Seattle's very broad literary scene, the Titlewave readings are required. Nufer seeks out some of the more experimental writers in town, as well as people who have never read before. "I like to mix more established writers with writers who are relatively unknown, although some of these relatively unknown writers have been known to pack the house with relatives. Each act gets 15 to 20 minutes. We used to have occasional problems with people who read too long, but that hasn't been a problem since last Halloween, when I wore a black leather mask and threatened to cut people off with a chainsaw."

A Tale of Two Gated Communities

by Charles Mudede

IN THE SUMMER OF 1977, my sister and I (six and eight at the time) flew to Seattle to spend three months with my Aunt Sana, who was the near double of my mother. Due to medical complications, Aunt Sana was unable to bear children, and so we were loaned to her, to simulate the little family she desperately wanted. And as she was munificent, always lavishing money and brightly colored mall gifts on us, we agreeably played

WHITING TENNIS

the role, addressing her as nothing less than our own mother— better, in fact, than the real thing. This visit, the first of three, not only introduced me to a new city—Seattle—but also to the abundant world of the Nordstrom family, in whose Highlands gated community palace my aunt lived and worked.

If, as Fred Moody claims in his book *The Washingtonians*, the "old-fashioned Scandinavian Episcopalian" Nordstrom family "is the

Rainier of the Northwest's civic and cultural landscape," then what better introduction could I have had to this corner of the world than to sleep and play while breathing the air of a palace owned by people whose very name had come to epitomize the Northwest?

During that initial visit I never really left the royal residence. It was in this mansion's natatorium that I was first taught to swim by a very young Nordstrom, whose name and face are completely lost from my memory, but whose full figure in a blue-and-white floral swimsuit I have retained with sparkling clarity. And how thin the air was in that house. Nothing weighed you down. Indeed, with the super-rich there is a divine paradox: The more money they accumulate, the less visible money becomes. All objects, void of all the hindrances that frustrate the poor, seem to float in and out of one's way without a care.

The Highlands, a work of landscape art, was designed in 1907 by the famed Olmsted Brothers, who are responsible for the basic park system of Seattle. The Olmsted Brothers' father, Frederick Law Olmsted, invented the profession of landscape architecture in America and designed Central Park and Boston Commons. The elder Olmsted was a great advocate for the expansion of public space. He believed the rich could easily flee to the mountains to get a break from the noise and the pressures of the city, whereas the poor were stuck here with only cemeteries (America's first public parks) to ease the intensity of urban life. The Olmsted Brothers continued their father's legacy and designed numerous parks and campuses around America. Here in Seattle, we have them to thank for Volunteer Park, Magnolia Park, and the Arboretum, among many others.

> When one looks too closely, the truth about this kind of power and wealth is never pretty.

Coincidentally, next to the Olmsteds' Arboretum is Broadmoor, another famous gated community. Designed by the Puget Mills Company in 1927, it is also home to the very rich. Yet Broadmoor is quite different from the Highlands: It has the feel of new money, while the Highlands has the sedative ease of old money. The very location of these communities tells it all: On the east side of Seattle, Broadmoor watches only the rise of the sun, whereas the Highlands, on the west, is witness to its fall.

I never knew exactly how my aunt got to know and work for the very old Great-Aunt Nordstrom (as we were required to address her). I imagine it went something like this: My aunt's former husband (who left her for a younger, fertile woman) was then completing post-graduate studies in education at the University of Washington. He was running out of money for tuition, and so my aunt, attending the right church, talked to the right people—possibly dishing them the old story of how she and her husband were students trying to complete their education, so that they could go back to Africa and lead their benighted brethren to a prosperity similar to what had been accomplished in this country.

In the years to follow, Aunt Sana arranged for other relatives to live with the wealthy families of the Highlands—the Nordstroms, the Pattersons, the Isaacsons, the Andersons. This continued until 1993, when my cousin, Placidas Chiro, graduated from college and bitterly left America having not one pleasant word to say about her experiences in that secluded neighborhood. It seems that during her stay she had been disrespected by Great-Aunt Nordstrom, who, if the truth be known, on top of being senile, regarded my cousin, and all other Africans for that matter, as emotionally and intellectually little more than clever monkeys. My Aunt Sana, who came from extreme poverty, was willing to overlook these insults for the opportunities that glimmered in the future, but for my middle-class cousin, already in possession of a happy and comfortable past, the humiliation was excruciating.

It was during Placidas' final days in the Highlands that I made my last visit. I arrived at the guarded gate at around 3:30 p.m. An old man with silver hair raised it without a word. It seemed he was expecting me. Though the day was still alive for the rest of the city, here, because of the thick and towering firs and hemlocks, the dusk was deep. The little roads that led me farther and farther into this damp neighborhood boasted cheerful names like White Huckleberry, Spring Drive, and Cherry Loop. Occasionally, as I made a turn, a white patrol car—the Highland's private police—would approach and slowly pass by.

Suddenly, breaking from the trees, a massive palace appeared. The hazy Olympics, the darkening Sound, and the setting sun were visible above a row of cedars with tops evenly trimmed to accommodate this glorious sight. It was night now, and the windows and the mirrors in each large room reflected the guests' unlikely presence. We were happy as we relaxed and roamed the great house, until somewhere, somehow, we managed to come across a revealing photograph: The Pattersons standing next to a smiling Ronald Reagan. The former president had scribbled something, an encouraging word, at the bottom of their treasured memory. Indeed, as with our mirrored images, when one looks too closely, the truth about this kind of power and wealth is never pretty. We did our best to remain in the haze.

I heard that Great-Aunt Nordstrom died recently. I was downtown in the deceased's family store applying for credit. Within 15 minutes my request was rejected, because, as the man behind the counter erotically put it, I was a "credit virgin." I had never officially borrowed money and was nothing in the eyes of big business. Feeling pity for me, he recommended I try the Bon Marché, which might be more lenient and overlook my virginity. As I left the Nordstrom store despondently, it seemed that all of the social and cultural distances between the great, mountainous Scandinavian family and my unknown, anthill African one had been fully restored. And the accident of our physical proximity, when we once shared that kingdom by the bay, would now be to my memory as substantial as the events of a vanishing dream.

Shopping

SEVERAL YEARS AGO, *THE STRANGER* tried to start a shopping column. We wanted to feature stores that catered to people of our economic persuasion, and so we ended up covering the Princess Market convenience store and all kinds of used-furniture stores. It wasn't long before we realized we were too embittered by our poverty to do Seattle's burgeoning boutique and designer industries any justice. Seattle's an easy place to shop if you're one of the nouveau riche; otherwise, it takes a little more dedication. This guide, therefore, focuses on the quirky, the cheap, and, of course, independent businesses.

Bookstores

Bailey/Coy Books
Capitol Hill
414 Broadway Ave E, (206) 323-8842
Sun-Thurs 10 am-10 pm, Fri-Sat 10 am-11 pm
Bailey/Coy Books is one of *The Stranger*'s favorite independent bookstores, offering an impressive selection of gay and lesbian literature, as well as an inviting art section located near the front of the store. While Bailey/Coy's other departments run from the incidental to the vestigial, the best reason to drop in here is to linger over the tables of new hardcovers and paperbacks, which showcase dense displays of the best mainstream titles in fiction, poetry, history, and cultural criticism.

Beatty Book Store
Downtown
1925 3rd Ave, (206) 728-2665
Mon-Sat 11 am-5:45 pm

SOMYA GUTSHALL

Beatty's: Crusty yet trusty

The city's most interesting general used bookstore may be Beatty Books, where a pair of conjoined storefronts and some generous real estate offer a pleasant assortment of standard used-bookstore fare with one important eccentricity—the bookstore's scattered holdings of 19th- and early-20th-century hardcovers. Many of these would be in rare and antiquarian bookstores were it not for slight damage. So, beyond the few books the store's owners deem marketable, old books here— though rare—are not antiques, art objects, or curios under glass; they are simply old books, meant to be dusted off and actually read. Additionally, Beatty's has a tidy selection of French-language literature, a table packed with outdated scientific pamphlets, and a decent supply of paperback fiction, with several sections running through the old, windowed listening booths. For curious bookhounds who strive to live lives enriched by ephemera, Beatty's is the best kind of used bookstore Seattle has to offer.

Beyond the Closet
Capitol Hill
518 E Pike St, (206) 322-4609
Daily 10 am-10 pm

For the city's largest selection of gay, lesbian, bisexual, and transgender titles in all fields, head to Beyond the Closet, which stocks nothing else.

Cinema Books
University District
4753 Roosevelt Way NE, (206) 547-7667
Mon-Sat 10 am-7 pm

Cinema Books shares space with the U-District's Seven Gables Theater, offering a large selection of film biographies, criticism, and published screenplays. There are so many books in her store, the lovely owner behind the counter sometimes has to search for the hidden cash register.

Confounded Books
Fremont
3506 Fremont Ave N, (206) 545-0744
Daily 11:30 am-10 pm

Fremont's Confounded Books is the closest you'll come to finding a reason for book-browsing in the neighborhood; the nearby branch of Twice Sold Tales has a dismal selection, and Confounded's range of comics leans even more toward the photocopied and stapled than Fallout's. A small selection of countercultural investigations and renegade how-to books complete the scene. It's also a video-rental store.

Elliott Bay Book Company

Pioneer Square

101 S Main St, (206) 624-6600

Mon-Thurs 10 am-10 pm, Fri-Sat 10 am-11 pm, Sun 11 am-7 pm

Elliott Bay Book Company is one of Seattle's largest independent bookstores, and the city's unchallenged leader in bookstore-centered literary culture. The store's extensive holdings are now supplanted by a welcomed annex of used books, and a cafe downstairs offers food that complements the bookstore's warm-wooded interior. Near-nightly readings offer little fluff; and free tickets, available at the front counter, can disappear fast.

Fillipi Book & Record Shop

Capitol Hill

1351 E Olive Way, (206) 682-4266

Tues-Sat 10 am-5 pm

This used bookstore, which opened before I-5 was built, began with a romance. Ted and Kits Fillipi, parents of today's brother and sister co-owners, met in San Francisco. Ted escaped the family farm in Nebraska, and wanted to start a bookstore; Kits wanted to go into radio. She convinced him that there were too many bookstores in San Francisco, so they moved to Seattle and opened

---

BIO

Brenda Fillipi

Who is she? She runs the Fillipi Book & Record Shop on Capitol Hill.

How did you get started?
"I grew up in Madrona, where, during the war, my parents operated a bookstore out of their home. I grew up surrounded by books, with a lot of great music, and my folks had a lot of interesting friends; it was a very unorthodox way to grow up. You don't start a business in the middle of the Depression and expect to launch a success. We have a great location, and since my parents were able to buy the place in the '60s, we have the luxury of space, and can afford to carry a lot of variety. There's a charm to small spaces, but it's great to be able to spread out a bit, too."

What do you think of Seattle as a "books town"?
"Seattle is such a wonderful city for bookstores, with a generous audience of book buyers and record collectors. Not every city has as many bookstores as Seattle does. People have an instinct to collect, but some things, like books, move from hand to hand."

shop in 1935. Ted bought and sold books; Kits took care of the records. Today's store occupies an enormous space, with high ceilings and plants thriving in all the natural light. In 1960, the Fillipis were able to buy the building, which had gone through various incarnations: a body shop, an upholsterer, a Chinese laundry. The selection of books is huge, and they offer great prices on reference books, art books, cookbooks, and literature. Fillipi's two and a half rooms house a record collection with more depth than any other store in town. A good place to find last week's bestseller and your Dad's favorite song.

Half Price Books

University District
4709 Roosevelt Way NE, (206) 547-7859
Sun-Thurs 10 am-10 pm, Fri-Sat 10 am-11 pm
Half Price Books is a strange store. Downstairs, there's an odd collection of oversized art and coffee-table hardcovers, among which the occasional gem can be found. And they do have an awesome travel section downstairs, too. Upstairs, though, is where the real treasure lies: Besides a surprisingly well-stocked fiction section, Half Price has one of the only used computer-book sections in the city. This is the first place to look if you're trying to school yourself in computer languages or other practical matters.

Horizon Books

Capitol Hill
425 15th Ave E, (206) 329-3586
Mon-Fri 10 am-10 pm, Sat-Sun 10 am-9 pm
A short walk from Capitol Hill's main drag, this jam-packed bookstore offers an Asian-centered history section, a strong selection of literary biographies and criticism, and a well-stocked theater section. Literary first editions are also available. The bookstore is much bigger than it looks from the outside.

Left Bank Books

Pike Place Market
92 Pike St, (206) 622-0195
Mon-Sat 10 am-7 pm, Sun noon-6 pm
Perhaps Seattle's most satisfyingly visionary bookstore is downtown's Left Bank Books, located on the edges of Pike Place Market. Bypassing the magazine section at front (itself the best source for left-leaning and radical magazines and workers' newspapers in the city), a quick look at the next two sections that present themselves—Fiction by Men and Fiction by Women—offers a glimpse of the many conventions of critical reading this bookstore prides itself in challenging. The entire store merges its new and used collections together (no self-respecting progressive would segregate books by price), and features excellent sections of gender and cultural studies, politics, philosophy, and media studies, each modest in its size but authoritative in its selection, with an overflowing zine display-stand

rounding out the corpus. Whatever books may be found here, people usually leave with a heightened awareness of a bookstore's function as an information center. The fact that this store can continue to exist at the feet of one of Seattle's premier tourist destinations is itself a sign that critical reading is one of the city's deeply rooted enthusiasms.

SOMYA GUTSHALL

Zines at Left Bank: Giving a voice to misanthropes everywhere

Magus Bookstore

University District

1408 NE 42nd St, (206) 633-1800

Daily 10 am-9 pm

Magus Bookstore plays Socrates to the University of Washington's legion of inquiring minds. The store may survive based on its currency as the best place to buy English lit texts secondhand, but its proximity to the neighborhood's most pensive coffeehouse (Allegro) and the owners' own interests make the store's window-display recommendations its greatest asset. If you have any interest in fiction, literary theory, social criticism, or history, we defy you to walk by without stopping, to stop without looking, and to look without seeing something you'd really like to read.

Marco Polo Books, Maps & Accessories

Capitol Hill

713 Broadway Ave E, (206) 860-3736

Mon-Thurs 11 am-7 pm, Fri-Sat 11 am-8 pm, Sun noon-5 pm

Travel is Marco Polo's specialty, but the store's owner, Laura Ingham, has proven that the best travel bookstores offer more than just travel guides. Entering Marco Polo is enough to make you feel as though you're already headed somewhere and, in a limited sense, that you've actually arrived. Browse the shelves of indigenous poetry, essays, and new and classic fiction within regional travel sections, or look through thematic coffee-table books of ancient maps, and you can't help but wonder why you haven't already traveled the entire globe. Located at Broadway and Harvard, this store is easy to miss at the end of the Broadway commercial drag, but well worth a visit.

Open Books: A Poem Emporium

Wallingford

2414 N 45th St, (206) 633-0811

Tues-Thurs noon-6 pm, Fri-Sat noon-7 pm

On the fringes of Wallingford, Open Books: A Poem Emporium has been serving up nothing but poetry for the last seven years, with an additional nine years as a bookstore under its current ownership. The store aims to encompass all the classic, canonical, and contemporary poets represented by major publishing houses, broadening the picture through a heavy dose of local authors, small-press publications, and hard-to-find poetry books, chapbooks, and poetry magazines.

Peter Miller Architectural & Design Books
Downtown
1930 1st Ave, (206) 441-4114
Mon-Fri 10 am-6 pm, Sat 10 am-5:30 pm, Sun noon-5 pm
This stylishly constructed store collects contemporary architectural- and design-theory books and shelves them alongside what seems to be every architectural coffee-table book ever published. Get there early in the year to order the coolest giant-sized wall calendar.

Revolution Books
Capitol Hill
1833 Nagle Pl, (206) 325-7415
Hours are infrequent and change often, so stop by or call ahead
Revolution Books picks up the party slack on Capitol Hill, with a heady supply of Lenin, Marx, and Mao, but a less impressive range of contemporary thought. The bookstore also functions as a center for occasional speakers and poetry readings, and its answering machine alone is a megaphone for upcoming rallies, events, and speaking engagements.

Seattle Mystery Bookshop
Downtown
117 Cherry St, (206) 587-5737
Mon-Sat 10 am-5 pm, Sun noon-5 pm
This is the repository for all the new and used whodunit, suspense, detective, thriller, and spy novels anyone could hope for. This shop oozes with pulp, but it keeps abreast of the meta-fictional branches in the genre as well. A great antidote to bookish pretensions, Seattle Mystery Bookshop specializes in fandom: A great many of its books are signed by the authors, and the store holds signings and informal chats as often as twice a week.

Twice Sold Tales
Capitol Hill
905 E John St , (206) 324-2421
Mon-Thurs 10 am-1 am, Fri 24 hours, Sat 10 am-2 am, Sun 10 am-midnight
If your quest is subject- or author-specific rather than oriented toward the newest of the new, we recommend heading to the Capitol Hill branch of Twice Sold Tales—Seattle's definitive answer to the needs of great readers the world over. With an impressive overall collection of used books, Twice Sold Tales offers the city's best selection of used history, an exceptional selection of used fiction (with a striking emphasis on post-WWII authors), and a strong

mythology and religion section. And if that's not enough, the well-lit, three-room bookstore encourages loitering with plush couches and comfortable corners, and features a system of shelf-top runners and passageways designed exclusively for the convenience of the store's numerous kitties. And the store is open all night on Fridays.

University Bookstore
University District
4326 University Way NE, (206) 634-3400
Mon-Fri 9 am-9 pm, Sat 9 am-6 pm, Sun noon-5 pm
You can't miss the University Bookstore, one of the largest independent bookstores in the city and the biggest independent college bookstore in the United States. For its selection of classic and contemporary fiction, literary criticism, mainstream poetry, history, and children's literature, the University Bookstore is unbeatable. Browse through the overflowing tables of heavily discounted remainders in the main hall, and don't be afraid to wander downstairs to the textbook section—in the humanities departments, this rarely means textbooks, but instead an intelligent selection of university-press academic books clustered around specific topics, often in combinations that are themselves as intriguing as the best cross-disciplinary window displays. Many of these books are not available on the main floor in this or any other bookstore. Plus, we love the art supplies downstairs.

Wessel & Lieberman Booksellers
Downtown
208 1st Ave S, (206) 682-3545
Wed-Sat 11 am-6 pm, or by appointment
Wessel & Lieberman has a great, curious collection of rare books; truly invaluable, though, is its letterpress book section. This carefully curated store of local and national handmade books is stunning and irresistible, like coming across a library of stories never told, or only told in dreams. The store specializes in out-of-print, uncommon books—poetry, Northwest history, and any number of strange literary artifacts, all in great condition. But rather than the dusty, drowsy shop this might suggest, Wessel & Lieberman glows with purpose and energy.

Comic Book Shops

Comics Dungeon
Wallingford
250 NE 45th St, (206) 545-8373
Sun-Tues noon-7 pm, Wed-Sat noon-9 pm
Ever since Fallout got rid of most of their comics selection, it's been hard work finding a good source for the underground stuff. Besides Confounded

Books in Fremont (see Bookstores), another less likely venue for underground comics is the Comics Dungeon in Wallingford, which looks from the outside like another superhero haven, but keeps an impressive shelf of underground work. Filled with work by Lewis Trondheim, Dave Cooper, Brian

BIO

Gary Groth and Kim Thompson

PETER BAGGE

Who are they? The co-owners and primary editors of Fantagraphics Books, the nation's largest publisher of alternative comic books. Fantagraphics gathered up the late-'70s detritus of the '60s underground comix movement, when the head shops were regulated out of business. Starting with a magazine, *The Comics Journal*, Groth and Thompson helped spawn a second, more artistically significant arts comic movement. Currently the eighth-largest comics company in North America, Fantagraphics publishes a some of the most important cartoonists in the world, including Jaime and Gilbert Hernandez, Joe Sacco, Dan Clowes, Jessica Abel, Charles Burns, and fellow Seattleites Peter Bagge, Jim Woodring, and Roberta Gregory.

You've recently celebrated your 10th year in Seattle. How did you end up here, and why have you stayed?
Gary: "It's mostly Pete Bagge's fault. After expressing my dislike of L.A., he became a one-man Seattle Chamber of Commerce and kept lobbying for us to check it out. We did;

we liked what we saw; we moved. When we moved from L.A. to Seattle, it took four tractor-trailer trucks. Now, it would take 10. But inertia's not the only reason we've stayed. I like the scale of Seattle—large but not too large, busy but not too busy, cosmopolitan but not too snooty—and it's got everything a civilized city should have (bookstores, video stores, theater)."
Kim: "Also, we've put down familial ties, and can't conceive of a life without Scarecrow Video."

Is there a Seattle comics community, and if so, what's your place in it?
Kim: "I guess it's a community, although 'loosely knit' would be the kind way to put it. We're the drunken, bitter old uncle whom you humor because he might leave you in his will."
Gary: "The Seattle comics

community seems more scattered now than it did seven or eight years ago when it was really buzzing with portentous excitement. We've settled comfortably into our position as the old fogey hipster outfit who publishes old fogies like Peter Bagge and Jim Woodring."

Robert Crumb or Art Spiegelman? Defend your answer.
Gary: "Crumb. I think his brand of self-conscious cartooning yields greater truths than Spiegelman's brand of self-conscious cartooning."
Kim: "As a thinker, Spiegelman. As a drawer, Crumb. As an editor, Spiegelman. As a liberating force, Crumb. Ultimately, if pressed to the wall, Crumb—because without Crumb there probably wouldn't be a Spiegelman, but without Spiegelman there'd still be a Crumb."

Ralph, and other great, lesser-known underground artists, the alternative stuff coexists peacefully alongside the Marvel, DC, and Image titles. The store's selection of action figures is likewise well curated, and there are plenty of great odds and ends around, like Little Nemo collections and illustrator anthologies. Plus, the staff is just geeky enough to know the inventory, without scaring any regular folks off.

BIO

Peter Bagge

DAN CLOWES

Who is he? The cartoonist behind the seminal alternative comic books *Neat Stuff* and *HATE*, a former editor of Robert Crumb's *Weirdo*, the writer of the recent gassy D.C. kids' title *Yeah!* and an on-line contributor to *Suck*. Peter Bagge isn't just one of America's most successful alternative cartoonists, he's one of humor's most influential artists. Bagge is the post-underground artist who comes closest to approximating the mainstream humorist status of Robert Crumb or Gilbert Shelton. His work on the 1980s comic *Neat Stuff* was an obvious influence on animators like Matt Groening, John Kricfalusi, and Mike Judge. Bagge lives in Ballard with his wife and daughter.

How would you describe the Seattle comics community? I've been told you played a large role in its creation.
"When Joanna (my wife) and I first moved here in '84, we missed socializing with a rapidly evolving 'cartooning community' that we left behind in New York, so we tried hard to get some-thing similar going here—which was hard, since there were very few alternative cartoonists living here at the time. But as the years passed, many more artists moved here . . . way more than could even be fit into one group, in fact. But other than encouraging people to move here, I didn't really start anything."

What comics or cartoonists have had the greatest influence on you?
"Charles M. Schulz and other 'funny' daily newspaper cartoonists when I was a kid, as well as *MAD Magazine*. Later on I was very influenced by Robert Crumb and other underground artists. And I'm still inspired by some of my contemporaries, Dan Clowes and the Hernandez Brothers."

Your comic *HATE* received some attention as one of the important chronicles of young people's lives in early-'90s Seattle. Do you welcome that kind of attention?
"I welcome any kind of attention as long as it isn't violent. What do I think of the early *HATE*s myself? I think I did a good job of capturing what was going on in my own head when I was in my early 20s, which was the intention of *HATE* in the first place."

You write and draw funny comics; a lot of alternative comics are really serious. Do you see your kind of comics as something that's under-appreciated by comics readers?
"No, I don't feel under-appreciated, all things considered. The more 'serious' stuff is easier to praise and write glowing reviews for, but so few people read comics criticism to begin with. So few people read comics!"

What's the best thing and the worst thing about living in Ballard?
"Compared to the rest of the city, Ballard is fairly peaceful and quiet. The worst thing about Ballard is that it's peaceful and quiet."

Fallout Records, Books, & Comics
1506 E Olive Way, (206) 323-2662

Fallout was once one of the greatest comic shops in the country, combining a great collection of indie music with a rare collection of indie comics, zines, and various photo, fetish, and comics anthologies. The store was recently forced to cut back on its collection of comics and books, but even at reduced capacity, Fallout has enough titles from Fantagraphics and Drawn & Quarterly to remain crucial for underground comic readers. The zine collection is still going strong as well. Fortunately, Fremont's Confounded Books stocks most of the books Fallout had to abandon.

BIO

Jim Woodring

Who is he? One of the most highly respected cartoonists in North America and a well-regarded illustrator and designer, best known for his surreal, lushly painted stories starring a character named Frank. In Seattle art circles, his work is treated with silent awe. Woodring's body of comics work, it's been written, is one of the three or four most likely to be remembered 500 years from now.

A lot of the younger cartoonists enjoy having contact with cartoonists like you and Peter Bagge. Do you think you have a specific role in the Seattle comics community?
"I like to think of myself as an opinionated, insecure Dutch uncle who can't wait to lecture someone. I love to talk shop. And it's important for younger cartoonists to see what this kind of 'career' can do to you; with my ruined physique and totally

JIM WOODRING

desiccated social skills, I'm a valuable object lesson."

In terms of alternative comics, your work is idiosyncratic. Can you describe briefly a few of your important influences in and out of that medium?
"Boris Artzybasheff, R. Crumb, Harry McNaught, T. S. Sullivant, Dali, Satie, Herriman, Henry Miller . . . that bunch."

As a lot of your work is based on very personal symbolism—what do you think people get out of reading it?
"I don't know, but I hope it's something akin to what I

get out of putting the work together, which is a feeling of love for a world that offers such rich opportunities."

I've seen some of your illustration and design work, and I know you've also worked for Microsoft. Has Seattle been a good place to explore those kinds of opportunities?
"Sure! This town is just bubbling over with fascinating business. But it's becoming like Los Angeles in the sense that straightforward, humane deals are getting harder to come by. It's painful to watch sweet old Seattle become just another playground for vulgar sharpies."

You once described your Ravenna neighborhood as the best in Seattle—what makes it so?
"It's the best neighborhood for walking, that's for sure. The houses are loaded with personality, and there's an incredible range of plant life. It has thick, sticky moods and millions of tiny vistas."

Golden Age Collectables Ltd.

Pike Place Market
Second level, below ground, (206) 622-9799
Mon-Thurs 9:30 am-6 pm, Fri 9:30 am-6:30 pm, Sat 9 am-6:30 pm, Sun 10 am-6 pm

Golden Age bills itself over the phone as "world-famous," and while it may be difficult to prove this claim, the store is surely renowned as a local landmark. Children's dreams are made of the junk Golden Age carries: toys, baseball jerseys, Pokémon, Star Wars, and of course, comic books. And Golden Age is a one-stop geek shop: graphic novels, action figures, and sci-fi art. The store seems to have a policy that, if an item will entice just one more customer to enter the gates, it shall be offered for sale at Golden Age. Employees are well versed in the popular vernacular of children's toys, but from the looks on their faces, you know they'd rather be reading their comics.

Zanadu Comics

Downtown
1923 3rd Ave, (206) 443-1316
Mon-Tues, Thurs, Sat 10 am-6 pm, Wed & Fri 10 am-6:30 pm, Sun noon-5 pm
University District
1307 NE 45th St, (206) 632-0989
Mon-Tues & Thurs-Fri 11 am-7 pm, Wed 10 am-7 pm, Sat 10 am-6 pm, Sun noon-5 pm

A local fixture for over 25 years, Zanadu offers very little in the way of drama or pretense. It is what it is: a comic-book shop. And we wouldn't have it any other way. Carrying comics and comic-related merchandise nearly exclusively (the one exception being the vintage *Playboy* collection at the downtown store), Zanadu exists for geek boys (and the rare girl) who run down every Wednesday afternoon for their fix of four-color melodrama. This is not the store for the casual browser unaware of the comics subculture—walk in at your own risk, and walk out richer for the experience.

Newsstands

Bulldog News

University District
4208 University Way, (206) 632-6397
Daily 8 am-9 pm
Capitol Hill
401 Broadway Ave E, (206) 322-6397
Sun-Thurs 9:30 am-10 pm, Fri-Sat 9:30 am-11 pm

Bulldog News offers a generous selection of magazines, from literary journals to instructions for model-railroad builders. Some notable titles: Paul Krasner's *The Realist*, *The Utne Reader*, *Adbusters*. Bulldog News is a neighborhood institution; after opening its U-District store in 1983, Bulldog opened a second shop in the Broadway Market in 1989. The Broadway Market store recently moved into a 1,300-square-foot location, after spending 11 years in the 225-square-foot kiosk under the stairs. The still larger U-District store offers more than 1,500 titles, and sells organic, fairly traded coffee as well.

Mag Daddy

Belltown

2237 2nd Ave, (206) 441-9880

Mon-Sat 11 am-7 pm, Sun noon-5 pm

Mag Daddy, attached to Wall of Sound Records, has a fairly small selection of magazines, but the collection features a number of cultural- and film-criticism magazines and small-press journals that don't even show up on the radar of any other rag store. They even have a rack of Belltown-specific zines. This place is supercool.

Read All About It International Newsstand

Pike Place Market

93 Pike St, (206) 624-0140

Daily 7 am-7 pm

Perched at the corner of First Avenue and Pike Street, this newsstand has all the energy of a New York minute. The roped-off and crowded racks hold an impressive array of newspapers from around the world, as well as glossy, hard-to-find mags on obscure subjects. The stand has been in operation since 1979, and on those days when you feel Seattle's provincial aspect like a painful cramp, there's no better remedy than to stand around here, look louche, and eat a hot dog from Wonder-Freeze.

Steve's Broadway News

Capitol Hill

204 Broadway Ave E, (206) 324-7323

Daily 8 am-midnight

Steve's Fremont News

Fremont

3416 Fremont Ave N, (206) 633-0731

Sun-Thurs 8 am-10 pm, Fri-Sat 8 am-11 pm

Steve began his newsstand experience 20 years ago at Read All About It in the Pike Place Market, and still acts as a partner there. The Broadway store opened in 1987, nourishing Capitol Hill's well-read clientele. Many titles are suggested by customers, such as *Nest*, *Wallpaper*, *Q* (a hip British music magazine), and *Asian Cult Cinema*. You can also find a good selection of international magazines and newspapers. The Fremont location, open since 1996, offers another place to stroll in from the street and find unusual, obscure, fascinating reading.

Record Stores

Bedazzled Discs
University District
4742 University Way NE, (206) 985-2990
Daily 12 pm-10 pm
If you want a generic album by what's-his-name superstar served to you by a perky teenager, go to the mall. If you want music—not just something to boom from your Jeep—Bedazzled Discs is the place. As with anywhere on the Ave, used CDs are picked over, but with entire sections devoted to Olympia labels Kill Rock Stars and K, you can walk into Bedazzled with a little over 10 bucks and go home with actual music. Enjoy.

Cellophane Square
University District
4538 University Way NE, (206) 634-2280
Sun-Thurs 10 am-10 pm,
Fri-Sat 10 am-10 pm
Capitol Hill
130 Broadway Ave E, (206) 329-2202
Mon-Sat 10 am-11:30 pm,
Sun 10 am-10 pm

C. TAYLOR

Future DJs of America

The first Cellophane Square was shmushed into a modest little storefront on NE 42nd Street, and it was the ideal off-campus music source: Vinyl bins jutted out from under stuffed shelves of used cassettes; CD racks bristled with the good stuff; and there was only enough room for about two clerks and five customers at any given time. Perfect. The inventory strain finally grew too much, though, and Cellophane relocated farther up the Ave in a shop three times as large, and opened another store on Broadway. The U-District shop is still good for browsing; they stock mostly used CDs, and good collectors still sell to them. They also have order bins, cheap cassettes, and a steady supply of oddball special boxed sets and whatnot. There's also a corner of the store that occasionally serves as a stage for short acoustic sets: X, Vic Chesnutt, and Harvey Danger have all performed free little gigs there. For some reason, the Broadway store is hardly worth checking out; the store just can't seem to reliably stock anything.

Easy Street CDs & Tapes
West Seattle
4559 California St SW, (206) 938-EASY
Mon-Sat 10 am-9 pm, Sun 11 am-7 pm
As West Seattle's original population of Scandinavian family folk continues to drop like flies, Seattle's young, poor renters and home-buyers are beginning to realize that West Seattle's only a bridge away—and it's as cute as a button. Plus, it's the home of Easy Street CDs & Tapes, one of the best music stores in the Northwest. For dedicated music hounds, Easy Street is a required sniffing spot for hard-to-find albums; the collection isn't enormous, but it's very well curated. Posters, flyers, and flats are tacked to every surface; it's a record store that lends itself to hanging out, running into friends you haven't seen since the Elf Power show, and catching up on indie-rock gossip.

Fallout Records, Books, & Comics
Capitol Hill
1506 E Olive Way, (206) 323-2662
Daily noon-7 pm
Located on the most awkward slant of Capitol Hill, this itty-bitty store is loaded with the most important underground comics, a healthy stock of vinyl, and a historical display of old and current rock posters (since you can't hang a fucking poster in this town). When you first move to Seattle, this is the place everyone tells you about, and if you're going to continue to live here, it should become one of your city habits. And if you're a zine fiend, this is where you get your *Cometbus*.

Orpheum
Capitol Hill
618 Broadway Ave E, (206) 322-6370
Daily 10 am-12 pm
Orpheum's window displays alone are worth visiting the store for: You never know what bizarre props have been scrounged up to illustrate the essence of the Murder City Devils or Built to Spill or Heather Duby. Inside, a great collection of independent music awaits, in CD form on the main floor and on vinyl in the upstairs loft. It's sandwiched between the Princess Market (where you can play Twilight Zone pinball) and the Jade Pagoda (where you can get the best burger in town and a double shot of gin for just over five bucks). If you hit all three, you've had an honest adventure. Orpheum stays open late and is packed until closing during the summer months. If your tastes glide from hiphop to indie to soul, it's all here. The cashiers aren't stuck-up music aficionados, so they don't mind if you've slipped a Tone Loc album between your Cat Power and Blonde Redhead.

Singles Going Steady

Belltown

2219 2nd Ave, (206) 441-7396

Mon-Sat 11 am-7 pm, Sun noon-6 pm

Even at the better record stores, punks and indie rockers have to part the seas of major-label dross to get to the records they're looking for. Not so at Singles Going Steady, a well-curated (and surprisingly complete) store that specializes in punk and indie 7-inch records. The only other store in town that seriously stocks 7-inch records is Fallout Records, but even Fallout can't compete with the boxes and boxes of vinyl at Singles. Electronica is mercifully absent, which is nice, though you might have to put up with the occasional swarm of window-shopping crusties. This is the first place you go for the rare songs in your search, and a great place to sample music you've been meaning to get around to. Singles Going Steady works so well it makes you wonder why every store doesn't have a decent singles collection.

BIO

Mark Sullo

Who is he? Owner, Wall of Sound Records; visual artist

How long has Wall of Sound been open?
"We opened in 1990, on Memorial Day weekend. At that time, the Belltown space we're still in was occupied by a cool art bookstore called Art in Form, which also sold a bit of music. They offered to turn that side of the business over to my ex-partner and me, so we shared the space for a couple of years, until the bookstore called it quits in '92. Our stuff was featured along one of the store's walls—hence the name 'Wall of Sound.' People often assume that it refers to Phil Spector or the Grateful Dead, but it's quite the literal reference. We started out VERY small."

What sort of stuff were you selling back then?

CURT DOUGHTY

"From the very start we sold lots of music from other cultures, or 'world music,' if you will, along with a wide array of other styles that tend to fall through the cracks, from vintage blues to avant-garde jazz to electronic music. However, we've never really believed in categories. Sure, certain types of music get hot from time to time, such as cocktail-lounge or Afro-Cuban, and we can't help but reflect these trends, but our philosophy remains the same: Wall of Sound has always featured what we, and our customers, think are the best recordings out there, regardless of genre. Anything goes, and all of it can be listened to in-store."

Anything goes?
"Well, yeah, anything but bad music. Local DJ extraordinaire Darek Mazzone put it best when he said, 'There's no crap!' I'll add that our space limitations have naturally led us to focus mostly on good music of the hard-to-find variety. We're very careful about what we buy, and so are our customers. Wall of Sound is still around because our staff, which includes Rob and Jeff from the Climax Golden Twins, has big ears for both listening carefully to people's interests and tracking down good new releases and labels. We all do a good job balancing these two driving forces. In other words, I think we run a damn fine record store."

Sonic Boom
Fremont
3414 Fremont Ave N, (206) 547-2666
Mon-Sat 11 am-8 pm, Sun 11 am-6 pm
The rock talk couldn't be better anywhere in the city—this store is often crowded with members of Death Cab or Sleater-Kinney. And for the music geek, Sonic Boom completes the fantasy checklist of what you would do if you opened your own record store/temple. It's airy; the bells chime when someone comes or goes; the playstations have easy-to-follow directions; and the hardwood creaks as you shift from one leg to the next, searching for the vinyl copy of your boyfriend's sister's new album. Stopping by on the chilliest days of winter or the hottest afternoons of summer makes you feel like you're really onto something in this city. Jason Hughes, the owner of this lovely store, used to be a DJ on KCMU and The End. He extends his store's mission to support musicians by sometimes producing their records; Sonic Boom Records co-released Death Cab for Cutie's first album with Barsuk.

Wall of Sound
Belltown
2237 2nd Ave, (206) 441-9880
Mon-Sat 11 am-7 pm, Sun noon-5 pm
Serious collectors all over the country (and some spots around the world) know about Wall of Sound. The store is without a mainstream; the closest you can come to commercial music is to buy Sonic Youth's instrumental work. If you need to find the music that accompanied Seattle's World Fair, recorded in 1962, at the same time you're looking to pick up folk songs of Croatia, there is no other place in Seattle. Don't ask the desk clerk about Nurse with Wound, though, because if you don't know who they were, when they were, and what they were, he'll go cold until you've left shivering.

Clothing (New & Used)

Alhambra
Downtown
101 Pine St, (206) 621-9571
Mon-Sat 10 am-7 pm, Sun 11:30 am-6 pm
The recommendation is to window shop here or for a once-a-year splurge; this is way out of *The Stranger*'s budget. But much like walking into the real Alhambra, walking into this store makes you go silent for beauty's sake. The women's clothes, the jewelry, the decadence are all imported from countries you've never been to (though the truth is, you could probably refrain from buying their Turkish exploitations and fly to Turkey with the savings). The clothes are incredibly unique and delicate creations, so

when you throw down three C-notes for a mesh top, you do believe you've gotten your money's worth. These clothes are beautiful enough to be passed down as family heirlooms.

Atlas Clothing Company

Capitol Hill
1515 Broadway, (206) 323-0960
Mon-Thurs noon-7 pm, Fri-Sat noon-7:30 pm, Sun noon-6 pm

Although Atlas started out as a used- and vintage-clothing store, in the past few years it has added an excellent selection of indie-designer wear, including T-shirts from Emily and pants from Suburban Girl. The prices here are so low they're disarming, and it's possible to shop from boutique wear and from

Atlas' still-stellar selection of very hip used clothing, sneakers, and jewelry at the same time. They also have a big ol' bowl of some of the coolest patches to sew on your backpack or jeans.

ANNIE MARIE MUSSELMAN

Atlas Clothing: Everything old is cool again

Betsey Johnson

Downtown
1429 5th Ave,
(206) 624-2887
Mon-Sat 11 am-7 pm,
Sun 11 am-6 pm

She got her start outfitting the Velvet Underground and Andy Warhol films, so even though she's a big-shot designer with a chain of stores all over the world, *The Stranger* can't help but recommend Seattle's own tiny Betsey boutique. The sales are fabulous here, and for most women it's fun to own just one Betsey Johnson.

Buffalo Exchange

University District
4530 University Way NE, (206) 545-0175
Mon-Sat 11 am-7 pm, Sun noon-6 pm

Buffalo Exchange, which sells used clothing, is a wonderful place to fill the void of contemporaries in your closet. Along with a recently tossed BCBG dress, you can get your wallet chains, spikes, leopard handbags, and Punky Color hair dye, if you're into that kind of thing. Caveat: Selling your clothes here can be a bit of an embarrassment, since the checkers will not hesitate to comment on the outdated styles you're trying to pawn off on them.

Crossroads Trading Company

Capitol Hill

325 Broadway Ave E, (206) 328-5847

Sun-Thurs 11 am-7 pm, Fri-Sat 11 am-8 pm

Where other used clothing stores get fancy, Crossroads keeps it real by stocking a huge selection of basics. This is the place to go if you need to find a crisp cotton button-up shirt or an orange corduroy skirt. The buyers favor designers who are on the fringe, and they frequently spotlight local thread-makers, but you'll also find good-quality used shoes. Crossroads is also a good place to sell: They pay better than most of the consignment shops, and they won't try to shame you when they pick through your old dirty clothes.

Delphinium Clothier

Wallingford

1705 N 45th St, (206) 548-0880

Tues-Fri 11 am-7 pm, Sat 11 am-6 pm, Sun noon-5 pm

Delphinium is an absolute garden of designer wear, but the jewelry is the real score here since it is often on sale and therefore much more affordable than the clothes. Owner Julie Draper's favorite designers tend toward clean

lines and functionality; she favors Daryl-K, James Perse T-shirts, cocktail dresses by Sue Wong, and shoes by BCBG and Rocket Dog. Draper also carries a great line of French lingerie.

SOMYA GUTSHALL

Isadora's

Downtown

1915 1st Ave, (206) 441-7711

Mon-Thurs 11 am-6 pm, Fri 11 am-8 pm,

Sat 10 am-6 pm, Sun noon-5 pm

Isadora's is an adorable time capsule of vintage couture. The shop has been around for years, and has a well-deserved reputation for finding those bits of

Wig, scarf, sandals: Don't be afraid to accessorize!

arcane history that will always stay beautiful—plush scarves, dangly bracelets, silver compacts, silk kimonos. If you're looking for a vintage bridal gown or cocktail dress, this should be your first stop.

Le Frock

Capitol Hill

317 E Pine St, (206) 623-5339

Mon-Sat noon-5 pm

Le Frock is a consignment store, but you would hardly know it—owner Diane Stone is able to ferret out current designer wear that's hardly been worn at all. There are racks of dresses and suits from such names as Mikimoto,

Prada, and D&G. Le Frock also specializes in vintage wear, including silk lingerie and some jewelry. The men's suits are awesome.

Les Amis

Fremont

3420 Evanston Ave N, (206) 632-2877

Tues-Thurs 11 am-6 pm, Fri-Sat 11 am-7 pm, Sun 11 am-5 pm

Fremont is becoming more French by the minute: The posh boutique Les Amis offers a selection of French-milled soaps, glass-bead jewelry, lush cashmere, linen, and fabulous silky lingerie. The prices reflect the fact that this is somewhere you go to treat yourself and to mumble "Ma cherie" over and over, practicing bedroom eyes in a handheld ivory mirror.

Mario's

Downtown

1513 6th Ave, (206) 223-1461

Mon-Fri 10 am-7 pm, Sat 10 am-6 pm, Sun 12:30 pm-5 pm

The Stranger has to suggest this as a window-shopping experience, since its prices leave our means in the dust. Say you actually sold your Amazon stock when it was worth something: Aren't you sick of your casual wear and isn't it time you got yourself a decent suit? Mario's collection is pure high-end NYC, and you'll have no problem dropping a couple thousand bucks to pick up an exquisite new D&G four-button suit and a Hugo Boss shirt. Mario's is the place to have your first muy rico shopping experience for one reason only: You've got to be fitted out by Mario's tailor to truly feel like you've earned your suit. He's got a pack of Pall Malls in his breast pocket and a measuring tape over his shoulders, and with his thick Eastern Bloc accent he mutters and measures and teaches you the history of the perfect fit.

Powder Room

Downtown

101 Stewart St, (206) 374-0060

Mon-Thurs 10:30 am-6:30 pm, Fri-Sat 10 am-7 pm, Sun 11 am-6 pm

The clothes here are tacky urban fare—it's the perfect place to pick out your next New Year's Eve party outfit. Everything's tight, shiny, plastic, and poorly made, but nothing is too expensive. They've got a great selection of Chinese Laundry shoes. And even though the girls who work here look better in these teenager styles than you ever will, they're incredibly friendly.

Private Screening

Fremont

3504 Fremont Pl N, (206) 548-0751

Mon-Sat 11 am-6 pm, Sun 11 am-5 pm

Fremont's vintage vocabulary reaches back a bit further than most other parts of the city—the whole neighborhood is crawling with vintage stores, and all of them seem to be focused on clothes and ephemera circa the '20s and '30s. Private Screening definitely represents this era with its hats, suits, and jewelry, but its collection includes a broad swath of time. Prices are reasonable if not thrifty, and it's worth stopping in regularly just to keep an eye on the store's collection of jackets. The proprietors are friendly without being aggressive, and they obviously put in the time repairing and rejuvenating the clothes before putting them on the rack.

Red Light Clothing Exchange

University District
4560 University Way NE, (206) 545-4044
Capitol Hill
312 Broadway Ave E, (206) 329-2200
Mon-Sat 11 am-8 pm
Buy/sell/trade: vintage, some contemporary, cash or in-store trade

No vintage store in Seattle is more thorough than the Red Light; practically every beautiful and ugly piece of clothing from the last eighty years can be found on these racks. The coolest thing about the store is its organization; everything is separated into decades, so you can really focus on your own specific nostalgic bent. It's also a history lesson in fabrics to brush your fingers along each rack and feel the particular textures of a decade. The Red Light also stocks plenty of contemporary junk: new, cheap knockoff clothes, glitter wallets, hair dye, etc.— to round out the corners of your wardrobe.

BIO

Joan Jones

Who is she? Manager of the Red Light, a vintage- and new-clothing store.

How did you start working at the Red Light?
"I've been working with Niz Marrar, the owner of the Red Light, for five years. I started at the Lola City Shop, which was mostly '60s and '70s stuff, very poppy. The store burned down in a three-alarm fire in 1998. We were looking for another location, and the Red Light owners were looking to sell, so we

CURT DOUGHTY

took over the U-District store in March of 1999."

Why vintage?
"The clothes are just beautiful: the way things were made back then, the

craftsmanship, the feel of the clothes, the fabrics. Now you wash something once and it falls apart. I'm just in love with the '30s and '40s. Everybody was gorgeous in ball gowns. People spent time dressing up with hats and shoes and handbags. It was a ritual to get all dolled up and just walk down the block."

Is your closet enormous?
"Oh, if I ever stopped this, I could open a small museum. You wind up owning a lot of clothes. It's not just the retail pull, but the love of vintage clothing. And it's easy to justify things when they are so cheap."

Rockin' Betty's

Capitol Hill

401 Broadway Ave E, (206) 709-8821

Mon-Sat 10 am-9 pm, Sun noon-6 pm

This is definitely *The Stranger*'s favorite cheap pop fashion store. Upstairs at the Broadway Market, it's a hidden stretch-fabric fantasyland. Only synthetic materials are allowed and it's best this way. If you have to have every trendy little thing, there is no better place to spend an hour or two cruising

SOMYA GUTSHALL

Fabulous shoes at Rockin' Betty's

clothes. Plus, the purses and shoes are fabulous. Call your girlfriend or favorite drag queen (they stock big sizes) and say, "Let's go to Rockin' Betty's!"

Room Service Clothing

Wallingford

1717 N 45th St, (206) 675-8602

On the window of the boutique, there is a sign that reads: "Shop here, don't shop at the mall." Of course you should and it's so good to see that this store is so pissy about it. Everyone knows that the future of such wonderful little boutiques relies on such an ethic, but it is definitely good to be reminded. The store houses a triangle of exciting stock: weird beautiful jewelry, the sexiest lingerie, and some great ladies' clothing.

Stella Beam

Downtown

1535 1st Ave, (206) 264-9699

Mon-Thurs 10 am-6 pm, Fri-Sat 10 am-7 pm, Sun 10 am-5 pm

The stock is spare, but if you're looking for something nobody else will be wearing at your high-school reunion (and you've saved some cash), this is where to go. Gorgeous slip dresses, red leather pants, and strappy silk tank tops can instantly make you feel like you've been invited to the Oscars.

Zebra Club

Downtown

1901 1st Ave, (206) 448-7452

Mon-Sat 10 am-7 pm, Sun 11 am-6 pm

Skaters used to clutter the Zebra Club to pick up oversized shorts and Caballero Vans. The clientele and content has switched genres to accommodate the club scene; you can get your Ecko Unltd. and Diesel clothing here. This place is worth facing First Avenue's terrible parking scene for the men's shoe collection alone. And for women, the true purpose for stopping in is to gaze at the largest selection of Kiehl's products (that moisturizing lotion supermodels use) in the city.

Shoes

Edie's
Capitol Hill
319 E Pine St, (206) 839-1111
Mon-Sat 10 am-7 pm, Sun noon-5 pm
Owner Erin Dolan saw the lack of a shoe boutique in Capitol Hill, and *ba-boom!* she moved right in. And we love her for it. Edie's carries a small but well-chosen assortment of men's and women's casual shoes, and a few funky dress shoes, too. Here you can find the elusive Camper brand, along with Diesel and some accessories such as beautiful evening bags and jewelry.

Five Doors Up
University District
4309 1/2 University Way NE
(206) 547-3192
Daily 10 am-7 pm
Perhaps because students wear out their shoes so quickly, trudging up and down the rough surfaces of University Way, the Annex has been successfully selling funky, thick-soled shoes for years. The store's selection of boots can seem like the only reason to look forward to winter in this city; it offers Steve Madden, Chinese Laundry, and Diesel. For less funkified, more hippie-comfortable shoes, check out the big brother of Five Doors Up, the Woolly Mammoth, just down the street to the south.

J. Gilbert Footwear
Belltown
2025 1st Ave, (206)441-1182
Mon-Sat 10 am-6 pm, Sun noon-5 pm
The bleached blond cutie who works here can tell you exactly how far the owner goes to get just the right shoes in stock. The staff attends shoe conventions and the owner flies to Italy to hand-select beautiful temptations. Each pair is a rediscovery of style. Great women's shoe collections are rare in Seattle, and nearly mythical is the presence of more than one decent pair of men's shoes, but J. Gilbert has them, casual to wingtip.

John Fluevog Shoes
Downtown
1611 1st Ave, (206) 441-1065
Mon-Sat 10 am-6 pm, Sun noon-5 pm
Seattle, 1997: Robin Williams is spotted in Fluevog, buying a pair of yellow loafers to go with his green parachute pants. Only John Fluevog can satisfy the frenetic needs of footwear fetishists, and only in Seattle and San Francisco, on the West Coast. Fluevog's Angel shoes, which feature a wing shape

along the side and lug soles, have been a fashion staple for downtown hipsters for years. The quirkiness permeates service, however: The chance that Fluevog will stock the style you want in your size is only about one in three.

Ped
Downtown
1115 1st Ave, (206) 292-0660
Mon-Sat 10 am-6 pm, Sun noon-5 pm
Ped began its life as the shoe-store sister to Ardour, Dayna Grubb's clothing and jewelry storefront. When she consolidated into a single shop, Grubb made sure to bring all of the accessories Ardour had been famous for: hand-knit scarves and gloves, purses and bags, and semi-precious stone jewelry from small West Coast designers. Ped's stock of shoes, both men's and women's, is amazing: there will always be more than one pair you've never seen the likes of, and might never see again. You don't have to go to Barney's to indulge in bizarre footwear (which also means you don't have to pay upward of $350), and you aren't going to find patent-leather orange space boots anywhere else in the city.

Furniture & Home Accessories

Antique Liquidators
503 Westlake Ave N, (206) 623-2740
Mon-Sat 9:30 am-5:30 pm, Sun noon-5 pm
When winter gloom hits Seattle and there are no garage sales to be found, Antique Liquidators makes a more than suitable substitute. In fact, after discovering this three-floor warehouse of treasures, you may never waste your time at a garage sale again. Don't be intimidated by the dust and grime: Brush off the dirt and you may have yourself a prime piece of pottery. Most of the merchandise comes from estates, so you're as likely to find Grandma's mahogany dresser as her vintage ceramic bedpan. The husband and wife who own this place are legendarily talkative and friendly and almost always willing to negotiate on prices, making Antique Liquidators a popular source for a lot of other antique dealers in town.

Area 51
Capitol Hill
401 E Pine St, (206) 568-4782
Daily noon-7 pm
Furniture is always too expensive. That's what makes furniture-hunting so exciting: It's high-stakes. When you've found the perfect coffee table, somehow in your price range, the feeling is incomparable. Okay, so you probably won't find much in your price range here, but you can dream about the

egg-shaped chairs with built-in stereo systems. Area 51 started out as an affordable vintage store, but as the collection grew more rarified, the prices kept climbing. Now, the store's inventory is still beautiful and dreamy, but it works better as a museum of modernist design from the last century. At least you can pick up some of the style accessories the store has collected, such as 1960s *Playboys*, old 16mm films like "How to Clean Your Teeth," or Stevie Wonder vinyl. Note: After you're finished at Area 51, check out the cool, cheaper used-furniture place next door.

Area 51: Where UFO-shaped lamps are sighted

Chartreuse International

Capitol Hill

711 E Pike St, (206) 328-4844

Wed-Sat noon-6:30 pm, Sun noon-5 pm, Mon "by chance or by appointment"

A swoopy plastic chair sits on a patch of AstroTurf in the window; the interior of the store feels like a furniture gallery. Chartreuse is a collector's haven for those who want to revisit vestiges of their '70s childhood. A place to find fine design, famous-name chairs (like an Eames potato-chip chair), and that plastic set of plates you ate off of when you were five (they make them still, but only in white). Chartreuse also has a collection of new toy accessories: architecturally designed flatware and kitchen utensils, timers, and pepper shakers that look as if someone left kids' toys on the kitchen counter.

Current

Downtown

629 Western Ave, (206) 622-2433

Mon-Sat 10 am-6 pm, Sun noon-5 pm

Open 18 years, now in its third location on Western, Current is run by a man who began his business back when Paul Schell was trying to develop this part of downtown. Current carries gorgeously expensive couches, inventive lighting in a range of prices, fun toy appliances, high-end (mostly European) furniture, lamps that cross Issey Miyake with Chinese rice-paper lanterns, and cartoon salt-and-pepper contraptions by Alessi.

Decades
Capitol Hill
613 E Pike St, (206) 860-1664
Wed-Sun noon-6 pm
Decades is located in a beautiful loft space, with Danish teak dining sets and sideboards—curvaceous chairs and an unusual collection of glassware. It also features such fantastic artifacts as a chandelier that looks as though it was designed by a gyroscope, scrolled maps from elementary-school classrooms, fans that will cut your fingers off, heavy-handled rotary phones, and one lovely, glowing lamp.

Mint Modern Office Furniture Supply Co.
Downtown
91 Wall St, (206) 956-8270
Wed-Fri noon-6 pm, Sat-Sun noon-5 pm
Your office chair could be as sexy as a cherry '60s dragster. Shouldn't everything be? The women at Mint think so, and have hot-rodded their collection of industrial-salvage office gear accordingly. They've worked out a deal with a local auto painter to cover much of their inventory with lush, sparkly auto paint. Chunky modernist desks, lockers, and lamps look lickable in deep lavender, Cadillac pink, sharp orange, or midnight blue. Mint's painter considers this work his creative outlet, so he takes pains to do it right. The stuff isn't vintage-store cheap but, really, nothing is cheap anymore. Staff members love the store's collection of outdated staplers and 1960s office wastebaskets, and would be happy to tell you all about each piece's idiosyncrasies and history.

Mondeo
Downtown
1200 Western Ave, (206) 622-9426
Mon-Fri 7 am-6 pm, Sat 9 am-6 pm
Mondeo has the feel of a design museum, offering smart toys to populate your home with: miniature Eames chairs, a rubber tablecloth with a built-in fruit bowl, gorgeously curvy flatware,

VICTORIA RENARD

Mondeo: Smart toys

and clever lighting. The store also sells chairs, shelving, and custom kitchen systems. Mondeo occupies an architecturally striking space with high ceilings, and provides sensual objects and in-house baked goods to enjoy with your Illy coffee. Run by a couple who are educated in architecture and design, Mondeo offers Seattle a good and surprisingly cheap cup of coffee and some sweets (they also serve lunch: panini sandwiches and salads). What could be better than a furniture-store coffeehouse?

Urban Ease
Belltown
2512 2nd Ave, (206) 443-9546
Mon-Sat 11:30 am-6 pm, Sun 11:30 am-5 pm
We love the intense contemporary freaky furniture here but we hate the prices: couches are priced around the $3,000 mark. It's okay, though, to enter and pretend you've walked through your own front door; slouch into one of these pricey comfort zones for 10 to 15 minutes. Press the buttons on that imaginary remote control, keep pressing, pet your imaginary cat—until the store calls the cops on you.

Thrift Stores

Chicken Soup Brigade
University District
4542 University Way NE, (206) 633-5083
Mon-Thurs 11 am-7 pm, Fri-Sat 11 am-8 pm, Sun noon-6 pm
The U-District Chicken Soup Brigade store walks the thin line between thrift and vintage. Purist thrifters scoff at this place, but sometimes it's a nice change of pace having the employees sift through the godawful junk and rack only the good stuff. Plus, the prices are fair, the counter people are attractive, and the $1 bin may contain some real gems.

Goodwill
Rainier Valley/Central District
1400 S Lane St (just west of Rainier Ave, off Dearborn St), (206) 329-1000
Mon-Fri 10 am-8 pm, Sat 9 am-8 pm, Sun 11 am-6 pm
The sheer size of this store induces a panic of the heart-pounding, 11th-cup-of-coffee variety. It's best to have a plan—say, "I'm looking for sports equipment"—or you could spend an entire day just wandering through all the books, furniture, clothes, and general junk. The front part of the store features mostly clothes, while the back houses electronics, sports stuff (bowling balls, skis, tennis rackets), office equipment, books, kitchen stuff, and tragically beautiful bad art. The clothes can be hit or miss, but most hipsters worth their Dickies can find at least one good coat or pair of pants. Keep this heartbreaking fact in mind while shopping: If there's no price tag, you CAN'T buy the item.

Salvation Army
Downtown
1010 4th Ave S, (206) 624-0204
Mon-Sat 9:30 am-6 pm
Need more crap? Sift through the refuse in this large Salvation Army near Safeco Field. There's at least one good thing in this enormous store, and

it's your job to find it. Special SA memory: The store used to have a grunge section, replete with torn jeans and flannels. The attached gift store sells jewelry, books, and antique stuff at outrageously high prices.

Shop & Save
White Center
10014 15th Ave SW, (206) 762-8099
Mon-Sat 9 am-9 pm, Sun 10 am-6 pm

A wash-your-hands-after-you're-done kind of thrift store, the beloved Shop & Save has a bunch of the usual crap: stinky shoes, ugly furniture, Barbra Streisand records, and broken electronics—along with some good stuff: strange tools, funny T-shirts, and mysterious stapled plastic bags centered around themes like "orange buttons" or "fake flowers." This store is part of a trinity of White Center thrift stores—Shop & Save, Veteran's (rest in peace), and a St. Vincent de Paul (really bad crap, but worth a look), all within two blocks of each other.

St. Vincent de Paul
Georgetown
5950 4th Ave S, (206) 763-8729
Mon-Sat 9 am-6 pm, Sun 10 am-5 pm

Out in the middle of nowhere, this St. Vinny's rises out of the industrial wasteland to bring you weird old washers and dryers and refurbished mattresses. Less about clothes, this smaller store really packs in the books, household items, and furniture. Every once in a while, the store will haul all the stuff out into the adjacent parking lot for a gigantic sale.

Thriftko
Greenwood
124 N 85th St, (206) 789-5357
Mon-Sat 9 am-9 pm, Sun 10 am-6 pm

Thrifters' eyes glaze over in rapture when they hear the name Thriftko. Walk down the ramp and enter the battle zone. Ignore the "good stuff" case with overpriced dolls and VCRs—

Thriftko: 6 am, Sunday, just before the hordes arrive

Thriftko has better things to offer: clothes, knickknacks, household furniture, and bad art. Your competition is comprised of seasoned hipsters, moms and kids shopping for school clothes, and other bargain hunters.

Value Village
Capitol Hill

1525 11th Ave, (206) 322-7789

Mon-Sat 9 am-9 pm, Sun 10 am-7 pm

SOMYA GUTSHALL

Thrifting: It just might change your life

Thrifting logic assumes that thrift stores in hipster neighborhoods are far too picked over to be of any use. For some reason though, Capitol Hill's Value Village is consistently rich with good gear, and a visit here is likely to be as rewarding as a trip out to Tukwila. The big, big score won't happen here—the employees are too on top of it themselves—but there's plenty of great shit, and the prices are thrift, not vintage. It's huge, too: women's clothing on the first floor and men's upstairs, at least in theory. Even the furniture in the basement holds possibilities.

Two Special Mentions
If you're of the larger persuasion (size 16 and up) and would like to thrift for clothes, check out **Two Big Blondes** in Georgetown (1223 S Bailey St, 206/762-8620—right around the corner from Dewey's motorcycle shop). The store has a great selection of clothes in good shape and a variety of styles. **Venus** (in Capitol Hill at 1015 E Pike St, 206/322-5539) is another great plus-sized used-clothing store, with a wide selection and a specialty in sexy lingerie.

Auction Tips

by Novella Carpenter

University of Washington Surplus Auction

1117 NE Boat St, (206) 685-1573

Auction is held every couple of months; call for dates; cash only

If you're after furniture for the home and office at great prices, get thee to the University of Washington Surplus Auction. A wooden filing cabinet. A set of six institutional-looking chairs. Two pallets of Apple SE 30s. A glass "Biochemistry Department" sign. These are just a few of the things I've successfully acquired at the UW Surplus Auction. Sure, every UW Surplus Auction has been a gas, but I'll always remember my first time. . . .

I arrived at 8 am on Saturday (preview times are 8 am-3 pm on Friday and 8 am-10 am on Saturday), coffeeless and unprepared for the four-hour emotional obstacle course that is the Surplus Auction. I disappeared into

CAROL LAY

the warren-like building: room after room of low ceilings over metals desks, odd pieces of lab equipment, computers, pallets of office supplies, hospital beds. It seemed like only five minutes had passed before we were herded upstairs for the silent auction. I had to register (you always have to register at an auction), but I was already hyperven-tilating from object desire and a need to touch EVERY ITEM in the entire building. I became bidder number 118, and was let loose.

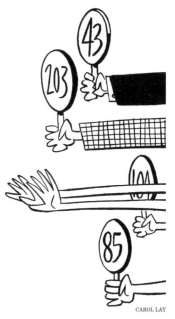

A silent auction means you have a piece of paper, and when your desired object comes up to the block, you write down your bidder number and how much you are willing to pay for the object. This is much, much more painful than it sounds. You don't want to underbid (you won't get the object) and you don't want to overbid (you look stupid and spend too much money). You just want to "win." The UW Surplus Auction is gambling. Period. "I just won a crummy, heavy, ugly file cab-inet," I shrieked. For five dollars. Yes!

After you've been once, the Surplus people begin haunting you every couple of

CAROL LAY

months with a flyer in the mail that lists items available at the next auction. It is a powerful, powerful thing. "Yes," you'll murmur, "I need some bowling pins and an infant incubator."

Tips

1. Bring a pen and a notebook. You'll get a sheet listing stuff for auction, but there isn't much room to write comments.
2. Move quickly—there isn't enough time!
3. Open all drawers to make sure they work.
4. Look at the object: Do you really want it?
5. Lift the object and ask, "Will it fit in my car?"
6. If you can't lift the object by yourself, ask, "Can I eventually burn this in my backyard?"
7. After the auction, you may go downstairs and purchase items that didn't get bids (this is how I got a beautiful orange chair set for 50¢—don't be afraid to be miserly).

Other Auctions/Surplus

Pacific Auction Galleries, 2121 3rd Ave, (206) 441-6919 or (206) 441-9990; call to find out about the next sale. This is the place where people's stuff goes after they die. Usually Pacific Galleries focuses on the high-end merchandise such as Persian rugs, antique furniture, and art, but they also carry odd things like stuffed animals or double waffle irons belonging to the deceased. Minimum bid is $5, and the auctioneer often starts with a price higher than you want to pay; but who knows? You could score some good stuff.

Just down the street is **Bushell's**, 2006 2nd Ave, (206) 448-5833. This auction house has cool, creaky floors and that old wood smell to it. The auctioneer's voice is so smooth and soothing it should be recorded and played back to insomniacs. Even though the stuff is just so-so, the people-watching is divine—check out the neurotic antique-hags bidding on Japanese battle swords, and marvel at that GQ model–type bidding for Christmas-scene sculptures. It's as if the whole world has lost its mind.

Quinn's Boat Sales & Auction, 3568 W Marginal Way SW, (206) 938-9830. This place can set you up with a leaky old sailboat or yacht, for cheap. The fact is that boats are expensive to moor, and people often abandon them, so Quinn's wrangles them up and has an auction about once a season. It's just fun to go out to W Marginal Way and check out these old vessels. Boisterous Quinn will fully support your plan to sail to South America.

Not scared of Kent? Head to the exotic **Boeing Surplus Retail Store**, 20651 84th Ave S; (425) 393-4065. The pro-scrappers head over during the week (Tues-Fri 10 am-5 pm) for their reamers, dial indicators, orange jumpsuits, and engineers' desks. Come Saturday (9 am-4 pm), it can get pretty ugly and crowded. Go out into the metal scrap yard and pick up some of those weird orange boxes that used to hold god-knows-what, but remember: All sales are final.

Finally, if you're looking for a cheap, possibly broken-down, piece-of-shit car, check out the heavily advertised **Woodinville Public Auto Auction**, 13820 NE 195th St, Woodinville, (206) 628-6445. Here, almost every Saturday morning, a parking lot of beaters await. However, the auction doesn't let you drive the car, and you can't bid $1, because the sellers get to set a price beforehand. But if you're looking for parts, this might be good.

The Stranger's Favorite Specialized Shops

Amour on the Boulevard
Tukwila
5301 Southcenter Blvd, (206) 248-5085
Mon-Wed 11 am-9 pm, Thurs-Sat 11 am-10 pm, Sun noon-8 pm
This tri-level porn shop is almost exactly the opposite of Toys in Babeland—completely tacky—and that's why we love it. The top floor is the art gallery: bronze statues of women pulling their nipples into erection, nasty Nagel-type prints of women ejaculating, photographs of Josephine Baker. The ground floor is full of "silks and satins": lingerie and the mildest SM gear. But the lower floor is where the action is. As Amour's card says, "Finally, a place that really DOES have it all." The lower level has four HUGE walls packed with vibrators for men and women, cock rings, those beads you stick up your ass, plastic doll heads (modeled after the real faces of porn stars) for simulated blowjobs, every brand of piña-colada lube, etc. The video/DVD collection is insanely thorough (you can purchase or rent). We do encourage you to buy your toys at Toys in Babeland whenever possible, but if you are on the poorer side, Amour has just incredible prices (sometimes half the price of Toys). You won't feel so sex-positive walking out of here, but at least it's not like any of the sex-store dumps downtown, which make you feel like the loneliest masturbator on the planet.

Archie McPhee & Co.
Ballard
2428 NW Market St,
(206) 297-0240, www.mcphee.com
Mon-Sat 9 am-7 pm,
Sun 10 am-6 pm
Fundamental Western logic dictates that for a thing to be manufactured, it has to serve some kind of purpose. Otherwise, why the hell make it in the first place? Archie McPhee's specializes in finding those funny little things that violate this principle. The store then gathers them all in one place and lets the cash registers ring. The result is undeniable: While you'd never consider buying a propeller beanie, life-

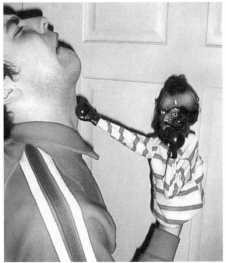

DAVID BELISLE

Archie McPhee: Toys that hurt

sized animal decals, or a boxing-nun puppet from Fred Meyer, the sheer vastness of Archie McPhee's collection of useless stuff might well convince you to at least buy a box of the world's smallest tarot cards. Just be warned: Almost everybody else in town gets their weird stuff here, too.

Bedrock
Magnolia
1401 W Garfield, (206) 283-7625
Daily 10 am-6 pm
It's difficult to explain the bounty of strange, desirable objects at Bedrock. If you've got a proclivity for the picturesque, this is where you go to get broken statues to add to your overwrought garden. There are also oil drums filled with carefully sorted, smooth-tumbled glass fragments of all colors. Glass (this is mainly a glass-blowing place) is cheap here, and there's nothing else like it in the city. This is a great place to pick up an armless statue of St. Francis and a couple of beautiful glass coasters for your sister's wedding.

Chubby & Tubby
Greenwood
7906 Aurora Ave N, (206) 524-1810
Rainier Valley
3333 Rainier Ave S, (206) 723-8800
White Center
9456 16th Ave SW, (206) 762-9791
Open daily; hours vary by location
Despite its various cracked-cement environs, Chubby & Tubby not only qualifies in our book as a boutique, but it beats the hell out of Restoration Hardware. A real hardware store, plus a plant nursery, plus a great selection of sneakers and jeans make Chubby & Tubby the preferred post-hangover-breakfast Sunday stop. You can find Dickies here, and New Balance shoes, alongside comfy hooded sweatshirts and really cheap metal shower rings that would cost you $40 at Pottery Barn. Go Chubby!

Columbia Plaza, the Shopping Place
Rainier Valley
Rainier Ave & Orcas
Mon-Sat 10 am-7 pm
You can't miss this place when you're driving down Rainier. It's the green monolith with the incredible parking lot. Everyone who migrated to Seattle from California must miss the giant flea markets. Fear not—Columbia Plaza has all the lovely junk you'd find at a California Mexican flea market (okay, maybe it's lacking everything Mexican, but all the good junk is here). There's a dollar store, a beauty supply store, a pager/cell phone island, an incredible sneaker alcove, a car stereo corner . . . baby, it's all here. Buy the cheapest cigarettes, the greatest, coolest pair of Adidas

that you can't find elsewhere, and pick up a hooded sweatshirt and Dickies while you are looking through the "underground rap and R&B" collection of CDs.

Continental Store
University District
5014 Roosevelt Way NE, (206) 523-0606
Mon-Fri 9 am-6 pm, Sat 10 am-6 pm
Ah yes, the Continent. Focusing on most things German, the Continental Store offers nutcrackers, a variety of German magazines and cookbooks, and even a German book exchange. The real fun begins downstairs, though, where a frau stands behind the counter—practice your German with her, or just order a sandwich made with head cheese, bologna, salami, or liverwurst. There's pickled herring, bratwurst, blood sausage, and a wide variety of cheeses in the deli case. The shelves buckle with jars of German mustard, sometimes Milka chocolate, and that perennial German favorite: bottles of red cabbage pickled with vinegar and sugar.

European Vine Selections
Capitol Hill
522 15th Ave E, (206) 323-3557
This a cooperatively owned wine shop, which makes it automatically cool. Talk to any of the employees here—they're very friendly and they know everything there is to know about wine. At European Vine, you feel like you're actually learning something, experiencing a little bit more of life when you buy your wine here instead of grabbing your Gato Negro from the shelf of Safeway while your car is still running in the parking lot. You should see the store's scandalous ad (only shown at the Little Theatre), in which a woman in a bathtub pours red wine all over her naked body.

C. TAYLOR

Won't you take me to Funky Town?

Funky Town
Rainier Valley
3818 S Graham St,
(206) 725-4906
With a name like Funky Town, it's got to be good, right? Yes and no. The owners are remarkably rude, but the stuff is awesome. Check out the amazing gold and silver selection, which features things like humongous crosses, cubic-zirconia-encrusted crucifixes, and—strangely—bull dogs. Gold cleaning costs $2 per piece. In

addition to the jewelry, Funky Town carries a ton of Dickies clothes, faux-lizard sports jackets, and big-lady dresses.

Hardwick's Hardware Store
University District
4214 Roosevelt Way NE, (206) 632-1203

Hardwick's is heaven. It's the perfect shop—a den of mysteries and surprises, all the more exciting because it poses as a mere new-and-used hardware store. Inside Hardwick's is labyrinthine, and packed with just the stuff to fire your creative impulses: spools of clear plastic tubing; chains of all different heft and textures; strange, heavy tools; clips and knobs and knockers and deadbolts and fixtures and hand drills and wood awls and . . . more than the eye can absorb. There are aisles of old telephone bells, anonymous circuit boards, switches, switchboards, and voltage meters—many of them beautifully rusted by their years of outdoor service. There's a room full of stacked wooden furniture, a stranded stovetop, and maybe a grid of apartment mailboxes with the tenants' names still attached. In another room, hundreds of scarred, unmarked wooden drawers are sorted for transistors, conductors, little working motors, calculator keypads, watch batteries, or faded brass letters. It's like a library of lost and forgotten things—not even the staff knows what's in all those drawers.

Hawthorne Stereo
University District
6303 Roosevelt Way NE, (206) 522-9609
Mon-Fri 11 am-8 pm, Sat 10 am- 6pm, Sun 11 am-6 pm

Hawthorne's philosophical foundation is radically, almost militantly, opposed to that of its Magnolia Hi-Fi neighbors. For starters, Hawthorne is the only stereo shop in Seattle that sells both new and used equipment. The new stuff is a collection of high-end British gear such as Naim and Roksan (prices for a record player can go up to $12,000). Still, Hawthorne is one of those great stores in Seattle that stays true to the sensibility of a small, local business. There's a careful selection of good equipment for a real-life budget, and a room that is nearly a curated gallery of used gear gleaned from various trade-ins. You can get the coolest amplifier with big, fat knobs and heavy switches from 1972, and the thing will work better than any Sony you'd pay triple for elsewhere.

Everybody who works at Hawthorne is a dedicated music listener—"as opposed to audiophiles, who will talk about 'soundstage,' 'depth,' and 'imaging,'" says staffer Tony Limtiaco dismissively. This has got to be the only store in town where the boys helping you listen to the stereo will argue over the choicest cut from personal LP collections—and sit and listen to the music with you.

Helpful Hint: They have a truly great website, www.hawthornestereo.com. Besides a list of gear for sale, the site is full of earnest, convincing essays written by the staff. Don't miss "Specifications and Other Nonsense." You will believe.

Hello Gorgeous
Downtown
1530 Post Alley, #5, (206) 621-0702
When Theresa or any of the other cuties answers the phone with "Hello, Gorgeous," a feeling of goodwill washes over you. The store's wares make you gorgeous, too. Hello Gorgeous features a mix of new stuff—days-of-the-week underwear, cool T-shirts, pink kitty-shaped bathmats—and hand-picked vintage items such as jean jackets, fur coats, and 1950s dresses.

BOOTSY HOLLER

They've got it all . . . including saggy undies!

Jukebox City
South Seattle
1950 1st Ave S, (206) 625-1950
South Seattle's industrial district used to be just that: huge lots and warehouses filled with the raw metal and machinery used to construct the city's undergirding. Now that Safeco Field has arrived and downtown is pushing south, this area is undergoing some inevitable upscaling, and those old print shops and factories, with their strange and beautiful detritus, are beginning to fade away. Luckily, there is Jukebox City, a rare and wondrous shop filled with yesterday's jukeboxes, neon signs, and ephemeral junk. This is no junk shop, though; it's the shop of a craftsman whose specialty is the painstaking restoration of bygone items. The jukeboxes aren't the showy collector's artifacts you might be used to seeing in antique shops: These are the chunky glass-and-metal boxes that sat in bars all around Seattle, now cleaned up and repaired for service. The thousands of 45s on sale for a dollar all around the room are perfect jukebox specimens: Cutting Crew, Stevie Nicks, Linda Ronstadt, Bobby Bland, and other barroom favorites.

Kiki's Candy Land/International Model Toys
International District
601 S King St, (206) 381-9152 and (206) 682-8534, respectively
Both of these shops are buried in a tiny mall experience. They sit across from each other, and ought to be seen as a pair. At Kiki's, every jelly candy imaginable is available—one of the best is the chocolate-covered jelly grapes (who knew?). Kiki's is the one place in Seattle where we've found Kinder eggs, the

popular European chocolate egg with a model toy in the middle. And Kiki's is cheaper than Uwajimaya. International Model Toys is an anime toy store with its own model competition. And without a hint of Hello Kitty, the store has plenty of cutesy stickers and key chains.

Lipstick Traces
Capitol Hill
500 E Pine St, (206) 329-2813
Mon, Wed-Sat noon-8 pm, Sun noon-6 pm

An unassuming storefront on Pine Street houses Lipstick Traces, where owner Jenn Gallucci fills her carefully arranged shelves with handmade, must-have accessories, including lotería-card-bedecked journals and purses, weird jewelry, soaps, homemade guitar straps, and gift books from Taschen and Chronicle. It's the coolest. She even stocks cool things made by the kids at Northwest High School, which is just up the street.

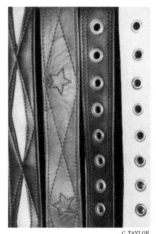

C. TAYLOR

Belts at Lipstick Traces: Local artists make good

Loud Music
Fremont
223 N 36th St, (206) 547-1981, www.loudmusic.com
Wed-Sat noon-7 pm, otherwise by appointment

"I'm a cheap guy," Loud Music owner Rob Skinner declares. Skinner (and Max, his dog) recently celebrated his third anniversary of eking out a living by selling used gear, making repairs, supplying local studios with vintage equipment, and otherwise making himself indispensable. His shop is a tiny single room with a bare heater and a heap of fixed-up vintage guitars, amps, keyboards, pedals, and hard-to-find parts: a sustain pedal for a '70s Rhodes keyboard, for instance; a late-'60s Baldwin traveling electric piano; a mid-'60s Premier gold sparkle kit; and boxes full of strange tubes and pickups. Loud Music looks more like a collector's basement than a proper shop, but therein lies the charm: absolutely no music-store pretentiousness, no music-store noodlers, no sales-guy schtick, and really good prices on vintage equipment. Skinner scavenges for cheap gear every single day, searching through every pawnshop, thrift store, flea market, and junk shop in the Pacific Northwest—so you don't have to.

Nancy's Sewing Basket
Queen Anne
2221 Queen Anne Ave N, (206) 282-9112
Mon, Fri, Sat 9:30 am-6 pm, Tues-Thurs 9:30 am-8 pm, Sun 12:30 pm-5 pm

Enter the land of silk and ribbon: Nowhere in the city will you find as many cool designer fabrics. There's something so sexy about rolls and rolls of imported fabric. Nancy's might be the only reason a person should travel up to Queen Anne, ever. Almost hidden in the back room are hundreds, maybe thousands of ribbons, many of which are antique. Even if you don't know how to turn on a sewing machine, Nancy's is worth checking out. Many of the staffers are fabulous designers (Aaron Lafferty is our favorite): If you ask nicely and can pay the price, you can order a custom suit or wedding dress.

One Wilde Night

Capitol Hill

(206) 325-6833

By appointment only

One Wilde Night, formerly known as Custom Corsets, operates very much like an old-fashioned tailoring shop, and offers the rare luxury of a piece of clothing made to fit your body and your taste. The shop's clientele consists of brides, people looking for costumes for holidays and Renaissance fairs, ultra-hip young women (and men), male cross-dressers, the leather community, and people interested in waist training. One Wilde Night is run by a man who's been making costumes for 25 years and corsets for the past five years, working from a desire to make historically accurate clothing to fit modern bodies. A corset, once you're laced in, keeps your back straight and your belly flat, and, if designed for your body, should be perfectly comfortable.

Paperhaus

Belltown

2008 1st Ave, (206) 374-8566

Mon-Wed 10 am-6 pm, Thurs-Sat 10 am-7 pm, Sun noon-5 pm

If you need a cedar clipboard with brushed aluminum casings, or you must have those special spiral Italian paper clips (an easy addiction, really), then this is the only store that can satiate your high urban style. If you're a photographer, graphic designer, or architect, you might consider investing in one of Paperhaus' beautiful oversized aluminum portfolios. The paper is of the city's highest quality, and the store allows you to imagine you live in Berlin or Milan, or anywhere else that has a greater design ethic than Seattle.

Toys in Babeland

Capitol Hill

707 E Pike St, (206) 328-2914

If every little girl on her 11th birthday could be marched in here with her mother and given a guided tour to pick out her very first vibrator, we would be living in a just and good world. Toys in Babeland is Seattle's premier woman-owned sex-toy shop, offering a treasure trove of items—from vibrators to butt plugs to hot lezzie porn—designed to provide even the most repressed with knuckle-biting, bodice-ripping, pillar-of-salt-shaking orgasms. Not to mention that Toys is one of the most successful lesbian community centers in the country. And to our benefit, they often offer informative workshops. For example, the strap-on workshop covers everything you ever wanted to know about the joys of wearing and using strap-ons, including picking out the dick of your dreams and choosing a harness, as well as tips on packing, positions, and techniques for those at both ends. They also teach Backdoor Basics (Anal Sex 101), a class that explodes the myth that the anus is an avenue of eroticism traveled only by sickos and inmates.

Uwajimaya Seattle

International District
519 Sixth Ave S, (206) 624-6248
Sun-Thurs 9 am-8 pm, Fri-Sat 9 am-9 pm
Uwajimaya's remodel has expanded the mind-boggling labyrinths of bubble-gum-colored cans, spiky fruit, and dishware that fill this Asian food mart/cheap trip. This place is an instant antidepressant, full of foodstuffs that inspire research, candy that defies our impoverished Western ideas of what is edible, and people speaking 13 different dialects. This is where you go to find your lime leaves, fish sauce, and Sanrio products. Take a crush, and make it a date.

Wigland

Downtown
1519 2nd Ave, (206) 623-4660
Mon-Fri 10:30 am-6 pm, Sat
10:30 am-5 pm
Forget about getting your wigs at pop fashion stores on Broadway or the Ave— get them here, where the drag queens spend hours making the owner pull down wig after wig. You can be anyone you want to

C. TAYLOR

Wigland: Get wiggy with it

be here: Catherine Deneuve or—if you must—Bettie Page. If the evening's success depends on your cotton-candy pink hair, Wigland has several nice varieties to choose from. This wig store makes the argument that Seattle is a progressive city; the wigs here are just as good as you would find in San Francisco or New York.

The Peninsula and Seattle: A Troubled Couple

by Matthew Stadler

DEVELOPMENT HAS ROBBED SEATTLE OF THE TWO GREATEST PLEASURES OF CITY LIFE: entering the city, and leaving it. Hong Kong has its enormous jumbo jets plunging into the throat of the massive downtown, aimed at that deliciously dangerous airport. The trains which enter Paris from the north and the south, crawl across pearl-gray districts to find their vast, hooded stations, from the portals of which exhausted travelers exit into the heart of that melancholy city. When one leaves Tunis, the city abruptly ends at a line of dirty gray buildings where the empty land rises up and claims the traveler, exiled now, expelled into the wasteland.

The traveler to Seattle faces a greater challenge. To the north, south, and east, the city does not end so much as it blurs and becomes indistinct. The government has taken to posting signboards throughout the city, announcing (in the midst of our blancmange of development and disarray) the names of the putative neighborhoods through which one is said to be passing. Similar signs mark the invisible north and south boundaries of the city itself, there being nothing else to distinguish them. To the east, Lake Washington briefly interrupts the bland compote of roads and houses and shops, but two major highways—comprising fully 20 lanes of high-speed traffic—have been laid across this helpless Lake, and one need merely yawn or turn attention for a brief millisecond to the radio dial for this watery glitch to pass unnoticed and the city's hastily woven fabric to appear to continue without rent or tear, on and on toward the distant mountains.

Ironically, Seattle's only satisfying boundary, the only proper path in or out for the questing wanderer or the exile, is to the west, across Puget Sound—to the Olympic Peninsula. The Peninsula and the city sit facing one another across a gray inland sea, like a couple at a table, a very troubling pair. On the one side: skyscrapers, fantastic new buildings, bold promising ideas, and a cosmopolitan future; on the other, a wall of mountains towering above scarred forests and the exposed wounds of a failed timber industry—the residue of the city's economic past. Standing amidst the bustle of downtown, "getting out" can only mean crossing that stretch of water and landing on the other side. The irony is how hopeless a direction this presents. At the terminus of westward expansion, the city's only focused regard points further west, into its heedless past, toward what Jane Jacobs calls "a supply region" of timber and fish, now nearly exhausted of its timber and fish. This is where we build our prisons now; tourists finger rusted steam donkeys at "timber museums;" more rain falls here than anywhere else on earth.

The Olympic Peninsula exposes the city's foundations, its repressed elements, and that is why crossing this last boundary makes the traveler fairly ache with portent and meaning. You cannot understand Seattle without going there. I suggest taking the ferry from downtown to Winslow and driving north and west to Blyn. If you have no car, get off the boat at Winslow and take county bus 90 to Poulsbo, then transfer to Port Angeles. Blyn is 35 miles short of Port Angeles, on US 101, just before the 7 Cedars Casino. Don't blink; there's nothing in Blyn except Dicky Bird's Tavern, but that is reason enough to go. Mountains gather right up behind the tavern's backyard (a kind of softball field with a few bleachers and a pig-roasting spit) so anyone with a hunger for hiking or vistas need merely stumble out of right field, past the drainage ditch, to become lost in woods which a justly-forgotten NPR commentator once called "God's gift to his hard working folk."

The natural beauty of the Peninsula is a commodity regionalists have cultivated and marketed for as long as the timber has been running out. The Peninsula is what geologists call "a domal uplift," a fairly young mountain range, formed in an abruptly rising kind of closed fist, from which twenty-one rivers run to the sea. It has always rained a lot, the rivers were full of fish, and Douglas fir, spruce, hemlock, and cedar used to cover everything up to the tree-line, about 5,000 feet. At least two-dozen different Indian tribes lived out here, always by the water, fishing and gathering berries,

TAE WON YU

sometimes going into the woods to find elk or other game. No one fought much; warring tribes, the Haida and Kwakiutl, came from the north, but on the Peninsula life was too bountiful. Food and materials were so abundant, the climate so mild and benign, Indians living here before white contact are said to have worked about 20 minutes each day securing basic needs; the rest was "leisure." 5,000 years of this kind of thing yielded cultures with highly-developed arts and an enviable economy of trade and gift-giving. Over this background of languor, ease, and sophistication, 150 years of grim Protestant work was then laid.

While a few whites began to settle among the Indians in the mid-19th century, the greatest influx came with the advent of commercial logging, around 120 years ago. The first mills went up along the Sound, and soon steam donkeys were being hauled into the woods of Gray's Harbor and Mason Counties. From there it's a short simple story: men cut trees and moved on. The industry boomed in WWI (the Army needed spruce for its new weapon—the airplane) and again during the housing boom of the 1950s. Along the way production climbed with every new technology, then sank as the best reserves ran out. Today we are left with an army of highly-skilled,

Ironically, Seattle's only satisfying boundary is to the west, across Puget Sound—to the Olympic Peninsula.

unemployed loggers (many of whom are being retrained to work as prison guards), some tree farms, a great reserve of protected forest inside the Olympic National Park, and a growing economy of recreation and tourism. The transformation of the Peninsula from vast commercial storehouse to cherished recreational playground parallels Seattle's transformation from an industrial to a more diversified service economy. Beginning in the late 1950s (around the time a handful of mountaineers founded an equipment cooperative to buy esoteric items like ropes and caribeeners and climbing boots—they called their small co-op R.E.I.), the city began to generate a class and culture that viewed mountains and trees as portals to a highly-prized, Romantic sublime. William O. Douglas wrote his remarkable book *My Wilderness*, praising the Peninsula and the ocean beaches in terms quite changed from the boastful hyperbole of loggers. Douglas spoke of "the cinema of the [river] whirlpools" and "the music of the ocean front" building a picture of nature's awesome art and "the challenges" that lie within it. These challenges were personal; solitary man in the cathedral of the wilderness—"My Wilderness"—discovering his own character through

Romantic communion. This rhetoric was not new. From Goethe and Rousseau, through John Muir, and a whole history of American Transcendentalism, "the outside," beyond cities and towns, has been forcefully cast as a surpassing work of art, the location of the sublime, where an enlightened man will find meaning, or a portal to God. But Douglas's essay came at a time, and reached an audience, that had been largely blind to this view of the Peninsula. My parents read it in 1961 and—unfamiliar with tides, storm surges, rogue waves, devil's club, or any of the other hazards of the coast—packed the scotch and beans in paper bags, put on their shorts and tennis shoes, and drove out there for a hike. Of course they nearly died, but they were not alone. To the city dweller gazing west, the Peninsula became a vast canvas; trips there would yield a treasure trove of natural beauty and physical challenges. The loggers became evil, enemies of the trees; the Peninsula's own economy and culture, formed around logging, was seen as backwards, even ignorant. Looking at the Peninsula, the city developed a classic relation to The Exotic—enchanted by its beauty and mysteries, yet derisive of its native intelligence and values. And, as Edward Said has observed of European ideas of The Exotic, this cherished, despised "other" began to function as a repository for all the city wished to repress in itself. Principally that has been poverty, dissolution, a kind of drunken solidarity, greed, empathy, and the violence of an economy that views workers as capital—interchangeable, replaceable, and less than human. While these realities are hidden beneath the bright face of our prosperous city, they lie in plain sight, exposed, amidst the open wounds of the Peninsula's collapsed economy.

An afternoon at Dicky Bird's will do you good. As evening comes on and the light gets sucked out the edge of the sky, board the bus back to Winslow so that you may enter Seattle the proper way—on a great lumbering ferry slapping across the gray waves of Puget Sound, drawing nearer and nearer to that bright, optimistic skyline, crossing into the city with your back turned to the past.

www.ellenforney.com

Diversions

IN A CITY MIRED IN WETNESS 10 out of the 12 months of the year, diverting oneself becomes a lifesaving necessity. Fortunately, there are all sorts of strange events and destinations to choose from throughout the year, from strip clubs to historical museums. And, because Seattle's majestic outdoors is the main reason 37.8 percent of the city's transplant population moved here, we have included many things to do to confront the outdoors, although you may have to leave the city for some of them.

Arcades

Hi*Score Arcade
Capitol Hill
612 E Pine St, (206) 860-8839
Daily 10 am-midnight

Certain people understand that the Western world reached its apex in the late '70s and early '80s. Not coincidentally, these people were kids or teens at the time, and were awash in the sea of pop-culture toys that only a surge of First-World prosperity can bring. The refinement of the pinball machine from a simple game into an amazing, whiz-bang overload happened during this time, and some of us will never recover.

Hi*Score is more than an arcade; it's an interactive museum of pop culture. Besides the 30-plus pinball machines and 30-plus video games, Hi*Score houses a ton of books, toys, 8-tracks, Atari machines and cartridges, and other detritus from this bygone era. Here you can find all the best pinball—Twilight Zone, Funhouse, and Theatre of Magic—next to all the best old video games: Galaga, Centipede, Tron, even Tempest, for God's sake. You can get a Coke and take a seat in the lounge, pick up a 007 "novel," and listen to the symphony of buzzes and clicks and moans as you revel in an adolescence without end.

Shorty's Pinball

Belltown

2222 3/4 2nd Ave, (206) 441-5449

Daily noon-2 am

C. TAYLOR

Shorty's is a little pleasure palace; on its premises are all of the ingredients for the happiest life on Earth. For starters— and most crucially—there are the pinball machines, a whole row of them, and they are beautiful specimens. Then there are the classic video games, Galaga and Defender chief among them. These are nourished by *Shorty's Pinball: Ding ding zort boop boop— winner!*

the presence of some good beer (although they no longer have Lucky lagers for $1) and Chicago-style hot dogs. Because it's officially a tavern, there aren't kids running all over the place, so patrons are at their leisure to smoke at the bar and flirt between games, free of young'uns. Periodic pinball championships separate the punks from the chumps, and they're a great spectator sport. Back in the even tinier Trophy Lounge—there can't be more than 15 seats in the whole room—happy drunks cheer on their favorite wrestlers on WWF night, or do Cartman imitations on South Park night. Though it's often used as a stopover between live music sets at the Crocodile Cafe up the street, Shorty's is a punk-rock heaven all on its own.

Basketball

B. F. Day Middle School Court

Fremont

4020 Fremont Ave N

The B. F. Day Middle School courts are the basketball heart of Fremont. The chain nets may give the raw rattle of Harlem's Rucker Park, but the pickup crowd is what you might expect from the crunchy Fremont district: The competition is whiter and a bit less polished than you may find in other neighborhoods. An added plus for the novice pickup player is that although the baskets are regulation height, the court itself is about 30 percent shorter than standard. That means less running and an eight-player maximum, so you might get more passes thrown your way than in a five-on-five game. The only downside is that on key summer afternoons, there is usually a two- to three-game wait to play on the main court. One jargon note: Any inexplicable basketball phenomena (rim-outs, uncalled bank-shots, toilet-bowl baskets) are greeted with cat calls of "Fremont, Fremont!" Don't be alarmed; the players are just paying homage to Fremont's reputation as a locus of weirdness.

Denny Court
Denny Regrade
Denny Way between Westlake Ave and 9th Ave
Located in the Denny Triangle on the northern border of downtown, this court is arguably the most integrated in central Seattle. It's a single court with some nice features such as a good surface and nylon nets, which offset the drawbacks: tight rims and a Honey Bucket courtside, a favorite for junkies who wish to escape the police state that is Belltown to the west. The level of competition for pickup is generally very high, with a good deal of showboating and beefing (yes, arguing) over various calls and non-calls. That means that the novice may learn a lot, but if you aren't assertive or don't know what the hell is going on, then you might not see the ball at all. Expect a long wait some afternoons.

Green Lake Court
Green Lake
7201 E Green Lake Dr N
This court is a magnet for superior talent from the neighborhoods north of Lake Union and west of I-5. The players tend to be real ballers, tall and lean and actually cognizant of what is happening on the court. If you can take the competition, Green Lake is a great place to play pickup games: The area is Seattle's undisputed recreation nerve center, and playing on its court makes one feel like a small part of a larger movement of youth, fitness, and constructive urban sweating.

Miller Park
Capitol Hill/Central District
400 19th Ave E
It took a long, hard fight with the city and various seedy elements in its own neighborhood, but the Miller Park community finally has its recreational jewel. Located on the east side of Capitol Hill at the edge of the Central District, this park includes tennis courts, a baseball diamond, rolling green lawns, the innovative Ron K. Bills fountain, and one single, perfect basketball court. It is less of a pickup court than Denny or B. F. Day, but you can still find games, and you can usually find a half of the court to practice on your own. Added bonus: The community center building also houses an indoor court, which can be especially useful during the winter.

Seattle Pacific University Basketball Court
Queen Anne
611 W Dravus St
Because this court adjoins Seattle Pacific University's Ashton Hall, tucked away on the north slope of Queen Anne, it scores high marks for scenery and availability. If you are looking for an empty half-court with clean nylon nets, surrounded by leafy trees and a small lawn, then this is the place. The only players you're likely to find are the cherubic undergrads who aren't looking for pickup players, but the good news is that the middle of the long court has been blocked with typical dorm debris (some stolen road signs and pieces of shag carpeting), so full-court games are a rarity. That means you can practice on your own or bring your friends to the court with little interference from the Free Methodist 20-year-olds for whom the court was built.

Bicycling

Around Lake Washington
The ride around Lake Washington is a sometimes noisy, sometimes quietly beautiful 60-plus-mile ride. Riding in a counterclockwise direction from downtown Seattle, you follow Lake Washington Boulevard south past Seward Park. At Seward Park, you can take a quick loop around the park either on the upper road, which is the site of weekly bike races from May to September, or via the lower loop, which hugs the coastline of the Bailey Peninsula, on which the park resides. To continue on the around-the-lake ride, take Seward Park Avenue up the hill, west of the park entrance, and follow it south until it crosses Rainier Avenue. Here you follow Rainier Avenue until you reach the far south end of Lake Washington and one of Boeing's many Puget Sound locations. Head onto the frontage road that parallels Rainier Avenue and runs along the airstrip, this road will take you around Renton Airport and head you north before crossing a small bridge, used mostly by aircraft. Pick up the bike trail there to the north, and then enter the maze of Boeing buildings as you make your way north and east until you reach Lake Washington Blvd E. The ride through this Boeing plant is surreal. You feel as though you've entered a *Truman Show* version of a NASA facility: lots of really clean, enormous machines and guys running around in lab coats and eye protection. Once you have gained Lake Washington Boulevard north of Boeing, follow it north all the way to I-405, where you can turn left just before the overpass and gain the frontage road for about two miles until it dead-ends, where you will find a bike trail taking you to Coal Creek Parkway. At this juncture you must decide if you wish to continue with your circumnavigation of the lake or cut out and cross the I-90 Bridge back to Seattle. If you decide to continue on, you will wind your way through the sprawling, high-tech wasteland of Bellevue, up through

bikini-clad Kirkland, and then over the mighty Juanita hill, back to the north end of the Burke-Gilman Trail in Kenmore, which you can then slowly coast south along to return to the gray splendor of Seattle.

Bainbridge Island

A short and entertaining half-hour-long ferry ride, and you can be biking in the relative obscurity of the west bank of Puget Sound. After you disembark from the ferry on Bainbridge Island, follow SR 305 north to Poulsbo. The ride is hilly and noisy (the Chilly Hilly ride is the traditional beginning of cycling season in Seattle, a ride that sees thousands of bikers weaving their way over these same roads in February), and drops you in Poulsbo, for Christ's sake. The Scandinavian feel of the town is ridiculous and oppressive. It's best to stop for a quick bite and turn back to grab the ferry home, or continue on all the way to Kingston, where you can grab another ferry to Edmonds.

Burke-Gilman Trail

The Burke Gilman Trail runs from Ballard (pick it up one block west of Leary Way NW and NW 45th Street) to Marymoor Park in Redmond, via the Sammamish Lake Trail (the Burke-Gilman turns into the Sammamish Lake Trail in Kenmore).This bike trail, winding through neighborhoods along Lake Union and Lake Washington, is a great way to see the city with minimal contact with car traffic. You may run into major non-auto traffic on the trail, however: It's a popular spot with bikers, skateboarders, joggers, and skaters. You must be careful and observe the speed limit (15 mph) to stay out of trouble.

Discovery Park

For a pleasant ride in the city away from all the traffic, head to Discovery Park. There are numerous roads winding through the park, off-limits to cars. Look for the bald-eagle nest, with the United States' only breeding pair of bald eagles within the city limits of a major city. It's then a quick ride over to the Ballard Locks, where you can see thousands of trapped fish get lovingly devoured by fat sea lions.

I-90 Bridge

From Lake Washington Boulevard you can catch the I-90 bike trail by taking Parkland Place up the steep hill to the I-90 lid; then drop down and start across the bridge at the west end of the bike tunnel. This bike path, separated from the cars by a large concrete barrier, takes to you some of the best riding in the Seattle area. Once you cross the first section of the floating bridge, after riding along the bridge with the water on one side (with the colorful array of waterfowl bobbing in the Lake Washington waves) and the speeding traffic a few feet away on the other, you come to Mercer Island. Once on Mercer Island, you can elect to continue along the I-90 trail and make your way to Bellevue, or you can take a right off the trail and do the famed Mercer Island loop. This 15-or-so-mile loop takes you around the entire island on Mercer Way. It's a fabulous ride, with gentle hills, curving lanes, and views of Lake Washington and the ridiculously lavish homes that make up Mercer Island.

If you elect to bypass the Mercer Island loop and continue along the I-90 Bridge, you will next hit Bellevue, which is worth avoiding. On the east side of Bellevue, however, a wonderful world of biking awaits. The I-90 trail ends at Lake Washington Boulevard E, where you turn south and join Coal Creek Parkway. Coal Creek Parkway takes you toward the west side of Cougar Mountain, a splendid hill ride if you are into a leg-burner, or stay flat going on to May Valley Road, which will take you along forested quiet roads and along some beautiful farmland all the way to Issaquah.

Bike Shops

Bikesmith
Wallingford
2309 N 45th St,
(206) 632-3102
Mon-Thurs 10 am-7 am,
Friday 10 am-6 pm, Sat 9
am-5pm, Sun noon-5 pm
Co-owner Val Kleits (the
guy with the handlebar
moustache) keeps his
store well-stocked with
collectible and vintage
bikes.

KELLY O

Bicycles: A must-have fashion accessory

Bike Works
Columbia City
3709 S Ferdinand, (206) 725-9408
Tues-Fri, 10 am-7 pm, Sat 10 am-6 pm, Sun 11 am-5 pm
Kids can earn credits for fixing bikes. Then they can buy parts or bikes with their credits. Cool.

Wright Bros. Cycle
Fremont
219 N 36th St, (206) 633-5132
Tues-Thurs 10:30 am-7 pm, Fri-Sun 10:30 am-5 pm
A one-time membership of $30 allows you to use their DIY tools and work-shop so you can fix your bike anytime.

Chaos Theory: Dead Baby Bicycle Race

by Wm. Steven Humphrey

AS A RULE, SEATTLE IS NOT A BIG FAN OF CHAOS. If the Mark Sidrans of our city had their way, Seattle would continue its lockstep toward a spit 'n' polished Happy Land where absolutely nothing out of the ordinary occurs. However, on a certain Friday night every summer, chaos comes to Happy Land and takes on a new name—the Dead Baby Bicycle Race.

Close to 150 bicyclists gather on the corner of 14th Avenue and Madison Street on Capitol Hill to compete in this annual and very illegal event. When the gun sounds at 8 pm sharp, contestants blast down the hill in an all-out race (traffic and intersections be damned) to the alleyway behind the Rendezvous lounge in Belltown. There are no set routes or rules—just get to the Rendezvous in the shortest time and, if possible, in one piece.

"Actually there's one rule," says Dave Ranstrom, owner of the Dead Baby Bicycle Shop. "No eye-gouging. Contestants are also asked to sign a waiver that says something like, 'I'm a badass motherfucker, and not a

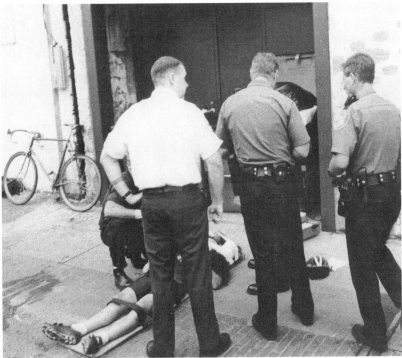

NICOLLE L. FARUP

sissy who would sue if I got hurt'—but that's pretty much all that's required." The Dead Baby Bicycle Race is kind of a punk-rock Critical Mass—but without the political agenda. Its sole purpose is to burn off the seemingly endless energy of bike messengers and their friends. And because of its illegal status, the race is strictly hush-hush and advertised by word of mouth.

"I mean, we would do it legally if we could. But it's just too expensive to hold a legal race in this town," Ranstrom says. "Once the city gets involved, there's permits, and insurance, and the roads have to be blocked off. So far we haven't had too many problems with the police . . . unless you count our first year, when we accidentally raced into the Torchlight Parade and knocked over a couple of motorcycle cops. They weren't so happy."

There are no set routes or rules—just get to the Rendezvous in one piece.

Though accidents have been rare in the race's short history, the race of 1999 ended in a doozy. Downhill winner Tony Reed, with arms held high, crossed the finish line in four minutes and 20 seconds, and was then knocked off his bike by a reeling drunk getting 86'd from the Rendezvous. Though Tony was taken away on a stretcher and strapped into a neck brace, he escaped with only a few stitches and a missing tooth. He was riding again by Monday. At this point organizers can only assume Reed will be defending his crown next summer—or (hush-hush) whenever the Dead Baby rides again.

Bowling

AMF Imperial Lanes

Beacon Hill

2101 22nd Ave S, (206) 325-2525

Mon-Fri 9 am-11 pm, Fri-Sat 9 am-2 am, Sun 9 am-midnight

Even though its business cards claim "AMF Always Means Fun™," Imperial Lanes hasn't been the same ever since AMF took the cool Imperial Lanes neon bowling-pin sign and replaced it with AMF's dumb blue one. The workers are different too, and are now clad in standardized blue polos. Still, you gotta bowl, and if Sunset Bowl and Leilani Lanes have lines out the door (or you live on Beacon Hill), this is the place to get serious. There are 24 lanes, many pull-tab machines, and a small, sort of expensive, yet exotic bar in the back, which serves Seagram's Wild Berries wine coolers and Cook's champagne. X-Treme bowling with lasers takes place on Friday and Saturday nights until 2 am. The only remaining vestige of old school stuff is the steel lockers you can rent for $15 a year.

C. TAYLOR

Leilani Lanes

Greenwood

10201 Greenwood Ave N, (206) 783-8010

Mon-Thurs 9 am-midnight, Fri 9 am-1 am,

Saturday 9 am-2:15 am, Sunday 9 am-11 pm

Bowling and pull tabs: Like gin and tonic

With Leilani Lanes' unspectacular location in Greenwood, you wouldn't expect it to possibly deliver the utopian dreamscape invoked by its name. But past the tranquil, gurgling, bowling-ball fountain in the entrance gleam 36 lanes amid a vaguely Hawaiian pastel décor. Sip a few tropical cocktails in the plush Tiki lounge (with fireplace!), and you'll swear you're in a bowling alley in Oahu. Rock-and-bowl happens every Friday and Saturday night. What this is shouldn't be described, but experienced. Hint: It's kinda like "couple skate" at a roller rink, when they turn the disco ball on and they shut down the lights.

Sunset Bowl

Ballard

1420 NW Market St, (206) 782-7310

Daily 24 hours

As good a place as any to bowl a few frames, the Sunset Bowl offers 26 lanes, a decent arcade, a full bar, and a restaurant. Add karaoke (Wednesday, Friday, and Saturday) and pin-shaped bottles of Budweiser enjoyed in the omnipresent and mildly depressing shadow of the state lottery racket, and you've got the city's grittiest bowling experience. Open an astonishing 24 hours a day for the benefit of speed freaks, shift workers, insomniacs, minors, and other folks who, for whatever reason, prefer to roll thunder at 4 am.

West Seattle Bowl, Home of the Glo-Zone

West Seattle
4505 39th Ave SW,
(206) 932-3731
Mon 10am-1am, Tue. noon-midnight; Wed 10 am-midnight; Thur 9am-midnight; Fri-Sat 10 am-1 am, Sun 10 am-11 pm

ERIKA LANGLEY

Sunset Bowl: Superheroes always bowl a strike

West Seattle Bowl would appear to be the no-nonsense counterpart to the city's more flamboyant bowling alleys. There's no fantastic tropical décor or unruly karaoke nights—just two 16-lane alleys, a modest bar, and a tidy, subdued atmosphere for optimally focused bowling. Yes, it's all very respectable, and it all disappears on Saturday nights, as West Seattle's only bowling alley becomes a frantic bacchanal for Glo-Zone Bowling, where the wild bowlers bowl themselves into a black-lit frenzy to the best sounds from the '70s to today. Because the Emerald City is always suffering from a shortage of bowling alleys, this place is good to know about when you can't get a lane elsewhere.

Lawn Bowling

Forget the smoke, the Coors, the stinky rented shoes. Lawn bowlers take turns throwing balls, or bowls, to the jack—a little white ball set about 100 yards away on the green. The player who comes closest in three tries wins. No special attire is required except smooth-soled shoes. White clothing is suggested for lawn-bowling tournaments. The game is played regularly at two Seattle hot spots: In the north, just off of Aurora Avenue N and N 65th Street at the Woodland Park (not the zoo!) Lawn Bowling Club; and in the south, on Beacon Avenue S in Beacon Hill.

Next to a roaring Aurora Avenue, with a view of Green Lake, the **Woodland Park Lawn Bowling Club** (6018 Whitman Ave N, 206/ 782-1515) has two well-manicured lawn-bowling greens. The greens, mowed to the quick like golf-putting greens, are fenced and lined with shrubbery, and a few benches and bleachers are sprinkled around for the weary. The Woodlawn Park Lawn Bowling Club has about 100 members, mostly of the older persuasion, but the club is open to everyone and offers free lessons on Fridays and Saturdays and by appointment.

Jefferson Park Lawn Bowling Club (4103 Beacon Ave S, 206/ 762-2490) offers a less tony atmosphere for bowling, with two greens behind the clubhouse at the Jefferson Park Golf Club. The bowling season starts in April, with games every Monday, Wednesday, and Friday at 10 am; and the club offers lessons at 10 am every Saturday. Call to confirm, though.

Boxing

Cappy's on Union

2002 E Union St, (206) 322-6410

Call for class schedule; bathrooms are big and clean, but there are no showers

Although Cappy's isn't the only place to box in the city, it should be—it's the ultimate girl jock experience (but boy jocks can also box here). It's cramped, it's sweaty, and Cappy herself will tape your knuckles for your first boxing lesson. Cappy's on Union offers two types of classes: "boxing fitness," which includes everything you saw in *Rocky* (except for drinking a raw egg and actually punching someone) and boxing lessons, which are just what they sound like. There are two reasons to go to Cappy's: The first is to glory in the full jock-fetish regalia, including Ace bandages, boxing gloves, and protective face gear; and the second is to be coached by the incomparable Cappy. Some coaches praise often and indifferently, as if they had a kind of positive-thinking Tourette's syndrome, but when Cappy says you show "good form," you believe it. She makes you want to be a better person.

Climbing

Inside Climbing

REI Pinnacle

Denny Regrade

222 Yale Ave N, (206) 223-1944

Stone Gardens Rock Gym

Ballard

2839 NW Market St, (206) 781-9828

University of Washington Climbing Rock

University District

Next to Husky Stadium, (206) 543-9433

Vertical World
Magnolia
2123 W Elmore St, (206) 283-4497

Outside Climbing

Deception Crags
Take I-90 east to Exit 38. Travel south for a half mile, until you see a stream to the south. The parking lot is north of the guard rail. The trail is to the west.

Little Si
Take I-90 east to Exit 320, take a left at the stop sign, then take the first right. Cross the bridge to a parking lot on the left. The path to the climbing area is on the right.

Marymoor Park Climbing Wall
Marymoor Park
6046 W Lake Sammamish Pkwy NE, (206) 281-8111

BIO

Carlos Barros

Who is he? A real live mountaineer. Age 26, born in Madrid, Spain.

What exactly is mountaineering?
"Mountaineering is like a raw version of sport rock climbing. Instead of climbing a fake rock in REI's lobby, mountaineers go to real mountains, set their own anchors, and hang out on glaciers or rocks way above valley floors. And mountaineers don't wear Lycra."

How did you get into the sport?
"Growing up in Madrid, my friends and I started climbing construction scaffolding, then [we broke] into bigger construction sites to climb them, too. After a while we wanted to climb legally, so we went into the mountains."

What's your favorite place around Seattle to go mountaineering?
"Washington Pass (in the North Cascades National Park) is beautiful, man. With peaks like Liberty Bell and Early Winter Spires, there are tons of things to climb. Also, Mount Rainier has great year-round glacier climbing-people even train there for climbing the Himalayas. Leavenworth is a little closer, but also has its good points."

How can beginners get into the sport?
"Call the Mountaineers in Seattle (206/284-6310). They offer a million classes, can help people get equipped, and have lots of structured climbing opportunities. It's definitely the best way to get on a mountain quickly."

Have you ever seen a Sasquatch?
"No, but there are little monsters who live under the glaciers who trip me every once in a while."

Organizations

Cascade Alpine Guides
2208 NW Market S, Suite 504, (206) 706-1587

Mountaineers
300 3rd Ave W, (206) 281-7775

Northwest Mountain School
5111 Latona Ave NE, (206) 634-3955

Flight

There is a height to Seattle that exceeds its tallest towers, a space overhead in which you are still a part of the city. This space is probably about as high as birds are willing to fly, and lower than the flight paths emanating from Sea-Tac International Airport; the only way to enjoy this rare dimension is by seaplane.

There is something literally dream-like about leaving or entering Seattle via Lake Union. You're downtown, amid the sidewalks, clubs, and apartments you visit every day. After an enjoyable short water-taxi ride in the small plane, you lift seamlessly from the surface of the city as you know it, to the rest of the city as you've dreamed it: viewed from slightly above, totally mobile and relaxed, in a motion more casual and infinitely more enjoyable than breezing onto an I-5 on-ramp headed north. You're in the middle of the whole city, and you can see each neighborhood conduct itself as always—then you're gone, swinging over the roofs of Fremont and Ballard for the open air above the coastlines, cliffs, and deep woods you'll never otherwise witness.

Kenmore Air on Lake Union (950 Westlake Ave N, 206/364-6990) offers flights to Victoria, the San Juan Islands, and the thickets of the tributaries that surround Vancouver Island. You can get from here to Victoria in less than an hour: Get up for a leisurely breakfast, drive on down to lower Belltown, and crack your first crab in a harbor-side Victoria restaurant before 1 pm has passed (or, if you've spent your whole wad on the flight, just smoke a good Canadian cigarette instead). Travel in Seattle is a harrowing duty rewarded only by the hope of a worthy destination; by seaplane, travel is a pleasing interlude before lunch.

Seattle Seaplanes (1325 Fairview Ave, 206/329-9638) leaves from Lake Union as well: The planes take off and splash down near the ZymoGenetics building on Fairview. While Seattle Seaplanes does fly charter planes out to the islands, it also has a 20-minute air tour of the city ($42.50 per passenger). The plane leaves from Lake Union and travels in a 35-mile circumference, drifting over the Seattle Center, the Space Needle, then down over Safeco

Field, Elliott Bay, and up to the University of Washington, the Ballard Locks, and Green Lake. The idea is not just to grab photos of landmarks—it's meant to be an aerial tour of Seattle's neighborhoods.

And when you return, you don't have to wrench back from your tour or vacation: You're just gradually here again, re-placed downtown where you left your old self and your old car. No passing through the cold, disappointing reality of Sea-Tac's terminals, traffic, and wearily memorized freeway connections—you're already back in the city as refreshed as you would be after a dream of flying.

Gambling

Diamond Lil's Poker Club
Renton
361 Rainier Ave S, (425) 226-2763
Daily 9 am-6 am
Diamond Lil's—hands down—wins for the best name in the gambling business. It's not a casino; it's a poker club, so the lights are brighter, the crowd is a little older and harder, the place is damn smoky—and, of course, the tables are limited to variations on poker. The people here couldn't be nicer or more welcoming. Security will answer all of your stupid questions. In the evening Lil's fills up, so you'll want to win the battle against your conscience early, and come here directly after work.

Drift on Inn Roadhouse Casino
Shoreline
16708 Aurora Ave N, (206) 546-4144
Daily 24 hours
When you walk into the Drift on Inn, you find yourself in a completely stylized '50s diner. Skip Debby's diner and walk down the stairs into the casino. Directly in front of you is "The LaFayette Antique Mirror Bar," the most beautiful bar in all of Seattle (well, Shoreline). Who the hell knows how a dive casino ended up with this kind of elegance? (The elegance, however, is very much challenged by the wall-sized television right next to it.) The bar was made in 1845 in New York City and is estimated to have cost $10,000 at that time. There are 250 mirrors and three chandeliers to dazzle you while you drink. As you lean into your drunkenness, you are actually leaning on an Italian marble railing and a solid piece of oak running the length of the bar (28 feet!). Two goddess statues are at the center of the bar, one representing air, the other water. Dealer Peggy is the other goddess at the Drift on Inn; she's the friendliest and sweetest dealer in town, and she's kind to newbies. Just sit at the table and watch her work. And then walk out flat broke.

Emerald Downs

Auburn
2300 Emerald Downs Dr,
(253) 288-7000
Racing season: April-September,
weekdays 6 pm on, weekends
and holidays 1 pm on; simul-
cast racing during off season:
9 am-9 pm

SHANE CARPENTER

Emerald Downs: Now family-oriented, so we won't make the obvious joke

It's time to put money down on something other than cards. And there's nothing better than putting your paycheck down on a sleek horse named Unturn the Screw or Adventure Begins or Twice Shy, especially with a funny short man sitting on top of the horse's lustrous back. Unfortunately, in the way that other former arenas of iniquity—such as Times Square and Las Vegas—underwent makeovers to make them more appealing to blue-collar Democrats and white-collar Republicans, so has Emerald Downs embraced a policy of inclusiveness. No longer just a haven for Bukowski-esque drunks and obsessive statistics-trackers, Emerald Downs now offers Family Days on Sundays. Kids will love the pony rides, face painters, and strolling clowns, while the adult crowd can still drop a sizable chunk of change waiting for their horse to come in.

Freddie's Club

Renton
111 S 3rd St, (425) 228-3700
Daily 24 hours

This place is the classiest casino in town. (Warning: somewhat hidden behind a Taco Bell.) And you know you're in the right gambling establishment when you walk in and—even though everyone is smoking—you breathe in deeply the over-oxygenated air. Yes, just like Vegas, they pump oxygen in through the rafters in the ceiling to make you feel good about yourself (and your hand). But before you start throwing dollars, sit down at the bar, get yourself a drink (they ain't coming around with free ones), and ask Connie, your bartender, just what the tricks are to Spanish 21, Let It Ride, or Pai Gow. Everyone who works here works the tables, too. Get yourself a burger or steak dinner, because this is the best lounge food in a gambling institution in the Seattle area. Once you're greased, fat, and happy, start at the $5 Blackjack table, where the odds are good and you don't have to know too much. But do stop yourself from staring at your neighbor's wad of C-notes. For the guy next to you, sitting at the table is his job.

Goldie's

Shoreline

15030 Aurora Ave N, (206) 440-8754

Daily 10 am-6 am

No atmosphere here; it's like a small warehouse. But this means it's airy and bright. And there's help-yourself coffee available to keep you going through the night. Goldie's is kind of a rough place. But if you've tried your hand at the Drift on Inn and Parker's already, Goldie's is on the way home, and maybe it'll give you a chance to earn it all back. Progressive Blackjack, Fortune Pai Gow, Let It Ride, etc. There's a wall of electronic darts and a few pool tables, too.

Parker's

Shoreline

17001 Aurora Ave N,
(206) 546-6161

Daily 2 pm-10 am

Across the street from the Drift on Inn, this is where you ought to come if your hand has gone sour over there and you need a fresh start. It lacks the personality of the Drift, but it is easier to focus in this plain, clean, upstanding gam-

SHANE CARPENTER

Come, join us—lose all your money

bling house—and this, for some, increases the odds in your favor. And Parker's is conveniently located next to the private strip club Sugar's. So if you're a member of Sugar's or you want to become a member of Sugar's, win your membership costs at a Parker's Blackjack table.

Riverside Casino

Tukwila

14060 Interurban Ave S, (206) 244-5400

Daily 10 am-6 am

Right across the street from the modest Silver Dollar is this glamorous, neon-twinkling, Wild West casino. This place is cool: wooden boardwalk and entryway, like they'd have in saloons, with painted pictures of old cowboy gamblers. The casino is spacious and airy—though stinky somehow—and the well-kept pool tables almost make up for the terrible live band onstage. The tables are generally good and friendly—well, almost friendly: If the person next to you stops playing when you sit at the table, and won't bet until you leave again, you'll know that these are serious gamblers who take your naiveté at the table to be just plain bad luck. They'll mumble to themselves while you're wasting their good earning hours; gamblers are the most superstitious people around, and it's best not to get in their way. Forget about the cafe. Yuck.

Silver Dollar
Tukwila
14027 Interurban Ave S, (206) 241-9526
Daily 10 am-6 am
If you stumble out of here at 6 am and still have a penny to your name, hit the espresso stand next to the casino. Or, if you won big, stumble into the 24-hour restaurant for a real Las Vegas–style breakfast: steak and eggs for $2.99! And if you come back for dinner, you can have another steak with your lobster for $13.99. With its *Dynasty* entrance, large-screen TVs, and walls covered in mirrors, you really feel like you're gambling in the comfort of your own home. Really, this is a comfortable place where the vibe's good and so are the dealers. And if you are really poor, this is the Taco Bell of casinos: Some tables dip down to single-dollar bets.

Skyway Park Bowl & Casino
Skyway
11819 Renton Ave S, (206) 772-1220
Daily 24 hours
Listen to this: Twenty-four brand-new lanes of bowling, an 18-hole pirate-themed miniature-golf course, a full casino, an arcade, a snack bar open until 3 am, a full-fledged restaurant open 7 am-10 pm, a large pull-tab island, a lounge, electronic darts, and karaoke! Fuck Disneyland! Now let's break it down. First, squeeze into a seat in the packed casino, and make some money at Caribbean Stud. Now go spend five bucks on some pizza at the snack bar, and spend your next five bucks making your way around those 18 holes. Throw some coins into the pristine fountains that riddle the golf course. Then take a break and lounge while you milk drinks with names like Royal Flush, Blue Dice, or Kings and Queens. Then it's up to you to decide whether or not you should sing Madonna's "Borderline" one more time at the karaoke mic. Finally! Snuggle up next to a security guard (this place is lousy with security!) and start pulling tabs with him. Oh yeah! Then go bowl!

Historical Museums

Bill Speidel's Underground Tour and Museum
Pioneer Square
610 1st Ave, (206) 682-4646
Mon-Fri at 11 am, 1 pm, 3 pm; Sat-Sun at 11 am, 1 pm, 2 pm, 3 pm, 5 pm
$4-$8
Seattle's got a dark, musty past, and that past is placed on glorious display in the late local historian Bill Speidel's hot-with-the-tourists-but-

still-compelling Underground Tour. Though much of the 90-minute tour is spent walking on improvised boardwalks, staring at dirt-covered walls, and suffering through the tour guides' bad puns and cheesy jokes, the Underground's unglorified approach to local history is refreshing. While strolling subterranean sidewalks, visitors are treated to tales of everything from early Seattle's sewage problems and political corruption to the "seamstresses" (whores) who populated our fair town in the early part of the century. The tour ends with a quite respectable museum at the tour headquarters—which includes the world's first "Thomas Crapper" flushable toilet!

Burke Museum of Natural History and Culture
University District
University of Washington, NE 45th St & 17th Ave NE, (206) 543-5590
Fri-Wed 10 am-5 pm, Thurs 10 am-8 pm
$2.50-$5.50

Occasionally a site of contention (e.g., its housing of the controversial "Kennewick Man"), the Burke normally plays the staid public-service role as the largest natural-science museum in the Northwest. The museum's current form is clearly geared toward children, offering lots of dinosaur skeletons, a rumbling volcano replica, an extensive collection of rocks and minerals, and a "bug wall" with individual light-up displays on each insect. But the museum's traditionalist leanings remain evident in such attractions as the Clovis arrowhead display.

General Petroleum Museum
Capitol Hill
1526 Bellevue Ave, (206) 323-4789
By appointment only
Free admission

VICTORIA RENARD

General Petroleum Museum: Grime-free service station artifacts

Founded in 1987 by the late longtime petroleum businessman Jeffrey Pedersen, this privately owned collection of "industrial archeology" is one oily delight. The General Petroleum Museum houses what is believed to be the largest collection of service-station artifacts and "petroliana" in the country, from rows of vintage gas pumps (prices averaging 20-35¢ a gallon) to Shell Oil jewelry and cuff links. The cappers: real men's and women's gas-station rest rooms, the latter complete with a 5¢ Kotex feminine-napkin dispenser and a sign with a flashing signal ("Please flip switch if rest room is found unclean or without necessary supplies"). Modern life should be so civilized.

Giant Shoe Museum

Pike Place Market
1501 Pike Place #424,
outside Old Seattle Paperworks
store on Level Four
of "Downunder" section of
market, (206) 623-2870
Mon-Sat 9 am-6 pm,
Sun 11 am-5 pm
$1 (four quarters)
to see all coin-operated
exhibits

DAVID BELISLE

Giant Shoe Museum: Peep at giant feet

The name says it all: This is a museum filled with giant shoes. The museum's founder, Dan Eskenazi, became interested in large sizes when a pair of huge boots (each measuring 28 inches long) suddenly disappeared from his grandfather's shoe-repair shop. Eskenazi began a fruitless search for the missing boots (he still offers a $1,000 reward for their return) and in the process he acquired the collector's bug for this curious hobby. His freakish obsession is our gain: Visitors to "the world's largest collection of giant shoes" are treated to views of some truly big-ass footwear, and the Coney Island peep-show set-up (25¢ a gander) only adds to the allure.

History House

Fremont
790 N 34th St, (206) 675-8875
Wed-Sun noon-5 pm
$1 donation

As the merciless fist of gentrification continues to pound Seattle's formerly vibrant neighborhoods into yuppie mush, the History House keeps our knowledge of the past intact. Founded in 1998 and run by locals who know their stuff, the History House is devoted to preserving the history of Seattle's quirky, distinct neighborhoods. Large murals vividly display the transition of particular city blocks; newspaper clippings shed light on each neighborhood's story; and unique exhibits on local pop culture from the '50s to the '70s chronicle such Seattle phenomena as Green Lake's Aqua Follies and the tragicomic story of Bobo the gorilla.

Klondike Gold Rush National Historical Park
Pioneer Square
117 S Main St, (206) 553-7220
Daily 9 am-5 pm
Free admission

If you think the aggressive hyping of Seattle began with the marketing of grunge in the 1990s, you've missed the mark by nearly a century. As the United States' smallest national park, this often-overlooked museum details Seattle's role in one of the greatest gold rushes in history—the mad dash for the Klondike River area in the Yukon Territory in the late 1890s. From the moment the *Seattle Post-Intelligencer* blared out the arrival of a gold-laden ship on July 17, 1897, local merchants began touting Seattle as the place to stock up for Klondike expeditions, and they reaped far greater rewards than the mostly ill-fated stampeders. Located in the old Union Trust Annex building, this tiny museum's photographic displays, newspaper clippings, and various artifacts offer a fascinating glimpse of one of the more tragic periods in the city's history. Visit on the first Sunday of any month for a showing of Charlie Chaplin's 1926 *Gold Rush*.

Maritime Museums
Of course, there's a buttload of them. None are destinations in their own right, but a maritime fan can spend an entire day bouncing from one water-happy museum to another.

The **Northwest Seaport Maritime Heritage Center** (1002 Valley St, 206/447-9800) is an umbrella foundation dedicated to the preservation of our region's maritime history, offering self-guided tours of the 1897 *Wawona*— the largest sailing schooner ever built in North America. Mon-Sat 10 am-4 pm, Sun noon-4 pm; additional hours in summer; admission by donation.

The nearby **Center for Wooden Boats** (1010 Valley St, 206/382-2628) is dedicated to the restoration of historic wooden rowboats and sailboats, and offers the opportunity to see, touch, smell, listen to, learn about, and—wouldn't you know it?—even rent some of the 100 or so boats moored here. Wed-Mon 11 am-5 pm, additional hours in summer; free admission, donations gratefully accepted; various charges for boat rentals.

The fancypants **Odyssey: The Maritime Discovery Center** (Pier 66, 2205 Alaskan Way, 206/374-4000) provides exhibits "packed with hands-on, high-tech, interactive experiences," revolving around various maritime topics. It's all very spiffy, and probably fun for kids, but compared to the opportunity to see real boats and fish, it's a soulless, cold, impersonal netherworld. Daily 10 am-5 pm; admission $4-$6.50.

Other places worth a look include the **Coast Guard Museum Northwest** (Pier 36, 1519 Alaskan Way S, 206/217-6993; Mon, Wed, & Fri 9 am-3 pm, Sat-Sun 1-5 pm; free admission), the **Hiram M. Chittenden Locks Visitor Center** (3015 NW 54th St, 206/783-7059; Thurs-Mon 11 am-5 pm, additional hours in summer; free admission), and the **Hydroplane and Race-boat Museum** (1605 S 93rd St, Bldg. E-D, 206/764-9453; Thurs 10 am-10 pm, Sat 10 am-4:30 pm, additional hours in summer; free admission; donations accepted).

Memory Lane Museum

Central District
1400 S Lane St, just west of
Rainier Avenue, off Dearborn St,
(206) 329-1000
Mon-Sat 10 am-8 pm,
Sun 11 am-6 pm
Free admission

You would hardly expect to find a museum in the middle of Seattle's largest Goodwill store. But there it is, right next to the store's Vintage Cafe ($2 egg-salad sandwiches and $1 onion rings). Open in 1968 with donated items, the Memory Lane Museum offers

DAVID BELISLE

Vintage toys: Space used to be so easy

a museum experience to those who might not otherwise visit a museum. After wandering through the long aisles of used clothing, you'll come to a display case containing Bruce the Bear—a huge (now taxidermied) Alaskan brown bear whose glamorous career in film and TV reached its peak with an appearance on *Northern Exposure*, then descended into a string of Les Schwab openings after a crippling sex addiction. Your attention will doubtlessly also be drawn to the Miss Bardahl World Champion Hydroplane, the WWII-era deep-sea diving suit, the exhibit of changing fashions over the decades (particularly noteworthy is the "Reagan Red" late-'80s red wool suit, named for Nancy Reagan), and an array of vintage toys, magazines, posters, cameras, TVs, typewriters, radios, record players, kitchen appliances and utensils, cosmetics, razors, and tobacco products.

Museum of Flight

South Seattle
9404 E Marginal Way S, (206) 764-5720
Daily 10 am-5 pm, Thurs until 9 pm
Admission $5-9.50

After coffee, heroin, and software monopolies, Seattle is famous for one other industry: aerospace. Founded in 1964, this massive paean to flight technology is the largest of its kind on the West Coast, and a dream come true for any airplane aficionado or concerned father hoping to instill jingoistic regard for the

American military in his sniveling, wussy son. Covering 12 acres on a corner of Boeing Field, the museum's enormous hangars contain more than 50 full-size aircraft, nearly half of which are suspended from the roof, six stories above. Also on display is a full-scale, hands-on air-traffic control tower. A large auditorium, named after former Boeing CEO William M. Allen, runs films such as *The Dream*—the museum's own take on the history of flying; the museum also runs temporary exhibits of interest (recent years have included Wings over Hollywood and Women and Flight). All this could easily be snoozeville for those whose interest in airplanes is confined to Real TV air-show disasters, but for any aviation freak it's the equivalent of blowing Chuck Yaeger.

Museum of History and Industry
Montlake
2700 24th Ave E, off south end of Montlake Bridge, (206) 324-1126
Daily 10 am-5 pm
$3-$5.50

MOHAI is the behemoth of Seattle's historical museums, with a huge array of permanent exhibits, including displays on the Great Seattle Fire of 1889, the settlers' initial arrival at Alki, a large maritime collection, and an interactive reconstruction of a street in 1878 downtown Seattle, where role-playing visitors can live out their dreams of pretending to have scurvy. MOHAI always has interesting temporary exhibits (recently including the newly restored, taxidermied Bobo, Seattle's beloved gorilla), as well as an accessible archive of more than 500,000 historical photos. Be warned that this is a particularly kid-friendly museum, full of rowdy little bastards hogging interactive exhibits such as "Salmon Stakes" (a hands-on simulation of the arduous gutting, slicing, and canning process). There are a few too many non-functioning bells and whistles at MOHAI, but the nearly 50-year-old museum still does an admirable job of providing an experience that "serves to dispel preconceptions and prejudice, that opens minds, and that creates understanding and tolerance," with its expressly multicultural history of the region.

Olmsted Interpretive Exhibit
Capitol Hill
Observation deck, top of water tower in Volunteer Park, 1400 E Prospect St,
(206) 684-4075 (Seattle Dept. of Parks & Recreation)
Daily 10 am to dusk
Free

Not only will you get great exercise (from climbing the exhibit's 106 stairs) and a panoramic view from the top of the water tower, you'll also have the opportunity to enjoy this pictorial/text exhibit on the history of Seattle's park system. In 1903, John C. Olmsted arrived in Seattle, and the legendary Olmsted Brothers landscape architecture firm was hired to plan the city's parks and boulevards. The exhibit includes newspaper clippings, letters, and picture postcards about the development of Seattle's parks and water system, as well as specific details about Volunteer Park (named in 1901 to honor the volunteers of the Spanish-American War). As the water tower is closed by park security at dusk, you need not fear involuntarily witnessing any of the park's famed homosexual trysts (that is, unless you want to).

Seattle Metropolitan Police Museum

Pioneer Square

317 3rd Ave S, (206) 748-9991

Tues-Sat 11 am-4 pm

$1.50-$3

Considering the Seattle Police Department's controversial reputation, the Police Museum's mission to "educate the public by 'demystifying' the police" would seem to be a challenging task indeed. Founded by Seattle Police Officer Jim Ritter in 1997, the museum uses glass-encased displays to present a wide variety of local police history from 1860 to the present, including anti-Chinese riots, mob lynchings, and opium battles. The display covering the 1934 Longshoremen's Strike includes a "Gas Gun," used to launch tear-gas canisters. The museum claims it will soon be adding

VICTORIA RENARD

Calling all cars: We've got a 420 in progress

WTO artifacts to that exhibit. We'll see whether they include the infamous photo of that poor guy being kicked in the nuts by Seattle's finest.

Wing Luke Asian Museum

International District

407 7th Ave S, (206) 623-5124

Tues-Fri 11 am-4:30 pm, Sat-Sun noon-4 pm

75¢-$2.50

Named in honor of Seattle's first Asian City Council member, elected in 1962, this pan–Asian Pacific American museum presents a wide range of displays. The permanent exhibits integrate the histories of 10 Asian Pacific American groups in Washington state (including a model of the Japanese American internment camp on the Puyallup Fairgrounds), and provide unique images of the early years of Seattle's International District. The tiny space is filled with photographs, clothing, and miscellaneous artifacts, including colorful kites painted in the image of various animals. The museum serves as a repository for many oral history projects, preserved in audio and videotaped interviews.

Ye Olde Curiosity Shop and Museum
Waterfront
1001 Alaskan Way, Pier 54, (206) 682-5844
Mon-Fri 9:30 am-6 pm, Sat-Sun 9:30 am-9 pm, additional hours in summer
Free admission
A tackier and more touristy version of the Memory Lane Museum, Ye
Olde Curiosity Shop is nevertheless worth a visit. "Daddy" Joe Standley
furbished this curio shop from 1899 until his death in 1940; subsequent
generations have continued the family tradition to the present day. Some
of the more popular items include "Sylvester," a well-preserved mummy
of a man shot in frontier-era Arizona; a pair of Siamese-twin calves; a
large collection of shrunken human heads; and other wonders both large
and small (a nine-foot blow gun, a six-foot crab, the Lord's Prayer
engraved on a grain of rice).

Kayaking

Downtown Waterfront
on Elliott Bay
Magnolia/Downtown Waterfront
For the most metropolitan kayak trip, try the downtown waterfront on
Elliott Bay. The best launch spot is from Smith Cove Park on W. Galer
Street in Magnolia—it's a bit farther than launching from Elliott Bay
Park, but the parking is much easier. From there, just hug the shore south
along the Port of Seattle. Among the highlights of kayaking in this area are
the great views of downtown and the opportunity to tie up at the Bell
Street Pier (Pier 66) and actually get some fish-and-chips with the feeble,
landlocked tourists. The drawback of the trip is that that you will be among
the very few kayaks out there amid heavy industrial traffic. Stay well away
from all ferries, watch out for electrical wires under piers, and you should
be fine.

Golden Gardens and Puget Sound
Crown Hill/Loyal Heights
Golden Gardens is the name of a beach just north of where Ballard meets
Puget Sound, and the waters offshore make for some of the best kayaking
in Seattle. If you have your own kayak or have done a take-away rental
from one of the outlets in Seattle (see Boat Rentals earlier in this
chapter), then you can access these waters by parking at Golden Gardens
and walking your kayaks to the public launch docks 50 yards to the south.
Large, rolling waves mean you should have some experience before
kayaking the Sound, but if you can handle the seas, there's a big payoff. A
buoy located about five minutes out in the Sound often serves as a nap-

ping spot for sea lions the size of Chevy Novas. In the distance, breaching whales can be seen, heard, and (unfortunately) smelled. Freight trains chug along the nearby shore. Huge sails from schooners and yachts frame the Olympic Mountains on the horizon, and on clear evenings, the sun sets just between the peaks, making you realize that you probably died earlier in the week and are now just kayaking through heaven.

Lake Union and Portage Bay
Eastlake/Montlake

The best attractions of Lake Union and Portage Bay (the part of Lake Union that lies east of the I-5 bridge) are convenience, the view of downtown, and the houseboats, in that order. The Northwest Outdoor Center, Moss Bay, and Agua Verde (on Portage Bay) all provide free parking and cheap kayak rentals (see Boat Rentals earlier in this chapter). As soon as you get into the water on Lake Union, you'll be amazed at the unobstructed views of downtown Seattle's skyline, as the southern end of Lake Union is a mere quarter mile from downtown. It's a rare combination of metropolitan grandeur and calm, friendly waters. The houseboat communities along Eastlake in Lake Union and the southern shore of Portage Bay also make for interesting ogling, as many of the houseboats are both eclectically designed and carefully maintained. The lake's only drawback may even be a plus for some: Lake Union always has a high volume of boat and seaplane traffic. If you're a fan of maritime transportation, great; if you're afraid of getting squished in your kayak, just remember to stick to the shore and paddle straight while crossing. Beware: the larger vessel always has the right-of-way.

Salmon Bay and the Ballard Locks
Ballard

The trip between Lake Union and the Hiram M. Chittenden Locks [note: this is the locks' official name, but I think it's okay to refer to it as the "Ballard Locks" elsewhere] in Ballard (the locks separate saltwater Puget Sound from the freshwater lakes) can take up to an hour and a half one-way in a kayak. If you plan on actually going through the locks (not allowed if you're renting your kayak), you can plan on waiting an additional 20 to 45 minutes to get through. The thing that makes it worth it is the maritime industry. Salmon Bay, just east of the locks, may sound pastoral, but actually, it's a great place to see the secret lives of Siberian trawlers, Alaskan cargo ships, and Washington gravel barges as they hole up for repairs or just sit there, rusting. As far as going through the locks, doing this in a kayak is a little confusing, but just heed the devilishly named "lockmaster" and things will go smoothly. What's more, the tourists loitering around the locks will be impressed that you are locking out with all the big boats, and you'll end up in many photo albums throughout the world. The wait and the large amounts of exhaust are but a small price to pay for glory.

Washington Park Arboretum and Foster Island

Montlake/Madison Park

A trip out to the Arboretum and Foster Island incorporates some of the best elements of urban kayaking. From land, the Washington Park Arboretum is a satisfying display of flowers, trees, and the occasional amorous couple, but from the water, it becomes a much wilder tangle of narrow sloughs, high grasses, and freeway underbellies. SR 520, which connects Seattle and the Eastside, meets the lake at the Arboretum, and its numerous on-ramps and off-ramps often hover less than four feet off the water. Just crossing under the bridge en route to the Arboretum is

ANNIE MARIE MUSSELMAN

The Arboretum: Nature's underbelly

an absolutely unique experience, and there's a strange quiescence in hearing the waves lap at your kayak 20 inches beneath many tons of moving cars and concrete. Foster Island is connected to the Arboretum with footbridges, but the best views of it are likewise from the water, where close encounters with statuesque geese, herons, and even sea otters are common occurrences. One word to the wise, however: The paths on the shore are secluded, and kayakers sometimes report middle-aged flashers carefully waiting, ready to show their stuff to the first group of boaters who come around the bend.

Boat Rentals

Agua Verde Cafe & Paddle Club

University District

1303 NE Boat St, (206) 545-8570

Daily 10 am-dusk

"Paddle Club" might be a bit of an overstatement, as Agua Verde offers the fewest services of any of the lakeside boat-rental facilities (kayak rentals only, for on-site use only). Its location on Portage Bay, south of the University of Washington, however, makes Agua Verde very convenient to Lake Washington and the Arboretum area; the trip around Foster Island will only take you from one to one and a half hours, depending on your need for speed.

The Center for Wooden Boats

Southeast Lake Union

1010 Valley St, (206) 382-2628

Wed-Mon 11 am-5 pm

The Center for Wooden Boats is actually a maritime museum, but unlike the Guggenheim, this museum will let you float around Lake Union on some of its exhibits. The center's fleet of available rowboats is small but wooden, and if that kind of thing excites you, then this place might scratch your itch. Additionally, it is the only place on Lake Union where you can rent a sailboat, provided you are competent at tacking, jibing, and docking.

Moss Bay Rowing and Kayak Center

South Lake Union

1001 Fairview Ave N, (206) 682-2031

Daily 9 am-dusk

Moss Bay is NWOC's only competition on Lake Union, but it splits its energy between kayaks and rowing skulls. All rowing-skull rentals require membership in Moss Bay's rowing club, as well as suitable rowing experience. Kayaks, on the other hand, don't require any experience, but even though Moss Bay has the same rental rates as NWOC, the larger NWOC offers more services and a slightly more convenient location than Moss Bay.

Northwest Outdoor Center

West Lake Union

2100 Westlake Ave N, (206) 281-9694

Daily 10am-6 pm

Since 1982, the Northwest Outdoor Center (NWOC) has been offering a full fleet of rentals, Seattle's largest kayak accessories collection, and classes that teach some 1,500 students annually everything from navigation to advanced rolling techniques. Take-away kayak rentals should be reserved at least a month in advance in the summer to ensure availability.

Seattle Sailing Club

Ballard

7001 Seaview Ave NW #125 (in the Shilshole Bay Marina, (206) 782-5100

Daily 9 am- 5pm

For the experienced sailor looking to see Puget Sound three sheets to the wind without lifting a glass, Windworks is the only place besides the Center for Wooden Boats that offers "bareboat" rentals of sailboats (meaning you're the captain). You'll need to demonstrate your sailing savvy before taking a boat out, but if you can get the full 9 am-5 pm day of sailing in, then the price is actually quite reasonable. Additionally, Windworks' location near Golden Gardens on Puget Sound is ideal: plenty of wind, lots of room to maneuver, and the possibility of making day trips out to Blake Island, Kingston, or even Poulsbo.

University of Washington Waterfront Activities Center
University District
Southeast corner of UW's Husky Stadium, on Montlake Blvd, (206) 543-9433
Daily 10 am-6 pm
The UW Waterfront Activities Center is a good spot for fumbling about in three-seater canoes and four-seater rowboats. Its drawbacks include the fact that you have to pay for parking in the Husky Stadium lot (except for Saturday afternoons and Sundays), and you are limited in where you can go. The center is located on Lake Washington and has good access to the Arboretum, but the canoes and rowboats aren't allowed to pass through the Montlake Cut into Lake Union. They stop renting boats at 4:30, so arrive before then if you're hoping to take an evening ride.

Parks

For more specific driving directions, bus routes, or other information about these parks, call the Seattle Department of Parks and Recreation at (206) 684-4075; there's a former cabdriver on staff with a velvet voice—he'll help you find the park of your dreams.

Alki Beach Park
West Seattle
You have to wonder what the first settlers who landed here would think of what Alki's become—low riders, bikini babes, and Harley hogs. It's totally So-Cal, especially in the summer, and it makes sense: Where there's sand, there's cheesy people. Alki Beach features a boardwalk, acres and acres of sand, and teenagers.
Directions: Take the West Seattle Bridge and take the Harbor Avenue SW exit. At the light, make a right turn onto Harbor Avenue SW, which becomes Alki Avenue SW. The park is on the right side of the road, just after Duwamish Head, and runs all the way to Alki Point.

Camp Long
West Seattle
A swampy little park reminiscent of a golf course, Camp Long offers a climbing wall, interpretive nature signs, and winding trails into the woods. There are musty little cabins for overnight rental. Reserve one by calling (206) 684-7434.
Directions: Take the West Seattle Bridge, exit at Fauntleroy, at the light take a left onto 35th Avenue SW, drive up the hill for three-quarters of a mile, then take the first left onto Dawson Street.

Danny Woo International District Park
International District
Works of outsider garden art are generated here: Elaborate string-bean fences are held together with pieces of brightly colored cloth; walls of snap

peas arch against odd bits of metal; and orderly rows of kohlrabi and garlic grow in dilapidated wooden boxes. The views of the city are amazing from up here, too.

Directions: On 6th Avenue S and Main Street in the International District.

Discovery Park
Magnolia

This park is so big that a stinky sewage-treatment plant smack-dab in the middle of it is barely noticed. That's right, at 534 acres, Discovery Park is Seattle's largest park. Fort Lawton used to be housed here, and you can see the scrody old barracks within the park. There are two miles of beach access (an ideal place for tripping), meadows, forest, and tons of trails to thrash through. The visitors center offers lots of natural history classes taught by volunteer naturalists; call (206) 386-4236 for more info. Discovery Park is also home to Daybreak Star Art & Cultural Center, a Native American center that hosts interesting art shows and enjoyable powwows. Call (206) 285-4425 for more information.

Directions: For some reason, it's impossible to find this gigantic park, or give accurate directions. Call (206) 386-4236 and they'll guide you to it.

Gas Works Park
Wallingford

This park will make your feet burn and your babies two-headed. Okay, that might be an exaggeration, but Gas Works Park (at the edge of yuppieville Wallingford) features gnarled old pieces of machinery, which, from 1900 until the mid-1950s, turned coal and oil into gas products. The resultant waste oozed into the soil and Lake Union. Though park developers knew the ground was tainted (they mixed the soil with sawdust, leaves, and—dear Lord—sewage sludge, then a layer of topsoil), they turned Gas Works into a picnic ground in 1976.

Directions: From N 45th Street, turn left onto Meridian Avenue N and head south. Continue until you hit the park.

CLAIR MORGANTINI

Gas Works Park: Re-defining nature

Golden Gardens
Crown Hill/Loyal Heights
Psst: There is a beach with sand just north of Ballard. Golden Gardens features 88 acres of fun, including a beach, a marina, railroad tracks, a grass-covered hillside, and the penis-shrinking cold waters of Shilshole Bay. Bonfires are allowed!

Directions: Go to Ballard and get on NW Market Street, headed west; Market Street turns into Shilshole Avenue NW, follow Shilshole until it dead-ends at Golden Gardens.

Green Lake/Woodland Park
Green Lake
One algae-filled lake plus 342 acres equals Green Lake fun. This park features lots of runners, in-line skaters, dogs, and children. Rowing and sailing are available through the Small Craft Center. Right next door is Woodland Park, 188 acres of playgrounds, a rose garden, tennis courts, athletic fields, lawn-bowling greens, and a big old zoo—which, even though it's very nice, still makes *The Stranger* cry.

Directions: From I-5 (north or south) take exit 169, the 45th/50th Street exits. Choose the 50th Street lane, turn heading west, proceed along 50th Street to a five-way stop light, where Stone Way N turns into Green Lake Way N, and turn right onto Green Lake Way N. Woodland Park abuts Green Lake to the southeast.

Harbor Island
West Seattle/Industrial Seattle
Not a park per se, but definitely something to see. Harbor Island is a man-made island that was constructed in the early 20th century, when the city of Seattle began filling in the vast tide flats south of Pioneer Square. In the early 1960s, the Port of Seattle constructed container-carrying facilities on Harbor Island. Today, you can marvel at the abandoned cars, rest among the rusting metal scraps, and identify petroleum reserves (hint: those big white cylindrical buildings with flammable warning stickers) on this big old wasteland.

Directions: Take the West Seattle Bridge, and get off at Harbor Island.

Kubota Gardens
Rainier Beach
Purchased from the Kubota family, these gardens near Renton blend Japanese–style gardening with native Northwest plants. There's an elaborate system of streams and ponds and unusual Japanese plants. The founder's house is still on the premises—ring the doorbell and you can hear it chime within—it's creepy!

Directions: Drive south down Martin Luther King Jr. Way S, turn left onto Renton Avenue S, drive until you reach 55th Avenue S. The park is to the right.

ANNIE MARIE MUSSELMAN

Parks: Full of bugs and Frisbees

Lincoln Park
West Seattle
This is one of the best parks in Seattle because it has it all: beach access, wide expanses of grass suitable for picnicking or outdoor sex, and Hansel and Gretel-type trails that wind through deep, dark forests. Vashon Island is just across the water, and you can watch ferries arrive and depart. There are a few baseball and softball fields, shelters for birthday parties, and a playground featuring a rope-swing ride that will cause small ones to wet themselves with glee.

Directions: Cross the West Seattle Bridge, take the Fauntleroy exit, and follow the signs to the Vashon Island ferry. The park is on the right, just before the ferry dock.

Madison Park
Madison Park
Apparently this park was THE place to go during the 1880s: There used to be drinking and gambling, a paddle wheel, a greenhouse full of exotic plants, and a cable car that ran directly from Pioneer Square to the park. Man, that must've been grand. Now this tiny park is cram-packed with tattooed hipsters who do cannonballs off the dock's diving board, lots of queers looking at each other, and families looking at the queers. It's like being at a bar, but outside, with grass—and no alcohol.

Directions: From I-5 headed north take the Madison Street exit. From I-5 headed south, take the James Street exit, make a left at 7th Avenue, head north to Madison Street and take a right. Continue on E Madison Street heading northeast for 2.6 miles; at 43rd Avenue E turn right so you are heading south—the park entrance will be right in front of you.

Magnuson Park
Sand Point

Yes, okay, Soundgarden got its name from this park's Sound Garden. Other potential band names: Kitschy Picnickers, Screaming Kite-Flyers, Dog Poop, and Blackberry Scratches. This park used to house Navy airplane hangars and runways in the 1970s, and now offers a public swimming beach, an off-leash area for dogs, and seas of grassland.

Directions: From I-5 north or south, take the 45th Street exit, head east on 45th Street NE, stay left onto Sand Point Way N, turn right on NE 65th Street, and you'll enter the park.

Ravenna/Cowen Park
University District

Ravenna, named after a town in Italy, is one of Seattle's oldest parks, filled with U-District joggers, hippies, and dog walkers. Cowen Park connects to Ravenna Park and is a squatter's paradise, especially during the summer.

ERIKA LANGELY

Ravenna/Cowen Park: Squatters and dogs

Walking through the ravine can be a lesson in human anatomy.

Directions: I-5 northbound: Exit at NE 65th Street. Turn right onto NE Ravenna Boulevard to 20th Avenue NE. Turn left on 20th Avenue NE. The parking lot is on the right side of the street on the corner of NE 58th Street and 20th Avenue NE. I-5 southbound: Take the N 85th Street/NE 80th Street exit. Follow the sign to NE 80th Street. Go east on NE 80th Street to 15th Avenue NE. Turn right onto 15th Avenue NE to NE Ravenna Boulevard. Turn left on NE Ravenna Boulevard. Take Ravenna Boulevard to 20th Avenue NE. Turn left on 20th Avenue NE. The parking lot is on the right side of the street on the corner of NE 58th Street and 20th Avenue NE.

Seward Park
South Seattle

Named after the secretary of state who was responsible for America's purchase of Alaska in 1856, Seward Park seems as big as Alaska sometimes. The park is made up of the Bailey Peninsula on Lake Washington. It has nature trails and a paved trail—frequented by annoying in-line skaters—that circles the park. Actually, annoyances are everywhere: If you swim in Lake Washington, watch out for schistosomes, or larval flatworms that cause swimmer's itch; and when thrashing through fern-covered hills, beware of poison oak. Less malevolent is the art studio in a converted bathhouse which offers instruction in pottery.

Directions: From I-5 headed south, take the S Albro Street/Swift Avenue S exit. Turn right at the light. Turn left at S Graham Street. Follow S Graham Street to Beacon Avenue S. Turn left on Beacon Avenue S. Follow Beacon Avenue S to S Orcas Street. Turn right on S Orcas St. Follow S Orcas Street to the entrance of the park.

Volunteer Park
Capitol Hill
Big ol' park for the citizens of Capitol Hill. Climb up to the water tower and learn about Seattle's Olmsted parks. Volunteer Park also features the Seattle Asian Art Museum, a greenhouse, teenagers presenting Shakespeare in the park, Ultimate Frisbee where there's room, and yes, cruising. Nubile boys. Go if you must.

Directions: From 10th Avenue E (the north end of the Broadway strip), turn right onto E Aloha Street, turn left onto 15th Avenue E, and it'll be on your left.

Washington Park Arboretum
Montlake
Wondering what witch hazel looks like? Go to the Washington Park Arboretum. With 40,000 species of plants, it can't be boring. These people treat plants like some people treat sex: They're obsessed; they can't stop thinking about it! Explore their website for more plant porn (http://depts.washington.edu/wpa), which offers photos of plants during their best season, taxonomic lists with photos of every plant on the list, and eco-geophapic plant collections—check out the New Zealand High Country exhibit.

Directions: From downtown Seattle, drive east on Madison Street to Lake Washington Boulevard E, then turn left into the Arboretum.

From east of Lake Washington, drive east on the Evergreen Point Bridge (Hwy 520) to the first Seattle exit (Lake Washington Blvd S). From the ramp, turn left into the Arboretum.

The Walker Rock Garden

by Stacey Levine

THE WALKER ROCK GARDEN IS THE WILDEST BACKYARD IN TOWN. If you've ever been subjected to a Rorschach test, you may recall that experience in this place—minus the sneering psychologist—because, in treading and retreading the garden's walkways, you invariably find new details and pictures in the stones each time.

This small dreamland in West Seattle is one of those off-the-map institutions that exists outside visible local culture. Clichéd sorts of questions ("Is it art? What kind of art?") tend to come up in the catalogs, articles, and

CURT DOUGHTY

guidebook pieces that have documented the garden, because the garden's creator, Milton Walker, was a self-taught artist. But academic questions about classifying the work as art, craft, kitsch, art brut, or "other" fall away when you see the place, because the garden, like a dream, presents itself wholly on its own terms, and defies easy description.

Walker, who died of Alzheimer's disease in 1984, wanted to create a tribute to nature, says his widow, Florence. In her nineties, she remains in the house where she and her husband lived since 1939. In 1959, Mr. Walker decided to make an imitation lake in his backyard and was apparently unhappy with the outcome; he began to embellish it with rocks, and the garden took off from there. For 20 years he continued this project, and today the yard reveals the intensity of his vision and work. During winters, he collected and sorted new rocks; springs and summers, he added these to the garden, building the place up like a nest.

The garden was like an organism its creator depended upon. "He was always working on it, every weekend," Mrs. Walker says of the former Boeing machinist. Entering through a gate alongside the Walkers' modest cottage-style house, you look across a landscape of mountains (caps painted white), pathways, slopes, and miniature lakes; looking closer, you see that everything here is entirely made of rock, mosaic-style. Bevies of ovoid river rocks line the walkways in rows; red, blue, turquoise, and green semi-precious rock and glass bits are embedded in the structures. Curved door frames, walls, arches, niches, steps, jagged hillsides, and an 18-foot tower sit behind the plain suburban cottage; the miniature lakes and stream beds (painted blue inside, filled with water) are meticulously lined with unending rows of rocks; stare long enough and they look like liquid. Crystal-lined, hollow, spherical rocks called thunder eggs abound; jewel-like stones also cover every crevice and ledge. The effect is staggering. Even the path beneath your feet is lined with smooth, caramel-colored petrified wood. This tribute to nature does not, of course, look "real"; its neatest virtue is that it looks hyper-real. As in Candyland, everything is made of the same stuff, suggesting that the world and its contents are all one, unified—which is true, in a way, and in another way, it's not true.

Over time, word about the garden spread. At first, neighbors and friends came to look; then people began calling for appointments; last year on Mother's Day, about 200 people made their way here. One article suggested that the high tower in the backyard bears a striking resemblance to work by Spanish architect Antonio Gaudí. "Milton was born in Eastern Washington, and he never heard of Gaudí," Mrs. Walker says. "He just had natural talent, and he never knew he had it until he started making the garden."

Visitors keep Mrs. Walker busy, and she insists that the garden keep its original spirit and intention—that it remain free of charge for anyone who wants to see it. She tries to explain her husband's motivation: "He was trying to make it like nature, and nature is heaven, I guess. He worked on it all the time." From the crevices of memory, she recalls days when she would help her husband. "We'd go spend weekends picking up river rocks, sorta everyday rocks, at the Columbia River. We'd spend the night there, and I'd have a pail. Then Milton noticed yellow rocks around there. I helped him collect them, and they turned out to be petrified wood. In those days you could bring home as much as you liked."

Mrs. Walker insists the garden keep its spirit—and that it remain free.

"We want nothing commercial about it," says Sandy Adams, the Walkers' daughter, who lives in the house and helps her mother manage the garden. "We don't want to advertise. Word of mouth is fine. If I see something highly advertised, I stay away. A lot of ads means there's something wrong." Ms. Adams' words are fresh and stark in a city that is more than ever about the urgent exercises of selling.

Note: Florence Walker has since passed away, but the garden is maintained by the city and is still free to public. It is open on the weekends in the summer only, by appointment; call (206) 935-3036.

Pool Halls

Garage

Capitol Hill
1130 Broadway Ave, (206) 322-2296
Daily 3 pm-2 am
$4-$14 per hour; Sun nights: ladies play free; Mon nights: $5/hour all night

Eighteen regulation-size tables, a full bar, and a damn fine menu add up to the best casual pool environment one might hope to find anywhere. Wait times for a table on a Friday or Saturday may be an hour or longer, but attractions abound while you wait: beautiful people, loud music, food and drink galore. While the hipsters line the walls, a quick glance around the room reveals the truth: It's safe to go in the water, as there are very few sharks in this wading pool. A pool hall to take your mother to on a weeknight—make her order the pear and gorgonzola salad, and she'll be happy. Guaranteed.

C. TAYLOR

Pool: It's more fun when you're drunk

Temple Billards

Pioneer Square
126 S Jackson St, (206) 682-3242
Mon-Fri 11 am-2 am, Sat-Sun
3 pm-2 am, open 365 days a year
$6-$14 per hour

Notice the wooden lockers on the wall (with beautiful silver plaque numbers) rented by the regulars who come to shoot after work. With such dedicated detail to the sport, Temple is the classiest pool hall in Seattle. Three straight regulation tables are elegantly offset by three tables at an angle in the main room. Four tables are hidden in the basement and one up top on the deck. The scene and décor are less gauche than the Garage, even with the same aesthetic at work. Go at 6 in the evening, the perfect time to avoid bumping your ass into someone at every shot. The panini sandwiches are great and can be washed down with some good beer. Plus, on deck #2, there's a couple of antique video games: Joust and Asteroids.

Skateboarding

Rain City Skate Park

Downtown

1044 4th Ave S, (206) 749-5511, www.raincityskatepark.com

Sun-Thurs noon-10 pm, Fri-Sat noon-midnight, Sat-Sun 9 am-noon Kids Skate

1 session member $5, 1 session non-member $8 (1 year membership $25)

Rain City is the best thing to happen to Seattle skaters in a long time. After a decade of city skate prevention, two hardy skaters, Todd McGuire and Marshall "Stack" Reid, took it upon themselves to build an indoor park with plenty of room to skate and socialize. Rain City Skate Park opened on February 20, 2001, and may not be in its current location for much longer, so get yourself, your board and your (required) helmet over to Fourth Ave S for a great vert ramp, a solid mini ramp, and an 8000 square foot street course. Rain City Skate Park goes all the way: it features a constantly changing calendar of events, including a bunch of day camps, as well as a fully loaded skate shop. It's intended for skaters of all types, so if you're a hotshot, you'll have some room to show your stuff, and you can spend some time teaching the newbies how to skate a vert.

BIO

Ryan Grant

Who is he? A local skate punk

Where's your favorite place to skate?
"Definitely Westlake Center [4th Ave, between Pike and Pine]. There's this thing in the middle of the plaza that they call a monument, but it's not. It's just a little marble thing that grinds real good. It's got a gap over water, too, and lots of rails. Somehow they just built a perfect place to skate."

What do you think of the Seattle Center Skate Park?
"It's cool, but the grinds are too metallic, too artificial. There's nothing like the feeling of good stone under

SOMYA GUTSHALL

your board. Marble's not too slippery; it just gives you crazy satisfaction. I'd take Red Square [at the University of Washington] over the skate park, too, because [Red Square] has lots of natural stairs and tabletops [elevated stones with flat tops]."

How would you rate Seattle's skating scene?
"It's obviously smaller than S.F. or L.A., but there's still a sick-ass scene up here."

What are the best bands around the skate scene here in Seattle?
"Well, Kool Keith, Brother Lynch, and the Misfits are sick, but for local stuff I'm into 500 Years and Elevated Elements."

What are the worst things cops do to skateboarders in Seattle?
"Especially at Westlake, the cops hired these random-ass goons dressed in green who call themselves "community organizers." They're these geeky, crazy-ass people, man; they just sit down in your path to knock you off your board. And lots of my friends have been taken to police holding cells in jail just for skating downtown."

Seask8 (Seattle Skate Park)

Queen Anne
5th & Republican, (206) 233-3959
Daily dawn-dusk
Free

Seattle's first skate park, Seask8's been around a long time, and it's been undergoing changes practically the whole time. It's had its share of golden moments (for awhile the park was actually open 24 hours a day!), and most local skaters have a good memory or two associated with the park. Today, it remains a good place to get up on the concrete: 8,800 square feet of ramps and bowls. The layout could be better, and traffic in the bowl gets way too heavy in the middle of the day (from about 3 pm-8 pm), but the park is free, open til 11:30 pm every night, and lighted. For the gruesome: helmets and pads are not required, but if you're seriously going to hit the bowl, you'll want them.

Snowboarding

Crystal Mountain

Enumclaw
Driving distance from Seattle: 4 hours (north face of Mount Rainier)
(888) SKI-6199 snow report, (360) 663-2265 main office; www.skicrystal.com

BIO

Jennifer Slack

KELLY O

Who is she? A local snowboarder

How did you get into snowboarding?
"I had been skiing since I was about two years old, even competitively, but somebody talked me into trying snowboarding about eight years ago, and I haven't put on a pair of skis since."

What's your favorite place to snowboard?
"Definitely Alpental [located off I-90 at the Summit at Snoqualmie].

It's got great runs and it's super-close to the city."

What makes Seattle a good place for snowboarding?
"The closeness to the mountains. It's just an hour to Snoqualmie from Seattle, so

you can hit the slopes after work or school or whatever."

Any jargon we should know about?
"The guys call girls 'Bettys' all the time. It actually pisses me off, because it's like when the skiers say 'snow bunny'—they're thinking more about your ass than your skills on the mountain."

Is it true what they say about Northwest snow-boarders and weed?
"Maybe so, but tell everybody that those skiers smoke just as much as snowboarders—we have a bad reputation, but we're not the only punks out there."

Mount Baker Ski Area

Bellingham

Driving distance from Seattle: 5 hours (Mount Baker)

(360) 671-0211 snow report, (360) 734-6771 main office; www.mtbakerskiarea.com

Stevens Pass Ski Area

Skykomish

Driving distance from Seattle: 2 hours (U.S. Hwy 2)

(206) 634-1645 snow report, (206) 812-4510 ext. 350 main office;

www.stevenspass.com

Summit at Snoqualmie Ski Area

Snoqualmie Pass

Driving distance from Seattle: 1 hour (I-90)

(206) 236-1600 snow report; www.summit-at-snoqualmie.com

Spas & Bathhouses

Basic Plumbing

Capitol Hill

1505 10th Ave E, (206) 323-2799

Mon-Thurs 6 pm-3 am, Fri 6 pm-5 am, Sat 1 pm-5 am, Sun 1 pm-3 am

Basic Plumbing is not a bathhouse per se, but a "private club for men" (wink wink). Drinking, drugs, and gum-chewing are expressly forbidden. In light of what is allowed at BP, it seems strange to exclude gum. Or anything else. It has a well-lit lounge near the entrance that plays mainstream movies, and a darker one in back that shows bad porn. In between lies a shadowy maze of dark corners and cul-de-sacs, where you may or may not find mysterious crotch-level holes cut in the walls. Everything is painted black and the lighting is virtually nonexistent—presumably to accommodate the more aesthetically challenged members. Keep in mind that a trip to BP is much like a trip to Goodwill: You have to weed through a lot of trash before you find that one cheap treasure.

HotHouse Spa

Capitol Hill

1019 E Pike St #HH (at 11th Ave, behind the Wildrose), 568-3240

Thurs-Sun noon-midnight, Mon-Wed noon-10 pm, $10

($9 if you bring your own towel), plus $1 locker deposit

Yeah, yeah . . . HotHouse Spa can be a really easy punch line: It's a partially hidden, women-only bathhouse behind and under the renowned Wildrose (a bar known for its, er, unofficial "ladies only" policy) on the Hill. But your giggles will subside as you enter this oasis, and see that it's not a lesbian meat market or a second-rate YWCA. With miles of immaculate blue tile and warm herbal steam wafting throughout the premises, this small, modest-but-beautiful spa is a beacon of serenity and pampering. HotHouse's women, all hushed tones and sleepy eyes, can relax in the swirling hot tub, pristine and peacefully communal. Then there's the steam room (with flowery herbal steam!), which will purge your pores and warm you to the core; and the cozy sauna, with its cedar sweetness, will form its own cocoon around you long after you walk home, sleepy and blissfully clean.

MELANIE RENECKER

Hot House Spa: Modest but beautiful

Outdoor Sex

by Trisha Ready

MOST SEATTLE GUIDEBOOKS TELL YOU HOW TO ACCESS THE LOVELY GREEN FEATURES OF SEATTLE: that glacial time bomb of a mountain, the bacteria-laden lakes, Olmsted parks, more parks, forest hikes, the winding open spaces of our concrete bike trails. The books recommend day excursions in which you follow hundreds of other like-minded weekend SUV-adventurers out of the city to "secret" hideaway vestiges of pure nature. And then what? Eat a peach at the top of Mount Si while someone's rottweiler pees on your backpack?

No, the way to really take advantage of the outdoors is to "do it": Reclaim your relationship with the elemental forces by having outdoor sex.

TOM DOUGHERTY

We've listed here a number of *The Stranger's* favorite places to do it out-doors. None of them are perfectly safe, and some of them are not hygienic—and be aware that by following this guide, you are leaving yourself open to a ticket for lewd behavior. This ticket is a fine mark on a person's character, though, and many otherwise law-abiding citizens have this offense trailing after them in their public record. You need to take responsibility for the risks, bring correct safety equipment, and watch out for unfriendly wildlife, which in most cases means the police.

Red Square and the entire campus of the University of Washington

For those of you who really want to risk full exposure, have sex in Red Square. Daytime in Red Square is a little tricky to pull off, but on a winter's night, the slippery red bricks and the lit-up library provide the outdoor-sex sportsperson with a fairy-tale scene. Straddle the steps of Suzallo, hold onto the railings (or slide down the railings), and begin and end with the sense that you're in an old Russian city, screwing the hell out of some young Russian. (Sometimes you can hear piano music coming from a concert in Meany Hall—how perfectly lofty it all becomes.)

The UW is also a favorite spot for men cruising younger men. You can lead young catches into the infamous Suzzallo Library bathrooms, or into an empty classroom where desks, blackboards, and wide-open windows make perfect props.

Volunteer Park Water Tower

It's so famous we have to mention it, but just because it's popular doesn't mean it's not good. The trick to the water tower is getting the whole structure to yourself. This necessitates either staying after hours to get locked in, or using a decoy to divert people. You can hire a friend to tell visitors that a senior citizen had a heart attack on the observation deck: Your friend could explain that an ambulance is on the way, and so the observation deck is tem-porarily closed.

After you have the winding metal staircase, the studded metal walls, and the observation tower to yourself, climb the stairs backward and crawl on your bellies. Lean each other over rails, leave your clothes on the steps. (Be careful not to injure your back here.) The metal is cold but should not be a deterrent. When you get to the top floor, there is a great view of the city. Play a game to see which section of Seattle inspires the biggest orgasm. The mountain? How about the Needle?

Arboretum

Everyone knows about the north end of the park: the part that resembles the Deep South, with willows and thick, lush undergrowth. Like most parks, it's a big cruising spot. And for some reason, it's got more flashers and wankers than any other park in the city, with the possible exception of Ravenna. The park's secrets are endless, and you can always find a path someone hasn't taken in a while. Give a show to boats passing by—but do watch out for geese. Early morning, before the bees start to bumble, is the best time to grind in this Southern wonderland.

Seward Park

Seward Park is the wild sister of Green Lake (one of the only outdoor places we recommend you never have sex in or near, because it is widely patrolled and it smells). The appeal of Seward Park is twofold: During the day, you can hike into its wooded center, listening to the panting of the runners on a Sunday morning while your bare ass rubs on the

People are occasionally found tied up naked to chain-link fences.

bark. Then, at night, walk in a bit farther on the park's circular path. If there haven't been any recent warnings about *E. coli* or dangerous levels of sketchy bacteria, then strip and fuck right there in the water. If you want to be totally careful about it, put cooking oil, baby oil, or some kind of greasy stuff on your skin to keep off bugs and chemicals. Oddly enough, this area is not patrolled heavily.

Woodland Park Zoo

So this is how the story goes: "Serge" sneaks into the zoo on a Thursday night. There's a hole in the fence, down near where the zoo fronts Aurora (you'll have to find your own hole; the zoo people have probably patched that one up by now). Serge brings along his semi-girlfriend, "Alana," who likes to take off her clothes whenever she gets the chance (she also likes nasty pictures of herself taken, then hung in public bathrooms). As the lovers head deeper into the zoo, rare beasts from all over the world screech and mutter to each other in the dark.

The two of them end up near the elephant compound, the one that resembles a scene from *The King and I*. Serge lifts Alana up onto a water trough, pulls her panties off, and spreads her legs: Serge says you don't worry about foreplay; you just fuck when you're at the zoo.

Train Tracks

Train tracks run through the city along the water. They offer all sorts of sexual possibilities; if you're really up for the whole hobo thing, sneak into the train yard down near Boeing Field and have sex inside a boxcar on a stretch of open track. Trains imply power, and their steady clicking rhythm is a complete escape. Dommes get busted here all the time; people are occasionally found tied up naked to chain-link fences, exposed to passing trains, below Elliott Avenue. To combine the elements and the industrial feel, go down to Golden Gardens, get sand in your private parts, and watch ferries and barges pass through the Sound as the trains blow around the cliff.

Strip Clubs

Centerfolds

Greenwood

8517 15th Ave NW, (206) 783-8534

Male dancers Thurs-Sat 8 pm-2:30 am

Let's face it: women have a much better time at strip clubs than men. Whereas strip clubs for men are always surrounded by some degree of ugly loneliness, a trip to Centerfolds is like walking into a party. This is a club where men do the dancing on the nights that count: Thursday through Saturday (women dance Monday through Wednesday). And these boys aren't dancing for other men: What the heterosexual ladies in this city lack in strip club quantity (this place is the only club for straight women in the entire state of Washington), Centerfolds surely makes up for in quality. Sure, you have to put up with constant bachelorette parties, but the men here are worth it. They are all perfect specimens, running the fantasy gamut: "Army Man," "Business-Suit Man," "Hardly Legal Boy," etc. All dancers have to be strong enough to climb upside down on a pole and hang there for a while. Oh, and there's a shower onstage.

Lusty Lady

Downtown

1315 1st Ave, (206) 622-2120

Dancers Mon-Thurs 10 am-2:30 am,
Fri-Sat 10 am-3 am, Sun 10 am-1 am;
videos daily 24 hours

Woe to those who neglect this labyrinth of desire! The Lusty Lady is the repository of all of your dreams, fluids, and flesh-based poems. The space itself is a self-conscious re-creation of the womb: velvet, moist, and welcoming, suffused with a distinctly baroque,

ANNIE MARIE MUSSELMAN

The Lusty Lady: We say, "Oui, oui"

vaguely dank accent of semen. Bring your laundry money. The interior of the space is given over to small booths, which overlook a roomful of naked sprites. These little rooms are sanctuaries in which one may take one's pleasure into one's own hands. There are also wee video rooms, where the naughty subconscious of our smutty nation is on proud display. All in all, the Lusty Lady is an oasis of masturbatory pleasure in the heart of a frigid, backward town. Photos of dancers at this women-owned sexual bastion were collected in a beautiful book by Erika Langley, who became a dancer herself to get the shots. The Lusty Lady's otherwise conservative neighbor, the Seattle Art Museum, was neighborly enough to exhibit the photos.

Sex and the City

by Charles Mudede

NOT SO LONG AGO, a glittering world of gentlemen's clubs, adult theaters, and sex shops thrived on Seattle's First Avenue. A brief description of this now-lost world is depicted in the penultimate chapter of Jonathan Raban's *Hunting Mister Heartbreak*, which details Raban's first impressions of Seattle when he paid the boomtown a visit in 1988. "Down on First Avenue," he wrote, "the Midtown Theater was showing *Depraved Innocent* and *Interlude of Lust*. The Champ Arcade (The Adult Superstore) advertised Live Girls, and around the corner was a club that boasted 50 BEAUTIFUL GIRLS & 3 UGLY ONES! Another sign alerted one to the fact that Nina Deponca, the XXX STAR, was playing Seattle LIVE IN PERSON!"

When you look down First Avenue these days, all you see are boutiques and condominiums. The only sex businesses still around from this glimpsed era of "pleasure and temptation" are the Champ Arcade, the Adult Entertainment Center, and the Lusty Lady—the rest have vanished. What happened to Seattle's bright world of flesh and fun? Or, to put it more crudely, why did our city obliterate its genitals?

Something radical happened in order for Seattle to become suddenly sexless, a city without a "reputation," without a district of earthly delights. It had nothing to do with our mild weather or our supposed Scandinavian tempera-

ERIKA LANGELY

ments, nor did it happen naturally, simply because patrons lost interest or were dissuaded by AIDS. It was a cold and deliberate action on the part of our city fathers and mothers, who, in their own words, saw "these establishments [as a] menace to individuals, businesses, and property owners."

So, where there was once a sign that read "Fantasy Unlimited," there is now one that reads "Seattle's Best Coffee," and where there was a sign that read "50 BEAUTIFUL GIRLS & 3 UGLY ONES!" there is now one that says "Pike Street Trading."

American cities deal with the sex industry in roughly three different ways, which, in a sense, mirror the stages of a city's physical and psychological development. The first is to ignore it altogether, to let it go unchecked: Cities in this stage are not even aware that they are entitled to enforce sexual mores, and tend to have only simple "lewd conduct" codes that are weak and rarely used.

The second stage is the ego stage (in the Freudian sense). At this point, a city realizes that it is a city, and sees itself in relation to other cities. This is a kind of awakening, akin to that of Adam and Eve, who upon realizing that they were naked, hurried to cover their private parts. A city like SeaTac is a great example: Before it called itself a city, the sex industry thrived! Along Pacific Highway South, which was known as "the strip," massage parlors, peep shows, and prostitutes prospered. Then, on the somber day of February 28, 1990, SeaTac declared itself a city, and like other "important" cities, it established an ordinance and doubled its police force. Within five years, the once vivid and vital sex industry was reduced to just one "all-nude dance club." In the preemptive days of the Bible, a city of sin would be destroyed by fire and brimstone from heaven. In our age, a city manager writes up a meticulous ordinance.

Although Seattle is not a sexy city, it does have a sexy law.

The third stage is when a city becomes so big and confident that it need no longer compare itself with other cities. It sheds its inhibitions and develops a distinct identity and lifestyle. This is the case with Los Angeles (the porn capital of America), Chicago, and, until recently, New York City (under Mayor Giuliani's reign, New York City has been reduced to an aspiring status it hasn't seen in 200 years).

In Seattle, we are in the "awareness" stage, thrown out of Eden and grabbing at fig leaves. Seattle became aware on November 28, 1988, when it passed its very first ordinance regulating adult businesses. Before this ordinance, there was only a "lewd conduct" code. The city didn't think it was so big then; conventioneers and fancy hotels did not rule the downtown core. Seattle didn't want to impress the world—it didn't care. It was as relaxed as a hippie in a pea patch. Then Seattle started getting ideas (the mirror stage); it started seeing itself in relation to other cities (Atlanta, Denver, Houston) and figured it wanted ed to become like these placeless cities, or placeless ideals, as novelist Matthew Stadler once called them.

Although Seattle is not a sexy city, it does have a sexy law. Because an aspiring city can't come out and forbid the existence of adult shops and clubs (that would be unconstitutional), it has to do the most perverse thing: create a law so elaborate, so dense, and so rigorous that it makes it impossible for anyone to operate such a business legally. In Seattle, this law is called Ordinance 114225. It was sponsored by our city mother, City Councilmember Jane Noland, and approved by our city father, then-Mayor Charles Royer; its function is "to regulate businesses, managers, and employers that provide adult entertainment" for the sake of "public peace."

Ordinance 114225—its obsession, its determination, its perfection, its round rhythms, perpetuated by the repetition of voluptuous and visual words like "vulva," "oral," and "areola"—creates a steady beat, not unlike that which drives "The Song of Solomon," the greatest erotic text of all time. This text, which is meant to destroy sex, to control it, to tell "sleazemeisters to get lost," as one zealous *Seattle Times* reporter put it, can also be read for the purpose of exciting the erotic imagination.

"Performance of a dance," according to one of my favorite passages of the ordinance, "involves a person who touches, caresses, or fondles the breasts, buttocks, anus, genitals, or pubic region with the intent to sexually arouse or excite the person." Fondling breasts, caressing the anus—my goodness! I hope my wife doesn't discover that I'm reading this steamy stuff.

Though Seattle's elaborate ordinance has not reached the level of literature, it is still hard to imagine that it is talking about the Seattle we live in. Rather, it must relate to some other fantastic city where thousands of people "simulate sexual intercourse, masturbation, sodomy, bestiality, oral copulation, flagellation" and use devices that forever stimulate the "pubic region."

Police officers act as the link between the written law and the individual—they are the interpreters and administrators of the text. But what happens when the police try to enforce a text that is purely fictional on a person or a situation that is not?

"They can do whatever they want," one dancer said. "The city of Seattle looks at the dancer the way they look at criminals. They handcuff us. Throw us in jail. It is harassment! Some nights I get tickets from the same cop, even if I didn't dance with him. But how can I make a case in court? Even the judges see us as criminals." The problem is not only with clubs but also with peep shows, which are harassed so frequently that so-called "sexual minorities" recently brought up the problem to the Seattle City Council, requesting a revision of the ordinance. They feel it enables vice cops to unfairly target and harass gay men who frequent certain "video arcades"—and indeed, every week, the Seattle police write up a heap of reports about "panorama" (peep-show) violations.

According to police data, between 1997–1999 adult businesses frequented by gay men (Love Boutique, Adult Entertainment Center) were raided 120 times, whereas those frequented by heterosexuals (Lusty Lady, Champ Arcade) were raided 47 times. And of the 73 arrests made at these adult businesses, 69 occurred at the Love Boutique and the Adult Entertainment Center. These figures are so extreme that they indicate not only harassment, but a vice squad that is addicted to a cruel game of power, erections, and handcuffs.

Who can break the cruel circuit of stupidity in Seattle—when will our city grow up and out of this morbid middle stage, this "banished from Eden" madness? No time soon, I regret to say. In 1998, Seattle imposed a moratorium on the opening of new sex businesses. It was extended in 2000 and at the meeting in which City Councilmembers agreed to the extension, our city mother Jane Noland said this of Seattle's businesses of pleasure: "The less said the better." Indeed, Mother, all we have to do is read your erotic text in the silence of our bedrooms.

Calendar of Events

January

Chinese New Year—International District; www.wingluke.com. Few things suck harder or more consistently than American New Year's Eve celebrations, so why not try your luck with the Chinese? This annual parade-centered celebration commemorates both the moon-loving Chinese and Vietnamese New Year, which means it'll be scheduled either in January or February.

Martin Luther King Jr. Day—Queen Anne; Seattle Center, (206) 684-7200 or (206) 684-8582; www.seattlecenter.com. The Seattle Center hosts a free series of tributes to a true American prophet. Celebrations include gospel, blues, and jazz performances, along with impassioned recitations of the Man's fine words.

February

Spring Fecal Fest—Phinney Ridge; Zoo Doo, Woodland Park Zoo, 5500 Phinney Ave N; (206) 625-POOP. As the majestic season of spring approaches, much of Seattle's tilth-oriented community looks for fertilizer for their anticipated monster gardens. Fortunately for them, the folks down at the Woodland Park Zoo have been assiduously collecting all their zebra, elephant, and orangutan poop and turning it into "Zoo Doo."

March

Kulturefest—Central District; Langston Hughes Cultural Arts Center, 104 17th Ave S; (206) 684-4757. Multicultural art goes bang at this ethnically focused arts fest, featuring everything from visual art to dance.

Motorcross—Tacoma; Tacoma Dome; 2727 E D St, (206) 628-0888. The nonstop, beer-swillin', exhaust-breathin' action includes professional racing, an extreme stunt-jumping showcase, and the wildly popular "Dash for Cash," a four-lap race with absolutely no rules and an unspecified cash prize.

April

Blak and Blu Ball—Denny Regrade; CoCA, in ConWorks, 410 Terry Ave N; (206) 860-5245. Poor spelling aside, the Center on Contemporary Art's spring fundraiser is usually quite the see-and-be-seen blowout. Past events have included a burlesque show, live music from local bands, and a raffle of donated items from many of Seattle's best shops and local artists.

Emerald Downs Opening Day—Emerald Downs, 2300 Emerald Downs Dr, Auburn; (888) 931-8400. This is the event that big-pocketed bookies and the compulsive gamblers who love them have been waiting for: the opening of Seattle's nearest and dearest horse track. Live racing occurs through September.

The Sound and the Fury—Sandpoint; Sand Point Naval Station, 7400 Sand Point Way. Professional, amateur, and unsponsored skaters showcase their latest mind-blowing tricks in the Northwest's largest annual "extreme" skateboarding contest, named, fittingly, after a William Faulkner novel.

May

Boating Season Begins—Lake Union/Lake Washington; www.seattleyachtclub.org. Which means the bridges will be clogged, people will be wearing white, and picnics will abound. Events include a regatta through the Montlake Cut, and a boat parade.

Northwest Folklife Festival—Queen Anne; Seattle Center, (206) 684-7200 or (206) 684-8582; www.seattlecenter.com. When it was free, it was free-to-be-you-and-me. Now, it's just another corporate-sponsored music event—but it is possible to catch some great acts you'd otherwise never see.

Pike Place Market Street Festival—Pike Place Market; (206) 682-1453; www.pikeplacemarket.org. Way back in 1971, a passionate bunch of Seattleites fought to save our beloved Market from the icky creep of gentrification, and this annual festival marks the anniversary of their triumph. All of the usual street-festival suspects—live music, craft vendors, beer gardens, and Market personalities—will be up and running to provide entertaining diversions for the Memorial Day weekend.

U-District Street Fair—University District; (206) 632-9084. While not exactly the Champs Élysées, the stretch of University Way from NE 40th Street to NE 50th Street (known both disparagingly and lovingly as "the Ave") is an entertaining place to usher in summer. The strains of live music fill the air, the highest echelons of the local arts and crafts community peddle their wares, local farmers hawk fresh produce, and hopefully, that death-defying kid who rides a 12-foot-high unicycle while juggling will be there to blow your mind.

June

Fremont Fair/Solstice Parade—Fremont; Fremont Ship Canal, N 34th Street; (206) 632-1500. Funky Fremont's Solstice Parade is the most down-home and creative annual celebration in Seattle. Modern hippies of all stripes paint their bodies and don huge papier-mâché masks, musicians fill the air with joyful clamor, and a whole bunch of naked people ride around on bikes. (No, we are not making that up.) Plus, yummy food!

Seattle Dyke March—Capitol Hill; http://come.to/seattledykemarch; dykemarch@technodyke.com. The biggest dyke event of the year draws women-who-love-women from around the area. The usual marching festivities include live music, a drag king show, and often one or two bare breasts. Festivities start at Broadway and Pine.

Seattle Pride Day/March—Capitol Hill; (206) 324-0405; www.seattlepride.org. Depending on whom you ask, Seattle's (gay) Pride March is either homo heaven or a boring, bloated mess that has lost whatever sense of purpose it ever had. But love it or hate it, Seattle's largest show of gay and lesbian pride draws more than 75,000 participants annually and is followed by a rally in Volunteer Park, where uniformly shrill speakers and entertainers compete for the attention of the roving gay crowds with an array of food booths and hand-grabbing politicians. The parade itself begins at 11 am at the corner of Broadway and Pike and proceeds to Volunteer Park, where the rally continues officially until 6 pm.

July

AT&T Family Fourth/Fourth of JulIvar's—The Sky. Seattle's two big fireworks shows are traffic ball-busters, but you can strategically position yourself pretty much anywhere between Lake Union and Elliott Bay and see some pretty sparks (and drunken people).

Bastille Day Picnic—Lake Sammamish; Lake Sammamish, 3560 Lake Sammamish Pkwy SE; 206/443-4703. Bet you didn't know that Nantes, France, is one of Seattle's sister cities, and that the mayor of Nantes, Jean-Marc Ayrault, visits the Northwest to help us celebrate Bastille Day. Much like our own Independence Day, Bastille Day is a celebration of the victory of the ideals of proletarian democracy over a feudalist, decadent bourgeois ruling class, which in France famously culminated in the storming of the Bastille prison, and left a couple of the aforementioned bourgeois without heads. Enragé!

Bite of Seattle—Queen Anne; Seattle Center; (206) 684-7200 or (206) 684-8582; www.biteofseattle.com. Good food, good music, and with luck, great weather: The annual two-day Bite of Seattle is a haven for gourmets and a hell for claustrophobes. Packed with booths.

King County Fair—Enumclaw; (206) 296-8888; www.metrokc.gov/parks/fair. The usual fair stuff—rides, greasy food, show animals, and pie cook-offs—and a big old rodeo! Yee-haw! Enumclaw Fairgrounds, third week in July.

Pain in the Grass—Queen Anne; Seattle Center, (206) 684-7200 or (206) 684-8582; www.seattlecenter.com. Seattle probably has more traditional summer events per capita than any city on Earth, and this stupidly named annual series of free rock concerts at the Seattle Center is one of the best. Bask in the twilight shadow of the Space Needle and the landmark EMP while rocking to usually excellent local music.

Picnic for Puget Sound—Ballard; Golden Gardens Park; (206) 382-7007. Grab your beach blankets and head on over to Golden Gardens Park to chow down on corn on the cob, hot dogs, gelato, watermelon, and of course, clams—all for the sake of the environment—at this annual fund-raising picnic.

Seattle to Portland Bicycle Classic—Cascade Bicycle Club; (206) 522-BIKE; www.cascade.org. If cycling up Seattle's hills isn't masochistic enough for you, try this annual two-day ride to Portland! Rest assured, though—most STP riders are "not lean, mean, cycling machines." Registration includes food and souvenir vest.

August

Evergreen State Fair—Monroe; (206) 794-7832. The Evergreen fairground, 30 miles from Seattle in Monroe, is a hot spot for a variety of events: cattle sales, gun and ammo shows, the llama expo, and AA meetings. The Evergreen State Fair features a rodeo, musical acts like Roy Clark, and good old 4-H youngsters showing their animals. Go stoned. The fair is held the last week in August through the first week in September.

Seafair—Lake Washington, (206) 728-0123; www.seafair.org. Some local folks think this annual fest is the cat's meow. We wouldn't know, as we're too busy hiding under our beds, rocking back and forth in traumatic shock, to ever attend. The "stars" of Seafair are the jet-plane acrobats the Blue Angels, and whatever appeal this legendary festival may hold is annually obliterated by the ungodly, earth-shaking howls spewing from the butts of these hideous planes, which we hope will one day crash in mid-air and plunge to the ground, landing in a fiery wreck on the home or office of whoever keeps inviting these ear-splitting menaces to our beautiful city. However, the Seafair Torchlight Parade through downtown is sweet, and there are charming, smaller Seafair festivals that occur in Seattle neighborhoods during the week preceding the torturous main event.

September

Bumbershoot—Queen Anne; Seattle Center, (206) 281-8111; www.onereel.com. The mother of all Seattle arts festivals, Bumbershoot boasts a truly spectacular array of artists and entertainers—local, national, and international—cramming them all onto the Seattle Center grounds over Labor Day weekend. Crowds are huge, lines are long, but the art 'n' entertainment can't be beat. Numerous stages provide spotlights for authors, artists, rock stars, performance artists, folk musicians, and short films. Throughout Labor Day weekend.

Puyallup Fair—Puyallup; Puyallup Fairgrounds, (253) 841-5045; www.thefair.com. Seventeen days of fair fun, including a rodeo the first three days of the fair, big and not-so-big musical acts, and rides that'll turn you upside down and spill your change. Held the first half of September.

October

KUBE Haunted House—Queen Anne; Fifth Avenue and Mercer Street. It may be haunted by cheesy DJs, screaming teens, and a line as long as a Poe poem, but it's the first event of the Halloween season (usually opening the first week of October) and it's a whopper—20 rooms of "horror" to encourage your incontinence. Look for the big flashpot-lit edifice in the parking lot east of Seattle Center, Fifth Ave and Mercer St.

Northwest Bookfest—Sodo; Stadium Exhibition Center, (206) 378-1883; www. speakeasy.org/nwbookfest. Late October is an opportune time to turn to books, but the Northwest Bookfest is too often a commercial whorehound of an event. Go to meet the people of the good small presses, and for the occasional great staged event. There are readings and forums all weekend long.

Painting Marathon; Denny Regrade; CoCA, in ConWorks, 410 Terry Ave N; (206) 860-5245. The pressure's on at the Center on Contemporary Art's annual 24-hour "art marathon," which separates the real artists from the . . . guys who can, uh, paint. Watch, cheer, inspire, pose, or just be a nuisance as Seattle's top painters struggle to stay awake while producing pieces that will be auctioned off the very next day. (Coffee available at all times.)

November

Nothing happens in November.

December

Breakfast with Santa/Holiday Zoobilee—Downtown; Woodland Park Zoo, 5500 Phinney Ave N, (206) 684-4800. If overuse of the old "coal-in-the-stocking" threat has weakened its pre-Christmas behavioral influence on your kids, then here's all the extra oomph you need. First, solicit a lecture from Santa at a very intimate breakfast, and then head straight for Holidoo, "the zoo's sweet-smelling compost" (available in two-gallon bags, or four-gallon buckets for the real bastards).

Community Hanukkah Celebration—Mercer Island; Strom Jewish Community Center, 3801 Mercer Way; (206) 232-77115. The Festival of Lights features a traditional candlelighting ceremony, kids games, arts and crafts, and music. Wear your flame-retardant yarmulke.

Qwest Holiday Carousel—Downtown; Westlake Park, Pine Street between 4th Avenue and 5th Avenue. "Carousel lore has it that Dwight Eisenhower actually helped create the 36 original hand-carved wooden horses while working in the Parker factory." In fact, it's true . . . except that it was Dwight "Six-Pack" Eisenhower of Akron, Ohio, the illegitimate son of a circus clown and the sheriff's daughter. Sadly, nobody understood his parent's love.

Teddy Bear Suite—Downtown; Four Seasons Olympic Hotel, 411 University Street. Visit the Teddy Bear family in their special suite at the Four Seasons Olympic Hotel. Then, return home to your feculent apartment, prepare your nightly feast of Top Ramen and white bread, and weep as you curse Mr. and Mrs. Teddy Bear and their lavish four-star accommodations. Damn the injustice of it all.

Demolition Derby, Fourth of July

by Novella Carpenter

THERE IS NOTHING MORE BEAUTIFUL THAN ONE CAR CRASH-ING into another—especially when it's done on purpose, and it's Fourth of July, and there's a rowdy crowd behind you yelling for more damage, more! Welcome to the town of Monroe and its annual Evergreen Speedway Demolition Derby (17901 State Route 2; 360-794-7711).

Since you're going to spend hours at the derby, it's best to turn the whole thing into a picnic. I'll fry up some chicken—soaked in buttermilk overnight, then lightly dusted with flour, salt, and pepper, and deep-fried until dark brown—and bring it with me in a cooler. And sure, I'll shoot up a watermelon with vodka and take it, too. My man and I like to get there early and scope out a good seat under the roof in case it rains (it almost always does).

The folks at the Speedway begin the derby with radio-station personalities tossing T-shirts into the crowd, followed by a real car race. The only reason to come is for the car crashes, though. Every Fourth of July, hundreds of brave drivers from near and far assign personalities to their cars (one year there was a cow car that spurted actual milk out of its hood when the engine was revved) and then proceed to destroy them.

I don't want to ruin it by telling you all the surprises you'll encounter at the derby, but the highlights include a school-bus demolition race, a race on a fig-ure-8 track with many close calls, and a race in which three cars are chained together, with drivers in the front cars and brakemen in the back. The cars race and smash into each other.

The finale is always the balls-out demolition derby: The last car moving wins. Because I'm the betting type, my friends and I all put a dollar on the one we think will win. Invariably it's a station wagon that wins—those suckers are able to inch around the track while the other cars burn, drivers fleeing from the wreckage. Then the lights go out and Bruce, Neil, and Garth come out over the stereo system. The crowd sings along, and the whole place is lit up with flames and fireworks, and it all seems to burn.

When you finally stream out with the crowd to your car, people let off fireworks, and the smoke is thick in that grass lot. You have the urge to smash your car into someone else's just to see how it feels.

Directions: Get on I-405 heading north. Take exit 23 to SR 522 (the Snohomish/Monroe exit). Follow SR 522 to the end and take a right at the stoplight. Take another right at the next stoplight. You are now at the Evergreen State Fairgrounds; the racetrack is inside. Evergreen Speedway Demolition Derby, 17901 SR 2; (360) 794-7711.

Accommodations

CONTEXT IS CRUCIAL WHEN YOU'RE LOOKING for a place to put someone up—your visiting ex-dormie is going to have different needs than, say, your estranged billionaire father. With that in mind, accommodations in Seattle are divided into four categories: hotels, motels, B&Bs, and "other." Seattle's hotels, with very few exceptions, are found downtown, while motels cluster along the seething whiplash known as Aurora Avenue. The city's B&Bs are sprinkled, as is their wont, eccentrically throughout town. Plus, there are a couple of other options here for the traveler without much cash at all.

Hotels

Ace Hotel
Belltown
2425 1st Ave, (206) 448-4721
A great bargain; stay here even if you live in Seattle
The Ace is Seattle's answer to Euro style: trim, whitewashed rooms, some with '70s-style outdoor-scene wallpaper. It is located in Belltown above the excellent Cyclops Cafe. Parking will be a problem, and you must share a bathroom on each floor unless you're in a deluxe. You can put up your fancy gay uncle or your rock star sister here.

Alexis Hotel
Downtown
1007 1st Ave, (206) 624-4844
Expensive
The Alexis bespeaks business elegance in a way your snobby, wealthy aunt and uncle might appreciate. Near Benaroya Hall and the Seattle Art Museum, but you have to walk uphill for shopping.

ANNIE MARIE MUSSELMAN

Ace Hotel: It's a lonely life, but stylish

Camlin Hotel
Downtown
1619 9th Ave, (206) 682-0100
A bit pricey
Home of the famous Cloud Room, with its infamous piano player, the Camlin is wonderfully centrally located; a walk to the Paramount or downtown shopping is minutes away. The rooms, however, are sterile and charmless. Guests should spend all their time in the bar, anyway.

Claremont Hotel
Downtown
2000 4th Ave, (206) 448-8600
Pretty expensive
The Claremont, like some clichéd old maid, exhibits all its elegance on the outside; the lobby reeks of overstated old-style elegance. The rooms are surprisingly small, especially for the price, but there is a fancy ballroom. Quick access to Belltown and downtown.

Hotel Monaco
Downtown
1101 4th Ave, (206) 621-1770
Really expensive
Hotel Monaco bills itself as "Seattle's Hippest Hotel"—a moniker that really should go to the Ace. Monaco takes an adequate second place, though, and might even be a more comfortable place to stay.

Inn at the Market
Pike Place Market
86 Pine St, (206) 443-3600
A great deal

This utterly charming small hotel is decorated with a comfortable fanciness that your parents will fall for. The courtyard itself induces love at first sight. The views over the Market—of Puget Sound—are beautiful. Chocolates are placed on pillows with the evening's turndown service. Food is supplied by the four-star French restaurant Campagne. If you send your parents here, you'll score points in a big way. Make reservations early.

Marqueen Hotel
Queen Anne
600 Queen Anne Ave N, (206) 282-7407
Pretty good prices

The Marqueen is decorated with the kind of elegance your great-aunt might appreciate—lots of brocade and lace—and is housed in a brick building that dates back to 1918. Quick access to the Seattle Center and the excellent French restaurant Le Figaro, but not much else.

Sheraton Seattle Hotel & Towers
Downtown
1400 6th Ave, (206) 621-9000
Pretty expensive

So close to the heart of the downtown shopping axis that you might bloody yourself on credit card receipts, the Sheraton is Seattle's stolidly fancy holiday hotel—meaning that people stay here for the weekend just to "get away." The rooms are of fair size, decorated with absolutely no panache. The sky-high swimming pool/hot-tub room is a nice feature.

W Hotel
Downtown
1112 4th Ave at Seneca,
(206) 264-6000
Really expensive

ANNIE MARIE MUSSELMAN
Earth & Ocean at the W: Pricey luxury

Outrageously fancy, the W is where you send your parents if they're jetting in from Paris for the weekend. W Hotels are known for their attention to detail, like the little "W" embossed on your glass shampoo bottles, and stuff like that. Staying here is like staying in a Calvin Klein Home Collection display. Very expensive. Right downtown. Internet access available in the rooms.

Motels

Green Lake Motel
Greenwood
8900 Aurora Ave N, (206) 527-5000
Really good prices
A classic '60s-style motel distinguished by its nostalgia-inducing sign, the Green Lake specializes in apartment units. A good place to stay while you're looking for a real place to live.

Seafair Inn
Greenwood
9100 Aurora Ave N, (206) 524-3400
Cheap

Looking like a nice, sterile setting for an affair? The Seafair Inn is just far enough out on Aurora to be cheap, but not far enough out to attract prostitutes. It's a clean, basic joint, except on the Fourth of July, when it's overrun by fireworks viewers (this part of Aurora has a view of both displays).

BOOTSY HOLLER

Seattle Inn
Denny Regrade
225 Aurora Ave N, (206) 728-7666
Good prices

Motels: Bring your own sheets

Where Aurora Avenue exits to Denny Way, the Seattle Inn is perched like a slightly dusty, last-ditch landing pad, but it's not that bad a motel. Rooms are small but inoffensive. The indoor pool is quite large, and there's a Jacuzzi. Very near Seattle Center, adequately near Westlake, and extremely convenient to the Denny Way Déjà Vu strip club.

B&Bs

Bacon Mansion
Capitol Hill
959 Broadway E, (206) 329-1864
Expensive
With a super-fancy dining room, close to Volunteer Park, the Bacon (mmm . . .) Mansion is an extremely cushy place to house friends and relatives who are

visiting you on Capitol Hill. Please warn them not to walk through the park at night.

Chambered Nautilus Bed & Breakfast Inn

University District

5005 22nd Ave NE, (206) 522-2536

Pretty good deal

This popular, cozy U-District B&B looks slightly run-down these days, but it's still a solid and affordable accommodation for Huskies-fevered relatives.

Shafer Baillie Mansion

Capitol Hill

907 14th Ave E, (206) 322-4654

Cheap

Spacious, cheap, and kind of spooky-looking (in fact, it houses Halloween parties yearly), Shafer-Baillie is a notch above other, smaller B&Bs.

Other

Green Tortoise Backpackers Guesthouse

Downtown

1525 2nd Ave, (206) 340-1222

Cheapest

Tends to be hippie-dippy, but offers extremely cheap, extremely close-quartered accommodations, which attract backpackers from all over the world.

Hosteling International Seattle

Downtown

84 Union Street, (206) 622-5443

Cheapest

Like every other hostel—cheap and crowded.

Index